Written BY A Woman

ANDREA ANDERSEN

CONTENT NOTES:

This story discusses sensitive topics and is meant for readers aged 18 and up. WRITTEN BY A WOMAN contains foul language, explicit content between consenting and enthusiastic adults (after a slow burn), feminist themes, discussions of pregnancy and family planning, and a romance that develops within the workplace. If any of these themes can be upsetting or triggering, readers are advised to decide if they feel comfortable continuing to read this romantic comedy.

This is a work of fiction. Names, characters, and incidences are products of the author's imagination or are used fictitiously and are not to be construed as real. Any resemblance to actual events, locales, organizations, or persons, living or dead, is entirely coincidental.

FIRST EDITION, 2024

Cover art illustration and design by Sam Palencia at *Ink & Laurel*

Interior formatting and design by Andrea Andersen

Developmental edits by Yara Gharios

Proofreading by Kelly Andersen and Megan Merrill

Pronunciation Guide

Signe (see-nyuh) Lange (lang)
Zaid (zade) Ansara (ahn-sah-rah)

To those who know exactly what they want,
and have the courage to go for it

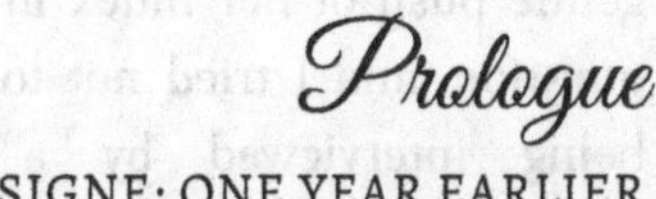

Prologue

SIGNE: ONE YEAR EARLIER

My name is Signe Lange, and I hate pretending that I like working.

I refused to believe anyone on planet Earth genuinely enjoyed clocking in for a nine-to-five office job. I was convinced that we were all lying through our teeth about how excited we were for the job opportunity during the interview process. In reality, we just wanted to ensure that we had a steady, reliable income.

"What made you want to apply at Sun Steer?" Jacqueline, the head of Sun Steer's Human Resources department asked with a polite smile.

I need money to buy food and books, by any means necessary.

"I thought this seemed like an enjoyable company to work for—" I was such a liar, "And I like the idea of working with a close-knit team, like the job description mentioned," another lie, I hated group projects with a deep fiery passion, "So since the commute was reasonable, I thought I'd shoot my shot."

Jacqueline's eyebrows rose a little at that turn of phrase,

so I tried to recover by pasting a friendly smile on my face. It worked, and Jacqueline's lips twitched a little at my blatant attempt to sweep "shoot my shot" under the rug.

She tucked one strand of dark loose hair behind her ear, the only strand of hair out of place from the slicked-back bun she wore. She nudged her glasses up her nose with a gentle push of her index finger as she asked me the next question, and I tried not to feel self-conscious that I was being interviewed by a woman as confident and professional-looking as Jacqueline. Her cream-colored pencil skirt lay perfectly without a wrinkle, and her light purple button-up blouse was flattering without being too revealing.

I felt underdressed, even though my cuffed jeans and striped button-up shirt were perfectly appropriate for this job interview.

Perhaps I was just worried that she would figure out that I had no intention of staying at this company long-term. I wasn't meant to sit at a desk in a formal office environment, doing reports for others. I was meant to sit at a desk in the comfort of my home (or more realistically, my couch) while I wrote about fictional characters falling in love and doin' it.

Sure, I wasn't published or anything, but that didn't mean I didn't have a ton of unfinished manuscripts saved on my personal laptop. I have been writing since I was in elementary school. It had always been a creative outlet for me. In the past few years, I have finally started taking my own writing seriously, fine-tuning my voice and my story flow. Occasionally, I posted whatever I wrote on online platforms for free, to see what kind of responses I got. Sometimes I got heart emojis, sometimes I got poop emojis. You win some, you lose some.

I wanted to be signed. I wanted to be published. I

wanted writing to be my full-time job. Not boring managerial work. I wanted to clock in in my jammies at my desk at home, not in an office that smelled like burnt coffee.

The interview finished smoothly. Since it was my second one, and because the job I was applying for was entry-level, even though the interview process was designed to make the candidate feel otherwise, I was offered the job on the spot. As if a handful of candidates were applying for the position of *General Office Manager* and we were all in competition with each other.

A few days later, I showed up, dressed in another pair of hole-less jeans and a comfortable but elevated sweater to accommodate the frigid air conditioning I experienced during the interview process. Workplace casual.

"This isn't your stereotypical office environment, you see," Jacqueline explained to me as she gave me the office tour, "Things are a little bit more relaxed at Sun Steer." I smiled and nodded because I quickly saw that she was right. The office space wasn't colored in grey and neutral colors that reminded me of a hospital. There were warm reds, oranges, and blues painted sporadically on walls. The company's logo colors. There were napping pods in a far corner, and Jacqueline showed me a sensory-friendly room designed for neurodivergent individuals. The lights in the room were dim, and the walls were a calm cream with a few plants in the corners. There was a hanging swing-like hammock with blankets and pillows and an essential oil diffuser.

Stereotypical office space, this was not.

The fact that there was also a mother's lounge designed for women who are breastfeeding confirmed Jacqueline's claim that perhaps this wasn't going to be as dull and stuffy of an office gig as I originally thought.

We passed an open concept area where Jacqueline introduced the software engineers. There were about a dozen desk clumps, covered with large monitors and colorful keyboards that made the loudest clicking noise I had ever heard. A woman with medium-length black hair and dark eyes lined with eyeshadow, complete with a septum ring, stood from her desk when Jacqueline gestured for her to do so.

The woman was wearing a cut-off t-shirt with a fishnet layer underneath that went all the way to her wrists, a studded black belt completed the outfit with loosely fitted black cargo pants and Doc Martens.

"This is Mary Jiang, one of our senior software engineers," Jacqueline introduced us as Mary held her hand out to me, and I grabbed it enthusiastically.

I already loved her.

"I'm Signe," I smiled, Jacqueline had already mispronounced my name a handful of times and I figured it was easier for people to learn how to say my name from the source.

"You're the new executive assistant," Mary's red-painted lips spread in a smile.

"Office Manager," Jacqueline corrected Mary before turning to me, "Though you will be assisting upper management with minor reports and tasks."

"Oh." This was something I was probably told during the interview process but promptly forgot about because I tended to check out as soon as the conversation became boring enough.

"I'll introduce you to some of the upper management team, I think they are in the office today," Jacqueline smiled as Mary wiggled her eyebrows at me and returned to her seat.

That solidified it, I wanted to be friends with Mary.

Jacqueline then walked me through a different open-concept area of the office where the sales team sat. It was much noisier because most of the people were on calls. They also seemed way more anxious and uninterested in introducing themselves, except for a small blonde woman who waved at me. She seemed friendly enough.

We passed by a large fancy-looking desk that had one monitor and a desk phone, located at the front of the office. It's the first thing people saw when they stepped off of the elevators. Jacqueline pointed it out as my desk space as we passed, turning the corner to where a small alcove of offices lined up.

"This is Brandon Moore, the CEO," Jacqueline introduced me to a tall stocky guy with short, perfectly groomed blonde hair. He was taking a sip from his mug. Upon hearing his name, he lowered his mug and smiled politely at me, diverting his steps away from the office he was heading towards. He held his hand out to me with a strained smile on his face, clearly wanting to get this social interaction over with.

"This is our new office manager," Jacqueline explained as we shook hands.

"I'm Signe," I noted how Jacqueline didn't attempt to say my name again as I cataloged the CEO. Plain t-shirt, slacks, and sneakers that reminded me of a brand that only tech-bros would wear.

Jacqueline said something to him, something I missed entirely but Brandon nodded politely at, before he lifted his hand in farewell and made his way back to his office.

The head of HR smiled at me before glancing at something over my shoulder and nodding, a gesture to tell me that I should turn around and meet whoever was approaching us. So I did.

And there he was.

The man romance writers dreamed of.

He wore a black polo shirt, with the top two buttons undone to show off a white undershirt and some defined clavicle. The sleeves of the polo shirt were snug around his biceps. His chest was wide, and I just *barely* had to look up at him to meet his dark eyes. I was a taller woman, around five foot eleven. A few inches taller than Jacqueline, and just a couple of inches shorter than this man.

As he shoved both of his hands into the pockets of his light grey slacks, I noticed how snug his pants were around his thighs as well.

Clearly, he wasn't a man who skipped leg day at the gym.

Right when I started to wonder how snug those pants fit around what I assumed was a tight ass, I caught myself, remembering that I was, in fact, in the workplace. I returned my attention to his handsome face.

Even with those thick-framed glasses he wore, it did nothing to take away from the sharp angles of his cheekbones, the thick black eyelashes, and the perfectly shaped eyebrows that made me suspect that a woman had shown him the importance of eyebrow grooming.

His jaw was framed by a closely cropped beard, thick enough to not have any patches, but short enough to still show off an unfairly defined jaw underneath. His beard was almost black, like the thick hair on his head that was styled perfectly out of his face.

I wanted to run my hands through it and mess it up.

"This is Zaid Ansara," Jacqueline explained while Zaid held his hand out for me to shake. I admit that I hesitated for a moment before clasping his hand with my own, because, *damn*, "The CTO of Sun Steer."

"Welcome aboard," Oh dear god, his *voice*. Zaid's voice was low. He had a voice that I knew would sell millions of audiobooks if he ever dabbled in narration. I could picture it now, hearing him attempt to growl or grumble like the manuscript would instruct him to do. And he'd be fantastic at it.

How did a guy that looked like *this* work at a tech company?

I wondered if he was some type of model or social media influencer on the side. I made a mental note to look him up online.

"Thank you," I smiled, barely remembering in time that he spoke to me and that it was now expected of me to reply, "I'm Signe."

Zaid nodded his head at me once before repeating my name perfectly, "Signe."

Say it again, the most desperate, unhinged part of my brain begged.

"Signe is going to be..." I didn't even acknowledge that Jacqueline had finally managed to say my name right. I was in shock. I was dumbfounded. Since when did tech companies allow actual models to work with us, normies? With us peons? Did no one else notice how attractive the CTO of this company was? Was I the only one who knew that he belonged on the cover of romance novels?

In the span of a few seconds, while Jacqueline spoke to Zaid filling him in on my job description (or whatever she deemed more important right now), I pictured Zaid on a white horse with a billowing shirt open and fluttering in the wind, exposing what I assumed was a sculpted and tanned, olive-toned chest. I pictured him doing the boyfriend doorframe lean. I pictured him caging in a woman against a wall with those tree trunks he called arms.

I pictured him shirtless, with his pants indecently low.

I blushed. I actually *blushed* in his presence because of how dirty my thoughts became, and how insanely attractive I found him.

He's literally just a guy. More importantly, your coworker and superior, I scolded myself.

He said only three words to me, mostly paying attention to Jacqueline at this point now. He would nod occasionally at whatever she said to him, with his hands still stuffed in the pockets of his slacks in a clear posture of someone anxious but trying hard to act casual.

Zaid was perfect.

The story just came to me in those moments, I couldn't help it.

"I hate to interrupt," Zaid lifted a hand to halt Jacqueline's sentence as he pulled his phone out of his pocket to frown at it, "But I have a lot on my plate. If Signe could get trained to help you and Brandon first, so that I can be left undisturbed for the next few days, that would be ideal."

Okay, well, sorry for breathing.

I didn't let his dismissive attitude get to me, everyone was allowed to have busy or stressful days.

Ignoring the hit to my ego from being so quickly dismissed by a solid ten, that night I started plotting. I started mapping out the love interest's character, his motivations, his drive, and his personality—which was much more friendly and charismatic than the inspiration. How he would react in the presence of a woman he was deeply attracted to and in love with.

I hadn't visualized a story like this in such a long time, so

I ran with it. I didn't want to waste this burst of inspiration and creativity that I had.

Whether or not anything became of this story, at least I was writing with intention. I was writing and excited to write, and also excited to go back to my office job the next day to see if I could become inspired even more. Were there other stupidly attractive people at my new job? Would this inspire spin-off stories?

A few weeks later, I had a couple of chapters drafted. I went back and edited them until I felt confident that I had *something*: a story that might be enjoyable to other romance readers. I wouldn't know until I tried. So, I posted the first chapter on a free-to-read website, mostly known for fanfiction, but original works were posted occasionally as well.

I was shooting my shot again, if you will.

The first couple of days I think I only had one or two readers.

I didn't think much of it, so I posted the next chapter. Same pattern. Only a handful of comments and shares.

I had hoped, obviously, but I never expected the response I ended up getting months later. The kind comments and feedback I received were the best surprise. It motivated me to keep going, to keep writing. To tweak things here and there, to take this story seriously.

I had something, and I fully intended to see it through.

Chapter One

SIGNE: PRESENT DAY

"I'M JUST SAYING, women's clothing sizes are arbitrary. None of it ever makes actual sense." I shrugged as I slurped down my coffee and stared at my friend and co-worker. She was leaning against the breakroom countertop, mirroring me. Her blonde hair was in a messy bun, and her petite frame was dressed in a one-piece green romper that she elevated with wedges to make it look a little more business casual.

Not that this office functioned like other offices.

Casual was welcome here, as long as everyone was comfortable and appropriate. That was fairly normal at a tech company. It wasn't like we were a hedge fund that had to put on an appearance in the workplace.

"I agree," Jamie nodded, scrunching her nose as her dark blue eyes stared at the coffee in my hands, "But it's still discouraging if I think about it for too long."

"Maybe," I shrugged again as she watched me tip my mug to my lips before continuing, "But you need to give yourself some more grace. You're human, you're allowed to lose weight, and you're allowed to gain weight. Your body is allowed to change."

11

She nodded, though I could tell her brain was struggling to make sense of my words. Jamie had just been telling me that she no longer fit in a pair of pants that she had kept around since high school. She had been in therapy for the last couple of years to help her with her unhealthy relationship with food, which was great, but the progress of that sometimes got to her.

The fact that she had been able to fit in pants that she wore in high school up until recently kind of blew my mind, though. She had gone up just one size.

"Who is gaining weight?" Mary asked as she entered the break room. Whereas Jamie Hansen gave off an aura of sunshine and flowers and rainbows, Mary Jiang gave off... whatever the opposite of that would be.

I sometimes liked to think of Mary as the office goth, but energetic and upbeat.

I had written some short stories about a character that was inspired by Mary.

Mary walked past both of us to reach into her stash of energy drinks I kept stocked in the breakroom just for her. They tasted like spray paint, though she'd fight you if you told her that, so nobody else drank them.

"Jamie," I nodded towards the blonde in the room, and Mary's dark brown eyes lit up as her grin spread across her face.

"Congratulations!" Mary tugged Jamie in for a hug, one that Jamie happily reciprocated, appreciating the immediate positive reaction. Mary was about an inch taller than Jamie, closer to my height, but she lifted the blonde woman up and shook her around.

"Thank you," Jamie mumbled against Mary's shoulder awkwardly before Mary set her back down, "I don't fit in a certain pair of jeans now, and Signe is reminding me that's okay."

"Of course it's okay," Mary bumped her hip against Jamie's, her studded belt poking Jamie's side, and snapped her energy drink open, "That just means we get to go clothes shopping."

"It does," I smiled, "I want to get a pair of jeans like yours." I nodded towards Mary's black wide-leg pants, loving how they were snug against her butt and thighs, but flared out near her calves.

"Let's go this weekend," Mary nodded with one arm around Jamie's shoulders. Jamie blushed as she looked back and forth between the two of us.

We sat in comfortable silence as we sipped our drinks. It was the middle of the workday, and we would be having lunch soon. I was grateful that I had found these two ladies to hang out with so easily when I started at Sun Steer. At first, Jamie and I were surface-level friends, meaning we only spoke at work and didn't even go as far as to exchange numbers. After a few months though, Jamie and I started to chat more and more. Eventually, we dived deeper at a company party when she had a couple of drinks. Thus, how I learned about her struggle with body dysmorphia.

At first, she was nervous to share with me because I was, well, bigger than her. Taller and wider. She didn't want me to feel uncomfortable about my body simply because she was speaking about her issues with hers. I, however, assured her not to worry about it. I was blessed with a mother who cared about what I was exposed to as a young child, so I never got to witness early two-thousands celebrities calling one-hundred-and-twenty-pound women "plus-sized" or anything else insane. My mother only ever spoke positively about her body and my own.

My mother was proud of her Scandinavian features, and now so was I. If anyone took a look at me and didn't like what they saw, that was their prerogative.

"I'm not doing anything Saturday night," I offered after draining my mug and setting it in the sink.

"Really? No dates?" Mary asked, pulling herself away from Jamie and smiling at the little woman. Her black tank top had the female symbol on it in white.

Nothing else.

Because Mary was iconic.

"Believe it or not, no," I smirked at Mary, who loved hearing about my dates with men because she couldn't believe half of the things I experienced as a straight white woman intentionally seeking out men for companionship. She was even more curious about my dating life since she broke up with her girlfriend about six months ago, and I had a feeling that Mary was distracting herself with my lack of a love life to fill the hole that her breakup left.

"Why not?" Jamie asked as she followed me to the sink to rinse out her mug.

"I don't know, after the last date I went on, I gotta admit I'm not excited to go on another," I replied.

Mary immediately started laughing, and Jamie gave me a sad smile as they both remembered what had happened.

The man took a hard look at my dark red hair, and somehow gained the confidence to ask me if the carpet matched the drapes.

Why, men?

My phone vibrated, and I pulled the device out of the pocket of my jeans to see the notification. I blushed and immediately pocketed the phone, not wanting Mary or Jamie to see it. I was a chicken, and I was worried that they would tease me if they found out how I spent my nights when I wasn't out on dates with disappointing prospects.

"You gotta get back on that horse eventually," Mary tipped her head back and drained her energy drink before tossing it in the trash can behind her.

"Only because eventually, I'll get bored of my DIY box." I agreed, staring pointedly at Jamie who I knew would blush at the mention of sex toys. She was a private person who wasn't as forward about her sex life, unlike Mary and me. But she was still friends with us, so we couldn't have been too immature for her to hang around.

As I expected, Jamie blushed again with an embarrassed smile on her face.

"God, you're adorable," Mary pinched Jamie's cheek, who quickly slapped her hand away while I laughed at them.

"I have been thinking about downloading a dating app myself, actually..." Jamie bit her bottom lip as her eyes bounced between the two of us, and Mary and I gaped at each other in shock.

"Are we going to hear stories about Jamie going on dates?" I asked Mary.

"I don't know if I'm ready for this." Mary looked genuinely distraught, but her laughter let me know that she was joking around like I was.

"Shut up," Jamie flipped us both off, making us struggle to compose ourselves, "I'm just inspired by Signe's tales and success rate."

"I don't know if I've had any real success." I countered.

"But you, like..." Jamie flapped her hand in the way that she did when she was struggling with which words to use, "...*go home* with men."

I stared at her.

Mary stared at her.

I broke the silence first with, "That doesn't mean that I'm 'successful' with men. Half the time I fake it, I finish things off myself after they leave."

"Oh my hell," Mary palmed her forehead, "Don't ever fake it with a man, that's your first mistake."

"But, like," I quirked my lips to the side as I leaned a hip against the counter to explain myself, "If I know that I'm never going to see him again, and I am nowhere near close, I might as well just rip the band-aid off and get it all over with."

"The attitude every woman wants with sex," Mary lifted a dark eyebrow with her sarcastic remark, her piercing shining in the harsh light of the breakroom.

I smiled and shrugged, agreeing with her.

This is the part of my life that doesn't quite make sense to me, which led me to believe that Mary and Jamie definitely wouldn't make sense of it either.

I went on dates, I had consensual casual sex, but I wasn't exactly going anywhere with any of it. Unfortunately, the last few men I had either gone out with or hooked up with had left me feeling...underwhelmed. I didn't exactly have a lot of reason to keep dating at this point. And yet, I did. I couldn't help it. I loved the excited feeling of getting ready, knowing that the chances of sex were high.

Sure, I only get off with my dates about fifty percent of the time, and if I knew they were just in it for a hookup or a one-time thing, I could almost guarantee that they weren't going to be able to get me off. And yet, I couldn't resist the possible creative inspiration I got by putting myself out there.

I *loved* romance. Anything from cutesy closed-door

romantic comedies to the most toe-curling monster erotica anyone can think of. If it has a happily ever after, I'm in.

Mary and Jamie knew I liked to read, but neither of them knew that I wrote, or how far I'd gone with it.

Because I was both ashamed and excited about it.

"I'm not going to argue with you, because you're right," I replied to Mary, "But I think that a small part of me just likes to get off on the fact that all I really have to do is swipe right a couple of times, and then there is a ninety-nine percent chance that I am going to get laid that night."

"Ahem," a throat cleared behind me, and I straightened from leaning against the countertop at the same time that Jamie and Mary stood taller. Their eyes widened in surprise. I squeezed mine closed and took a few milliseconds to hate myself before I turned around to see who had just walked in on our very inappropriate conversation.

Zaid Ansara.

Our boss.

Well, kind of.

Not directly.

He was just high enough in rank that he could fire us if he wanted to.

"Let's try to remember that we're at work," his low baritone voice rumbled throughout the breakroom, and I had two conflicting reactions to his words. The message he delivered made it feel like a cold bucket of ice immediately got dumped over the fun times my friends and I were having together.

However, because of how delicious his voice sounded, paired with his entire physique, I felt my skin start to heat in his presence.

Because Zaid Ansara was *hot*.

I know, I know. It was wildly inappropriate to say that

about the Chief Technology Officer at Sun Steer, but it was true, nonetheless.

Zaid was taller than me, a feat that not a lot of men could pull off. I wasn't bitter about being a tall woman and generally didn't have any problems dating shorter men (as long as their egos weren't incredibly fragile about it), but I would be lying if I said that seeing a man who was taller than me wasn't an immediate plus one in the hypothetical, "This makes you hot" column.

Zaid's tall. Maybe closer to six-three if I had to guess, but I digress.

His dark eyes were surrounded by thick, black eyelashes that he usually kept hidden behind glasses, but I still couldn't help myself and made direct eye contact with him almost every time we came face to face.

He was always the first to break eye contact with me. Every time. Without fail.

He held an empty mug in his large hand. Two thick veins curved up his exposed forearm before hiding under the rolled sleeve of his button-down shirt.

Huh, he must have had an important meeting today to justify a button-down. Usually, he opted for a black T-shirt or polo. I was convinced that he had hundreds of black T-shirts that he cycled through. It was very Roy Kent from *Ted Lasso* chic.

Breaking eye contact with me almost immediately, as usual, he turned and nodded to Jamie and Mary behind me.

"Will do, sorry about that," Jamie immediately apologized.

"Yeah, sorry," I repeated. Zaid didn't look at me as he walked past and set his mug down in the sink, rinsing it out and drying off the two mugs that Jamie and I had left in there. We both shared a panicked look as we watched the CTO dry the mugs that we left.

Well, Jamie watched him dry off the mugs.

I found myself staring at Zaid's incredible ass.

Because *of course* his tanned skin and black hair and unnecessary height weren't enough. He had to be physically fit, too. I swore his pecs always strained against his shirts. His butt probably never got sweaty in the summertime because the globes of muscle were raised and firm, something I was both turned on by and weirdly envious of.

I had yet to see him in a pair of pants that did negative things to his butt, even though he was usually in slacks.

One time I found myself staring at a picture taken of the two of us at a company holiday party, and even though an employee was standing between the two of us, I couldn't help but notice that it looked like his bicep was competing in size against my thighs.

I *loved* my thunder thighs. I loved all of my curves, and how I could easily crush the heads of my enemies in between them if I needed to. How my thighs looked when I was sitting in underwear or short shorts, and how the meat of my thigh created that cute little thigh line against my hips. I loved the feeling of a man's hand gripping the meat of my legs. And ass. And hips. Any part of me, really.

But Zaid could probably crush the heads of his enemies by flexing his biceps against his forearms in a strongman pose. Which my ovaries loved.

And because life isn't fair, Zaid didn't have one of those un-proportional upside-down triangle-like gym bodies men usually had when they focused on arms and shoulders too much. Nope. Zaid was tall, dark, handsome, muscled, and utterly perfect.

And also my superior.

Which made my silly little crush on him inappropriate.

Which, also, made my hobby outside of work *wildly* inappropriate.

"No worries," Zaid replied as he set the last mug in the cupboard. He then turned to leave the breakroom as quickly as he came in, barely giving us a nod as he marched off to do whatever it was that he had to do today.

Probably something techy, or businessy.

"Thank god," Mary wheezed, giggling a little as she rubbed her cheek in embarrassment, "If it was Jaqueline who had walked in—"

"Oh, that would have been horrible." Jamie nodded in agreement.

Jaqueline was a stickler for proper office conduct, even though our office was pretty relaxed, and a lot of the time upper management needed to tell her to calm down. Sun Steer was fairly new, only about five or so years old. The company had only recently been labeled as a company in "rapid growth" as Mary explained to me one time. From what I gathered, Jacqueline only started working here less than a year before I started and was used to working in more established organizations that had much stricter and more professional work environments.

"Praise be," I nodded as we all quickly sauntered out of the breakroom. We returned to our desks to wrap some things up before the three of us met again at the elevators for lunch.

My phone kept buzzing, making my anxiety rise in my chest just enough for me to struggle to focus for the rest of the day.

After wrapping things up at work and returning home to my studio apartment in Costa Mesa, I finally allowed myself to change into my comfy clothes and read my notifications.

After reading a few comments left on my last post, the excitement I usually felt when readers gave positive feedback on my writing, flooded my system.

> **Well done!**
> **I'm FERAL for this story!**
> **I need more of Zayne and Sydney!**

And at that comment, reading the names I gave my characters, a little bit of guilt came into play. I responded to a few comments, thanking everyone for the love and support they were giving the most recent chapter of the cute little romance I had posted, but I hadn't posted anything else for a few weeks.

Another message popped up on my phone, reminding me to grab my laptop and settle in on the couch:

> **Ready when you are.**

I clicked on the virtual meeting link my agent sent me and waited for the call to connect.

Soon a short, straight, blonde bob filled the screen, and the image of Michelle taking one last drink of her coffee before greeting me, made the corners of my lips tip up.

"Well, if it isn't the one and only, Signe Lange," Michelle grinned. This was the second time we had spoken over a video chat, all of our correspondence beforehand had been via email or phone calls, and I was glad to finally put a face to the woman who slid into my DMs and inquired about representing me for potential publishing deals.

"In the flesh," I grinned, excitement buzzing in my veins because I had just signed with her a few weeks ago. Gaining a literary agent before I even had a formal manuscript to pitch was almost unheard of, and I resisted the urge to pinch myself to see if this was real life.

"Before we get started, do you have any questions for me so far?" Michelle asked, clicking on her mouse as her eyes scanned whatever else was pulled up on her screen.

Many, actually, I wanted to say, *number one, how the hell did this happen?*

I had just uploaded the twelfth chapter of my little story to that website I found a year ago, celebrating the little wins I had gained by the handful of likes and comments readers were leaving for me.

I was thrilled because I was gaining traction, slowly but surely.

What I hadn't expected a few weeks ago, though, was to wake up to what felt like an endless number of notifications.

Because, somehow, romance readers from all corners of the internet loved the free drafts of my story and shared it with everyone and their mothers. I had created a new social media account, @ReadHeadedWriter, to update the small handful of readers who cared every time I posted a new chapter to the thread. My profile picture was just my name, Signe Lange, in fun colorful, seventies' style font. My account wasn't that interesting, yet; my posts only consisted of quotes from the manuscript, to entice new readers to give my story a chance.

And yet I had thousands of new followers.

"No," I shrugged, "Not at the moment, at least." I settled in, grateful that I could take a business meeting wearing my pajama bottoms, sipping on a warm mug of tea.

"Excellent, let me know if you do, but this meeting will be brief," Michelle nodded. Michelle couldn't have been more than a handful of years older than me, and yet she gave off this motherly aura with her kind eyes and soft smile that made me relax. As if she was in my corner, ready to support me when I needed it. To guide me through the clusterfuck that was traditional publishing.

"Alright," I replied.

"Now that you submitted your first draft of the story—well done finishing it so quickly, by the way," Michelle grinned at me, "The next step will be developmental edits, which Layla has already started on. She should be close to being halfway done with those." I felt my heart flutter in both excitement and panic at the thought of a real adult, a professional editor, reading and critiquing the words that I had slapped together for a romantic comedy.

"Cool," I nodded.

"Once she's done with that, you'll have a few weeks to provide feedback and make any edits you'd like after reading it over." Michelle nodded once to herself, clicking on something with her mouse. I could tell that this wasn't her first rodeo and that she had this conversation practically memorized at this point. Somehow, that knowledge made a spark of imposter syndrome bloom inside of my chest, an uncomfortable ache that made me want to slam my laptop closed in a panic.

But I wanted this.

This was always my goal, so I fought against my insecurity and listened in to what my super professional agent wanted to tell me, "After that, we will do another round or two of edits, including copy and line. That shouldn't take more than a few months, but the goal is to make the manuscript as polished and pristine as possible. Once we feel confident there, that's when we can start submitting the manuscript to publishers. See who is willing to bite."

I nodded and chewed on my bottom lip, "And...you think publishers might want to bite?"

Michelle raised her blonde eyebrows at me, giving me a look that reminded me of my own mother when she thought I was being ridiculous, but cute about it, "I can't say for sure, but based on how popular you already are, I'd say that publishers will be interested in getting in on your story's success, yes."

I tried not to wheeze at the compliment, even though my success was already a cause of my anxiety lately, but that had little to do with so many readers *liking* my story, as it had to do with *why* so many readers were liking my story.

The daily comments I was still getting made it clear that it was because readers loved the male love interest. I'd argue that the appeal of the male love interest was what originally hooked so many readers onto my writing and platform. The problem was, that Zayne Abdul was based on someone I worked with.

Someone with almost the exact same name because I was too lazy to come up with a name that didn't sound like Zaid Ansara. I didn't expect this story to be the one that took off in the online world. I had hoped, but also had realistic expectations. But now that so many eyes were on the story, on the characters and their backgrounds, I couldn't exactly go back and change the name without possibly severing the connection between thousands of readers and my story.

Because readers were *obsessed* with Zayne Abdul.

If only they knew how very real he was.

Within a couple of days, after my story took off online, I received two unsolicited character art pieces from artists who dedicate their craft to visualizing characters in books and bringing them to life. Both times, because apparently, I describe people way too well in my stories, both pieces of art illustrated perfect cartoonish images of Zaid Ansara.

Whoops.

Weeks later, it's only gotten bigger. I had more readers following me every day.

I was thrilled and nervous at the sudden attention, because I wasn't trying to be the next Jane Austen or Ernest Hemingway, after all.

I just loved writing love stories.

"That's...exciting and nerve-wracking," I sipped my tea while Michelle hummed thoughtfully.

"Usually, the submission process can take a while. More than a year or so before we get a deal that's worth taking. But I wouldn't be surprised if someone wants to snatch you up much sooner than that."

Would that mean I could quit my job within the next year or so? I grinned at the thought of not having to formally get dressed for an office every day, even though half the time I just wore jeans and sweatshirts. Michelle and I had spoken about what a good deal for me would look like, and we were thinking that a three-book series would be what appeals to publishers the most, unless they suggest otherwise after receiving my manuscript.

I didn't expect to be offered millions or anything, but I liked the idea of being able to make ends meet with writing alone, even if that meant budgeting and being more frugal with my expenses.

You don't become a writer to become rich, after all.

"That being said," Michelle added, making me focus back on the present instead of a hypothetical future, "You should focus on being more present on your social media accounts. Scheduling regular posts, interacting with readers, that type of thing. Oh—" Michelle grinned as she gave me a look, "You might even want to consider doing a face reveal."

I quirked my lips to the side as I thought about it for a moment before asking, "A face reveal? Really?"

"Yes," Michelle nodded, "You don't need to be posting selfies every day or anything. But it would be beneficial for readers to put a face to the name—speaking of, just wanted to double check, are you sure you want to stick with your real name and not a pen name of some kind?"

I frowned, "A pen name might have been a better idea," especially since using my name potentially made it easier for people I work with to find my book, though I suspected I was the only person in the entire office who was into romance novels, and was really banking on that assumption to not fail me, "But I'm worried that I've already established myself with my real name, considering it's been my profile picture this entire time."

Michelle tilted her head side to side though, weighing the pros and cons, "It's up to you, so if you're comfortable sticking with your real name, that's fine."

I shrugged, because it was more of a lazy, passive decision at this point, "Sounds good."

"But think about the face-reveal thing," Michelle pressed, "If you're already using your real name, there is no real harm in showing your face to readers, too."

She had a point.

Might as well go balls to the wall if I really wanted to do this.

"It'll be easier to promote and sell the books to readers if your social media following is already established," Michelle added, "Publishers might also want you to have professional headshots to put in the back of the book. A photoshoot might be a fun thing to plan for in the future, too."

"Hmm, I'll sit on that and let you know," was my non-committal response. The problem with plastering my face all over my author account was that, again, it wouldn't be hard for anyone I worked with to find out I wrote a book, read that book, and immediately know who I was writing about.

Especially if future cover art depicts Zaid's appearance as well as the fan art has so far.

Oh, dear god.

Perhaps I could hold off on revealing my face until after publishers wanted to sign with me, until after I could quit my job and try to blow off the Zaid/Zayne resemblance as pure coincidence, should anyone at work find out about it.

Double-checking that I had no future questions or concerns about the querying process, and lying to Michelle by saying I had no concerns at all at this point, Michelle and I ended the video call. I took a moment to internally squeal at the excitement of all this, the fact that I had an agent, that I had a big-kid editor combing through my story to make it better and did a happy little shimmy in my seat. I closed my laptop and turned on the TV to one of my favorite comfort shows to watch, knowing that my mind would be too all over the place to pay attention to anything new that night. After ordering dinner and blatantly ignoring my phone's newest social media notifications, I finally called it a night and went to bed, lulling myself to sleep with made-up stories in my head about two people stumbling into each other's lives at work and falling in love.

All while bending over backward to make the male love interest any other persona than the CTO at my job, and giving up hope, before finally succumbing to sleep.

Chapter Two

SIGNE

God bless the bookish community.

A week or so passed, and I was doing a decent job of staying active on my social media account like Michelle advised, but I still hadn't posted a selfie or anything. I did, on occasion, get inspired to write a spinoff sequel, of characters that were introduced in my first book, but wasn't sure who would get their own story next? I would sometimes get an insatiable urge to pull out a notebook and write an idea down. Or pull my laptop open and type out a scene that just wouldn't get out of my head. Perhaps feeling mildly successful after meeting with Michelle gave me more confidence to keep going.

This came to me more often now that I had supposedly gotten the bookish community's blessing to write a formal manuscript instead of posting chapters of my story online. People have been following me while begging me to post the next chapter. A few days ago I bit the bullet and posted about how I wouldn't be sharing new chapters because I was officially signed with an agent and was pursuing traditional publishing. I woke up the following few mornings with new notifications, comments, and tags all congratulating me on signing with an agent and wishing me luck on my adventure. They were all willing to wait for the revised and fresh aspects of Zayne and Sydney's love story. Most knew that traditionally publishing a book would take time and weren't bitter about it at all.

Keeping my handle something silly like @ReadHeadedWriter helped me feel hidden from the bookish community, even though my real name and picture were on my profile for those who cared because I officially decided that I wasn't willing to confuse myself with a pen name. I figured that if I was going to write something people loved, I wanted to claim those words proudly.

But mostly anxiously, because I still didn't want certain people finding out about this aspect of my life. Having people tag my account and seeing @ReadHeadedWriter instead of, hypothetically, @AuthorSigneLange also helped me feel like I was protecting myself from future humiliation.

Or future reprimand from Jacqueline, who would probably add a whole section to the Sun Steer Code of Conduct explaining how unethical it was to write smutty fanfic about members of upper management. I vaguely remembered Jacqueline mentioning something in my onboarding process about how Sun Steer had a right to look through any public social media accounts that I had, but I didn't have any active social media accounts at the time, so I didn't think much of it.

Now I did, but I assumed that Jacqueline wasn't about to follow up with me to see if I was randomly active on social media again or not. She had no reason to do that.

Plus, Zaid's inspiration for the love interest or not, my account had nothing to do with my day job. It was completely separate, if things worked out how I hoped.

There was no need to disclose my new author account to Jacqueline for any reason. Especially if I was going to quit if a publisher offered me enough money to do so.

And that's how I started wondering if showing my face to readers really was that risky at all. There were less than five women in the office, who hadn't disclosed their love for reading to me at all—and not to be totally sexist—but I really doubted any of the tech bros here read romance novels.

The only social media they were active on was probably Reddit or Discord.

Their feeds were probably just a bunch of posts about their noisy-as-hell mechanical keyboards.

"Heads up!" Mary called, making my gaze lift from my phone just in time to see a Rubix cube, that she had just tossed, flying toward my head. I yelped and dropped my phone in my lap to prevent my face from being impaled by the sharp edges of the children's toy.

"Nice catch," Mary smirked as she sauntered over to my desk and leaned her elbows over the edge.

"Amazing what the body can do when immediately threatened," I smiled at her as I gave the cube back to her.

"What are ya looking at?" Mary asked, leaning over more to look at my phone resting in my lap. I glanced down and saw the screen was black, so I just smiled and set it next to my keyboard.

"Just texting." I sighed, resting my elbows on the desk, and setting my chin on my fists. I ended up blocking Mary and Jamie from my new account as soon as I made it, as a precaution. The platform had just asked me if I wished to sync my contacts with my friends list, to which I aggressively answered *no*, and decided going the extra mile to block their accounts was worth it. I was just too embarrassed to admit that I love writing girly love stories in my spare time to someone as cool and kickass as Mary, and that my claim to fame involved readers loving a fictional man inspired by our superior.

"Ah, I, myself was just writing a long-ass message to Andres," Mary matched my position by resting her chin on her fists, "But I decided I didn't want to stare at screens anymore, so I came over and decided to harass the office manager with requests."

I lifted an eyebrow at her, my lips twitching with the hint of a smile as I waited for whatever request she was about to pull out of her ass, "You don't have a bug to fix or something?"

"I do," Mary responded with an eye roll. She was a senior software engineer, the only woman engineer on the team, "But, I'm waiting for fucking Andres to finish troubleshooting his part before I can work on mine."

I nodded.

I had little to no knowledge of how coding or troubleshooting worked, and whenever Mary or anyone at the company tried to explain the details of back-end coding to me, I could feel my eyeballs physically glaze over as they spoke. It was like speaking a different language. I tried to keep up, but I didn't go to school for software engineering.

"Ah," I nodded at her.

"Anyways, the snacks."

"The snacks."

"What if we got better ones?"

"Are you saying that the cheapest snacks that I could find online to stock the vending machines are not up to your standards?" I asked, knowing that she would prefer it if we had catered food every single day.

"Yes, you get it." Mary nodded.

"I do, and yet," I shrugged, "We have a budget. If you don't like the snacks, feel free to bring your own."

"It's the least the company can do."

I agreed with her. But I also didn't care about this place because I wasn't destined to stay here. It was unlikely for people our age to stay at one company long term anyway. Five years was generally the longest anyone was willing to stay at a company now because the only way to keep up with the cost of living in Orange County, California was to accept a new position elsewhere.

However, Sun Steer was breaking workplace stereotypes and norms by giving their employees fairly livable wages and providing significant benefits and bonuses. We were reaching the point, however, that they needed to do something again. Employees like Mary were starting to feel run down keeping up with all the demands people put on the software engineers, and usually, money was the only way to make an employee feel valued after putting in crazy overtime hours.

The elevators dinged. Loud voices and laughter echoed toward my desk as men started to waltz toward Mary and me.

"Oh, good, Nikhil is back." Mary stood up from my desk and waited for her manager to approach us. Nikhil was one of the nicest managers at the company, in my personal opinion. He always smiled and said hi, and asked how I was doing with genuine interest. He did that with everyone. He never let his position or status make other employees feel like plebes for not being high up in rank.

Something upper management (*I'm looking at you, Brandon*) could learn to do.

It sounded like Nikhil had just finished chatting about the vacation he took with his wife over the summer, where they visited his side of the family in India, and finally turned to meet Mary's eyes.

"Uh oh," Nikhil spoke, smirking at the way Mary was drumming her fingers on my desk with obvious impatience, "At least let me get to my desk before you come at me, Mary."

"But I've been waiting for you to tell Andres to hurry up!" Mary groaned, making Nikhil chuckle and shake his head.

Beside Nikhil, the two men he was speaking to watched the exchange with interest.

First was the CEO, Brandon Moore. The man who looked like every other man in his mid-thirties in Southern California. Tan, blonde, blue-eyed, obviously goes to the gym regularly. Unlike Nikhil, Brandon had no idea how to talk to lower-level employees. He kept his distance from people like Mary and me and preferred to have managers like Nikhil be a third party to filter communication. If Brandon ever needed something from me, he preferred to tell me via email. It was fine.

Then there was Zaid, barely towering over the two men, he stood just a step behind as he also watched Mary and Nikhil joke around.

I stared at him, waiting for him to make eye contact with me. I couldn't help myself; he was just *so* pretty. I forced myself to at least scan the faces of everyone else who had approached Mary standing in front of my desk, before finally looking back at Zaid again at the same time his eyes landed on me.

And then he immediately looked away.

Like always.

I felt my lips twitch a little bit at how predictable his behavior was at this point.

"...Can I?" Mary asked, making me blink and focus on my friend and the conversation she was having.

"No." Nikhil laughed at Mary right when he met my eyes. I had missed a sentence or two of conversation, "Can you do that?"

"I'm sorry, what?" I asked, blinking, and focusing back in. Damn, how long had I been staring at Zaid's beautiful, sculpted cheekbones?

"Simon is going to be out for a couple of weeks," Nikhil smiled, not irritated at all that he had to repeat himself, "And we are hiring two more senior-level engineers. Would you mind sitting in with me on the initial interviews?"

I smiled at Mary, whose arms were crossed over her chest in irritation, "Of course."

"Excellent." Nikhil reached out and patted Mary on the shoulder, "You won't ask fair questions and you will scare my interviewees off."

"Maybe you should interview more competent engineers then."

At that, Zaid's lips twitched a little bit as he fought a grin, before his hand came up to wipe across his face to hide it.

"I am trying, but we need to give them a chance to prove their competence in a friendlier environment," Nikhil jutted his thumb toward my direction, "Which is why Signe is sitting in instead of you."

"Ugh," Mary playfully rolled her eyes before starting to walk back to her desk and calling over her shoulder, "I'm still waiting on Andres!"

"I'll talk to him!" Nikhil gave her a thumbs up before turning back to me, "Jacqueline has already screened these candidates and helped me narrow things down. So we only have two or three short interviews in the next few weeks. I can't quite remember which day. Does that work for your schedule?"

I nodded, grabbing my mouse to click open my calendar to double-check, but my days were always flexible, "I think so."

"I'll send you the invites when I get them," Nikhil smiled and turned to Zaid, "Hopefully we can get these two hired and ready to go in time for the product team to calm down."

"Hopefully," Zaid's low voice agreed.

"This is Brandon..." The CEO suddenly answered a phone call and started marching off toward his office, lifting a hand to wave goodbye to the two men in front of me. I waved my hand goodbye, but he didn't acknowledge it. So I shifted my hand underneath my desk and flipped him off.

I then turned to glance back at Zaid and Nikhil, still chatting in front of my desk, only to see Zaid lifting his gaze from my lap, tipping one corner of his lips up a little bit. It was *almost* a smirk.

My whole body froze.

Did he just see me flip off the CEO underneath my desk?

Based on the knowing look in his eye before he turned to pay attention to whatever Nikhil was saying, probably. *Shit*. Like every other awkward interaction I had with Zaid, I pasted a smile on my face and got to work on my computer to pretend that nothing weird happened.

The method was tried and true.

Finally, Nikhil and Zaid continued towards their offices as they finished their conversation, something I tuned out because it involved more coding and development words that I didn't care too much about. What I did care about, shamefully, was getting my fill of Zaid's glorious backside as he walked away from me. If I found out a co-worker was staring at my butt as much as I stared at Zaid's, I would be fairly uncomfortable. And yet, here I was. I blatantly ogled him whenever I could because I was officially a huge hypocrite.

I just wanted to bite his hammies, nothing crazy.

I reminded myself in these moments that it wasn't like I *actually* wanted to sleep with Zaid. I hardly knew him beyond our roles in the office, but our first one-on-one interaction together had been...underwhelming.

Zaid was shy, that much was obvious.

As was the way he wouldn't meet my eye at all for the first few days of me starting here, even when I made sure to paste a friendly smile on my face every time we passed each other. I constantly remembered our first real conversation, where he basically told me to leave him alone until he was in the right headspace to train a new employee on how he liked his reports and presentations formatted.

I was an assistant to Zaid, the CTO; as well as Jacqueline, the head of HR; and Brandon, the CEO. Talks were being made about officially hiring a CFO here soon, but that hadn't happened yet. I had plenty of work to do for Jacqueline and Brandon when I first started, so I wasn't too disappointed that Zaid had dismissed me so suddenly, but it was still a *little* disappointing, nonetheless. Especially seeing how chummy the guy seemed to be with Brandon over the last year or so.

Mildly rude, business-obsessed, and introverted men were cute to read about in romance novels. Unfortunately, they weren't as cute in reality. This is where another spark of Zayne and Sydney's story came to me. I couldn't help myself. A man with the physique of literal perfection being shy and short with his words? All I had to do was write a sentence about how he was originally shy and short with his words because his brain just couldn't comprehend how *gorgeous* Sydney was, and boom. A tried-and-true romance was born.

The miscommunication trope has its problems, but many readers were suckers for it—every single time.

Personally, I liked a little bit more personality in my partners.

Not that I was against shy men, but usually if a guy was shy on a date, it was because, well, we were on a date. I had the motive to break through his shy walls and get to know him. A shy CTO that could sometimes come across as rude and demanding? I was *not* motivated to help him not be shy around me. We were both professionals and adults. If he wanted to be friendlier with me, he would. So far, he was a little friendlier, but not a lot. And that was fine by me. Boundaries, and stuff. Beyond the little *almost* smirks he would give me, or the eye contact he would break first every single time, it was clear that we would never be more than co-workers.

All of this to say, I also used these mental gymnastics I created for myself to justify writing the male lead in my romance novel. The male lead that thousands of readers were already obsessed with.

My phone buzzed, and I opened my account to see that I had passed ten thousand followers.

Whoa!

I bit my lip and made a little happy shimmy dance at my desk, only checking my surroundings afterward to make sure nobody saw me. But ten *thousand* followers? I quickly scrolled through my follow list, grinning to see that almost all of the followers looked like real accounts, not bots sent on a spamming mission.

Ten thousand *real* followers—readers—excited for my cute little story. I was doing it, I was really doing it.

That does it, I should take Michelle's advice. I thought, *Show the readers the face behind the story they're excited about. No more delays.*

I struggled to finish my reports for the rest of the workday, but I managed, and ended up getting a few emails back from Jacqueline and Brandon giving me the thumbs up on my work. I glanced at the clock and realized that it was already past six and that, based on the silence and emptiness I encountered walking through the office for my supplies check, most of the employees had cleared out already. Sometimes engineers like Mary would stick around if there was a bug they were trying to fix before going home, but as I strode to the break room to take inventory of everything, I saw that even the engineers' desks were empty.

I glanced around, thinking that there was a good chance that I was the only employee left in the building.

A phenomenon that happened more often than I originally expected when I started working here.

I finished taking stock in the break room. I was wondering where in my house I could set up a live stream, since I didn't exactly have a scenic backdrop like so many other influencers and authors had. My apartment was a studio, and I had lots of clutter. I wasn't the most professional person out there, but I also wasn't trying to live-stream all my unfolded laundry either.

Regardless of the state of my apartment, I was determined to go through with my impromptu face-reveal plan before I chickened out, and then realized that the blank walls that surrounded me were kind of...perfect. I glanced down at my nicer work clothes and played with my hair, remembering that both my hair and makeup were done.

Hmm...

I thought about the blankness of the break room as I tapped my inventory notes away on the company iPad I used. While I plugged the iPad in and stowed it away in my desk drawer (I refused to take work home with me), I thought more about the bright overhead lighting it provided. I didn't have a fancy ring light or anything at my apartment, either.

If I were going to do a spontaneous livestream and reveal my face to readers, the break room wouldn't be a bad place to do it. The internet speeds in this building were fantastic.

I did another walk through the office, not seeing anyone. Offices were closed, lights were turned off, and even a peak in upper management's wing showed the same. Nothing but the sunset outside the floor-to-ceiling exterior windows illuminating the open-concept floor plan.

I nodded to myself as I entered the breakroom again and shut the door behind me, for the unlikely chance that anyone else was still in the office. I set up my phone against a box of tissues to line up my shot. The lighting was directly overhead, so I had to change positions and angles to get the light to not create an insane shadow on my face. It took a few minutes for me to figure out what angle was best and which spot worked, but eventually, I set it all up and got ready to start my first livestream, deciding that the wooden breakroom door behind me was bland enough to be a non-issue.

Having never done a live stream before, I opened the app and scanned the button options, feeling like it couldn't be that difficult to manage. After a quick internal pep talk to myself, I leaned forward in my chair and pressed *start*.

Within seconds, I had a hundred people suddenly tuning into my stream.

"You guys!" I tried my best not to look at myself in the

image. Instead, I tried to focus on all the hearts and comments that slowly started to flood the stream, "Ten thousand followers? Are you kidding me?" I giggled at some of the comments that were typed in caps lock, cheering me on, "You're the freaking best!"

I settled in my chair and started reading everyone's comments, answering questions about Zayne and Sydney's story without giving away too much.

"I just wanted to pop on here and introduce myself to all the new faces who followed me recently," I smiled at some of the excited emojis that started to dance on the screen, "My name is Signe, and don't worry, I don't expect you to know how to pronounce it correctly the first time. Also, I'm *so* excited for this journey you all helped me on, and—"

The sound of the break room door opening made me snap my mouth shut and turn to look at who was walking in on my livestream.

I first saw the tanned hand with those two distinctive veins, and my heart sank when I saw the rest of Zaid's large body step into the break room. His head did a double take when he saw me sitting at the break room table, making me gasp and quickly turn around to mute my livestream and slam the phone face down.

I felt my face burst into flames.

Oh god no.

I quickly glanced back as Zaid walked through the breakroom towards the coffee pot, my eyes bulging out of my head when I saw him refill the container with water and grounds, brewing a fresh cup.

I was frozen. My mouth was opening and shutting, trying to figure out what to do.

Do I just end the stream? I glanced at the phone face down on the table, wondering if people were jumping off now.

Was this valuable? A muted stream with a black screen while I sat here and tried not to have a panic attack? But I didn't want to risk lifting my phone to end the stream officially and having Zaid see what I was doing.

"Were you on a call?" Zaid asked, making me jump a little in my seat. I leaned forward with my arms on the table, trying to look casual even though it was anything but.

"Um. Yup." I shot a nervous glance at my phone while Zaid's back was still to me, but I could feel his eyes as he turned his head to glance at me over his massive shoulder.

"Oh, I didn't mean to interrupt," Zaid replied, opening a cupboard to grab a mug, and brewing a fresh cup of coffee. I glanced at the clock on the wall above me, it was six forty-five.

What kind of monster brewed coffee at six forty-five in the evening? Did he not need sleep?

"No worries!" My voice was higher and squeaked a little bit, but I tried to hide it by relaxing my shoulders and casually drumming my fingertips on the table. Except the drumming didn't sound casual. I immediately stopped, but then pressed my lips together as Zaid leaned against the countertop to pull his phone out and scroll while he waited for his beverage.

I decided to turn in my seat to face him so that I could lift my phone and see who all had bailed on the muted, black livestream so far. This angle kept the screen facing me, and not him.

I was weirdly getting more viewers, so after mouthing a quick *sorry one sec* to those loyal homies, I decided to try to wait it out. I did, however, mouth the words *what do I do?* Which resulted in a lot of laughing and crying emojis.

"Are you still on the call now?" Zaid asked, making my heart thump against my chest with nerves. I widened my eyes at the stream and lowered my phone so they had a nice view of my nostrils, before I looked at him, remembering to relax my facial features. His lips were in a line, and his dark eyes darted between me and my phone behind his glasses.

"Oh! Um. No."

Zaid blinked at me, "It just looked like you were talking to someone still." The man had the audacity to lean a little to the side to get a better view of my phone. I quickly laid it face down in my lap.

"I am, but they, um, left the room to go get something." It was a blatant lie, and based on the slow blink Zaid gave me after my words, I had a feeling he knew I was lying.

"I see," he definitely thought I was lying, but didn't seem to care enough to push the issue. Silent moments passed. Excruciatingly silent moments, and finally he reached for his coffee that had finished brewing and turned to face me again.

I held my breath when Zaid said, "We need more filters."

"I know," I replied.

He took a step towards the door but hesitated after my words. God, Zaid was so handsome. Even as he hesitated a step towards the break room door, he moved gracefully. Heat burned through my veins simply from being alone in a break room with him.

Zaid furrowed his dark brows for half a second before smoothing them and continuing towards the door, "Just a friendly reminder, employees are forbidden from filming personal content on company property." Zaid stopped a step or two away from said door, and at his words, I felt my lips part in horror.

"Oh—oh god—I'm not—I mean, I am—but I didn't know—"

"I'm not reporting you or anything, just a friendly reminder."

He had one large hand on the doorknob, clearly intending to walk through it, but hesitating for whatever reason.

"Thank you, I'll wrap it up." I gave him a wide, apologetic smile. Hoping we could just blow past this situation, but he just studied me in that thoughtful way of his.

Ohmygodgothefuckaway, I wanted to scream.

Zaid's lips twitched again, one of his large hands coming up to mess with his hair as he shook his head and finally, finally let himself out of the breakroom. Shutting the door behind him.

I sat frozen in my chair, watching the door and listening for his footsteps to thump away from the break room before I released a very loud and very obnoxious breath as I set up my phone again, getting ready to professionally end the stream for what little followers stuck around—all for that *nothing* they just experienced.

"Oh my god that was so embarrassing," I slammed my elbows on the table and covered my face with my hands, before remembering to unmute the livestream. I had reached forward to do just that before I took a closer look at the mute button.

Which wasn't a mute button, but instead was just a button to add a filter. My face currently had digitized freckles on it.

That, and my stream had almost fifteen hundred viewers now.

Emojis, hearts, fire, and sweating faces were *flooding* the screen.

What the hell?

I smiled and used my index finger to start scrolling through all the comments that I had missed while Zaid was in the room, "Okay, where was I again?" I felt my eyes widen in horror as I read the comments people had left.

> **OH MY GOD WHO IS THAT**
> **Did I really just see Zayne casually walk into the room?**
> **Zayne?? That you, bro??**
> **Who is THAT, Signe!?**
> **That is the hottest man I have ever seen.**
> **Is he really that tall or is that the camera angle?**
> **How do I get him to narrate audiobooks? That VOICE!**
> **Zayne!!**
> **OMG IT'S ZAYNE!**
> **HOLD UP are you at work? Do you WORK with ZAYNE??!**

No.

No, no, no.

My face was beet red.

"Oh no," I mumbled out loud, my hand coming up to cover my mouth. I was frozen as I read the hundreds of comments people had left. What had I done? *Fuck, fuck, fuck.*

I quickly ended the livestream.

I almost had two thousand people tuning in, but it didn't matter. Everyone had clearly seen Zaid and noticed. They knew. The internet *knew*. The internet wasn't stupid. Everyone had seen the cartoonish fanart that people had created for Zayne and Sydney's story, so it was easy to see the living breathing Zaid and notice the similarities. I mean, based on their personalities I was pretty sure Zayne was wildly different than Zaid. Almost a completely different person, even. But in appearance?

They were the spitting image of each other.

Because I was a creepy, weird, pathetic person who wouldn't accept that I had crossed a boundary until it came back to bite me in the ass like this.

"Shit!" I ground the heels of my palms against my head, making me groan as I struggled not to panic.

Only about two thousand people tuned into the stream.

Not everyone who tunes into a stream actively watches it, which was good.

That was also not as much as my followers, so hopefully, it would blow over.

Also, nobody knew Zaid's name. I hadn't said it in the livestream, so his privacy was still pretty much protected. As far as I knew, he had no social media accounts. I knew because when I looked him up to see if he had a side-gig as a model or influencer, nothing came up.

I inhaled through my nose and exhaled through my mouth.

It was just a fluke, nothing serious.

I ended the stream before people speculated more.

People were probably already forgetting about Zaid appearing in my livestream.

I chanted these reassurances to myself as I finally packed up my things and rushed out of the building, desperate to curl up on my couch and eat my stress in potato chips.

ZAID

THE SMELL of allspice and coriander filled the air of my parent's suburban Irvine home, as well as the sound of laughing women. I winced, reminding myself that my mother's kibba was waiting and would be worth the noise level before closing the door behind me. I bent over to untie and remove my shoes before I set my laptop bag down and entered the kitchen. Following the noise and smell, I found my family gathered around the island that was, as expected, already covered with food.

Food that I had missed out on helping prepare because eight-hour workdays were a distant dream at this point in my life.

"Bisbous!" my mother greeted me when she saw me enter the room.

"Sorry I'm late," I spoke up just as my mother grabbed my face to pull it closer to hers. She planted kisses on both of my cheeks, making me feel more like a child than a thirty-four-year-old man.

"Don't apologize for working as hard as you do. But before I forget," my mother gave me wide, encouraging eyes as she clasped my hands and pulled me further into the kitchen where everyone else was standing, "I just saw another listing, just a couple streets over. You should look it up." She grinned and turned around before I could crush her hopes yet again. I only lived about fifteen minutes away from my family home, closer to the office, and yet my mother still complained that it was too far away.

"The home is only about three times the size you need for yourself, and probably three times the cost of your condo," my father chimed in, giving my mother a look that I had seen him give her many times throughout my life. The "he's a grown man" look, the "he's allowed to make these kinds of decisions for himself" look. My mother gave my father an innocent smile before getting back to dishing up plates.

"As long as I can keep your old room, I don't care where you live," my little sister, Raina, chimed in. She was washing her hands in the sink, eyeballing the plate of bread that sat in front of my father. Raina was about ten years younger than me, finishing up her art degree, and had turned my old room into a mini art studio as soon as I made the sudden decision to move out two years ago.

Like me, Raina was a mix of my mother and father. She had my mother's sharp facial structure, and my father's caramel-colored hair and hazel eyes. Whereas I had my father's more masculine facial structure, and my mother's dark brown hair and eyes.

"I'll check it out, Mama," I always did, just to keep up with how the housing market was doing. But everyone knew that I was comfortable in my condo, living on my own. Far enough away to where my family couldn't show up unexpectedly all the time. Where I could unwind in the peace and quiet after a long day.

My mother was still adjusting to the idea of her son moving out without having started a family of my own first. My mother lived with her parents until she married my father, and my eldest sister Salma didn't move out until she married her husband, Ben, a few years ago. Me moving out without so much as having a partner surprised her, even though I was thirty-two at the time and I felt like I was ready to be on my own.

"I see you timed your arrival perfectly," Salma raised a dark eyebrow at me as she scraped a cutting board of vegetables onto a plate, an expression that mirrored my mother's. Whereas Raina and I were mixes between our parents, Salma was practically the spitting image of our mother. They both had the same beauty mark on the right side of their lips, the same sharp bone structure, with dark hair and eyes. She was even the same height as my mother, and they had often been mistaken as sisters out in public.

"How do you mean?" I avoided her gaze as I snagged the piece of bread Raina was about to take, grinning at the annoyed huff she gave me at having to pick a new slice.

"We're just finishing up, we were considering keeping all the food in the oven to keep it warm until you finally managed to arrive," Salma gave me a teasing smile, but her words made my stomach churn with a small tinge of guilt. It wasn't like I enjoyed being late to dinner most of the time.

"Yeah, Zaid," Raina added, taking a bite of her bread and walking over to swing an arm around Salma's shoulders, "How do you feel about eating food that a pregnant woman slaved over all evening?" Raina used the bread in her hand to gesture to Salma's rounded belly, who responded by rolling her eyes and pushing a giggling Raina off of her.

"For the record," my father raised his glass and grinned

before taking a sip of his wine, "I told Salma to sit down and relax an hour ago, and what was your response?"

Salma smirked and replied, "Pregnant women are perfectly capable of helping cook dinner if they want."

"There it is," I took a seat next to my father, smiling, as my mother set plates of food in front of us, "Thanks, Mama," before she shooed Salma into her seat while she prepared the rest of the plates. I glanced at the other wine glass to the side of her, and asked, "Where is Ben?"

"He's laying Zeki down," Salma replied, scooting her husband's wine glass closer to her plate to make room for Raina and my mother to sit around the kitchen island as well. Whereas my sisters and I took after our mother, who didn't bother with alcohol, my father and brother-in-law often enjoyed a glass of wine with dinner. My father was Italian and owned his own restaurant on the other side of town, but my mother never made us feel like we weren't allowed to drink with him.

Similar to how my mother chose not to wear a hijab or raise my sisters with the expectation to wear one.

I glanced behind us towards the stairs that led up to the bedrooms, remembering that Ben was still laying their three-year-old down, and feeling bummed that the little guy and I couldn't watch a couple of episodes of his favorite superhero cartoons before bedtime.

"Where's Tariq?" I asked as we all sat and waited for Ben to join us before digging in.

"He could only stay for a little bit tonight," Raina replied, "He tried to wait as long as he could, but he's pretty swamped with the summer term." Raina met her boyfriend at her art school, and I was the only one in the family who hadn't officially met him yet. She wasn't in the habit of dating, let alone dating seriously, so when she told everyone that she had a steady, long-term boyfriend, we all were dying to meet the guy who convinced Raina to give him the time of day.

"Ah," I nodded in understanding, "Hopefully I can catch him next time." I felt my shoulders slump, a movement my father clocked by patting me on the back.

"You're just in a busy season of life," my father spoke, "It'll pay off in the long run."

I nodded, appreciating his words of encouragement.

"Sorry, sorry," we all turned toward my brother-in-law's voice, which sounded out of breath, echoing down the stairs along with his heavy footfalls, "Little stinker needed a lot of convincing."

"But he's asleep?" Salma asked her husband as he took the empty seat next to her.

"I believe so," he smiled at everyone and took a quick sip of his wine, relaxing in his chair before leaning around my sister to meet my eye, "Glad you made it." His blonde hair looked disheveled as if my nephew had tugged on it several times, and I noticed the dark circles of sleep-deprived parenthood lingering under his bright blue eyes.

"Thanks," I nodded.

"*Finally*, we can eat," Raina sighed, earning a tut from our mother in disapproval. Raina ignored our mother and scooped a large forkful of food into her mouth, letting out a satisfied groan as she chewed our mother's homemade cooking.

My father laughed at the youngest Ansara child, and soon we were all digging in.

After a few minutes of mild chit-chat about our week, how delicious the food was, and thanking my mother again for cooking (because while she was married to a professional chef, my father still enjoyed my mother's homemade Syrian meals more often than not), I saw my mother prepare herself for her upcoming question with a quick dab to her lips with her napkin.

As soon as her dark eyes landed on me, I prepared myself.

"Now that you're the only one who is single here, have you considered putting yourself back out there again?" I tilted my head at my mother, raising my eyebrows in a way to let her know that she should already know the answer to that question.

"If I'm barely able to make it to family dinner on time," I replied, mindlessly dragging my food around on my plate with my fork, "I don't see how I could possibly fit in time to date anyone," not that I was against the idea at all. Finding a life partner was definitely something I was interested in, but…logistics. I took another bite and chewed thoughtfully for a moment before adding, "The only people I interact with all day are coworkers."

At my words, Raina and Salma both lifted their heads to exchange a look with each other, and I felt something spike in my nerves at the secretive glance they gave each other. I would have missed it if I hadn't happened to look over at them myself.

"Have you brought up the idea of you stepping down again?" Ben asked, his eyes on his plate as he scooped another bite.

"I'm working on it," I nodded, "I even found some people that I thought would be a good replacement for me. I forwarded the names to Brandon earlier today." I had been sitting at my desk, after receiving the email that held the link to yet another investors meeting. A meeting that I loathed taking part of, because I found myself dissociating throughout them out of pure, mind-numbing, boredom. But that wasn't what made me pause at reading the email. No, what made me pause when I accepted the invite link was how used to these meetings I had become. How I didn't even tense or cringe at the thought of attending another. Instead, I was *used* to attending these meetings. These meetings were just a regular part of my work routine, and I had a moment where I realized how much I hated it.

So instead of carving out time to iron out the talking points I was expected to discuss during the meeting, I took an hour researching possible candidates for Chief Technology Officer on my own. I figured that I wanted to be involved with whoever replaced me anyway, to ensure that they were qualified and a good fit for the role.

Once I had several options listed, I checked Brandon's schedule to see if he would have time in the next couple of days to discuss my replacement options.

However, it looked like his calendar was completely packed, so I opted to just forward him the email with the subject line "Zaid's replacement" to hopefully catch his attention.

I understood the need for me to step into the role of CTO two years ago, how we wanted to look like an established company that people would be comfortable investing their money in. But we had just received a significant round of Series A funding, which meant that now the company was stabilized and prepared for growth for the time being, it also felt like a good time to hire someone prepared to be CTO long-term.

That way, I could go back to getting my hands dirty in the code I had personally written.

As much as I appreciated the monetary benefits of holding a title like Chief Technology Officer, I missed doing what I loved even more.

"Hopefully they can find someone to relieve you soon enough," my father nodded, "Though I don't mind when you decide to take your fancy meetings at my restaurant, either."

I grinned, "I'd much rather go to your restaurant to enjoy myself, not to schmooze people for money."

My father laughed, nodding in agreement.

"And then you can have time to open that kind heart of yours to love," my mother nodded once to herself, making Ben huff a laugh under his breath at my mother's desperation to see her only son happy with someone. I turned to give my brother-in-law a traitorous look but instead got distracted by seeing Raina and Salma exchange yet another glance between the two of them.

Something was up with them, and when Raina lifted her eyes to meet mine after having what looked like a telepathic conversation with Salma, she snickered to herself and shook her head before focusing back on her food.

Excellent, so their secrecy had something to do with me.

I didn't love that.

"Maybe," I replied to my mother before the conversation turned to what projects Raina was working on at school. The rest of the dinner went on uneventfully. My father squeezed my mother's hand to thank her and started to gather our dishes to wash. As my father left with our plates in his hands, I leaned back in my chair to catch Ben's attention behind Salma's back.

Do you know what that's about? I mouthed the words to him in a low whisper while my mother and Salma were distracted by their conversation.

Ben blinked his wide blue eyes at me, chewing his bite some more before swallowing and mouthing back, *yes, but* and then he zipped his lips closed with his pinched fingers.

I huffed and mouthed, *Because of your wife?*

"Of course," he replied at a normal volume, lifting one last bite to his mouth before gathering his own plate to follow my father to the sink.

Noticing the conversation happening behind her back, my sister whipped her head towards her husband, hissing between her teeth, "Did you tell—"

"No, my love," Ben shook his head and gently patted her shoulder, before standing and retreating.

"Good," Salma gave her husband's back a warning look, making him smirk at her over his shoulder and then at me before standing next to my father at the sink and grabbing a dish towel to dry the dishes.

I felt my heart start to race with nerves. My sisters were sneaky, and clearly acting suspicious tonight. I didn't want to overthink anything, but the fact that Ben was sworn to secrecy about whatever they were up to didn't bode well for me.

Finally, after chatting and laughing and wishing everyone a good night, I decided to excuse myself early to go home and sleep. It had been a long day, and I was desperate for at least a full night's rest without my phone blowing up with another issue that someone needed my immediate input on.

I embraced my mother and father before tying my shoes back on and shouldering my laptop bag, ready to sneak out the door just as my mother shoved containers of leftovers in my hands for me to take home.

"I'll help him carry those out," Raina chimed in, tugging the leftovers out of my hands, and elbowing her way out the door in front of me. I threw a curious look at Ben, who was now chatting with our father but gave me a subtle grin as he nursed the same glass of wine he had earlier with dinner.

"Oh, don't forget the bread," Salma added, following the youngest sibling out of the doorway, and leaving me in her dust. I released a tired sigh and followed them to my car, shutting my parents and Ben in the house behind me.

"What's going on?" I asked as my sisters carelessly tossed the leftovers into the passenger seat of my Model X. Thank goodness my mother bought quality Tupperware, otherwise, my car would be a mess now.

"Do you know a woman named Sig-nee?"

I halted in my step, freezing almost entirely as my sisters now stood tall with crossed arms and narrowed eyebrows. My gaze bounced between both of their suspicious ones and before I could think better of it, I felt my nerves start to get the best of me.

One mention of that woman, and my body immediately tried to betray me.

I found myself standing stock still, instead of relying on my go-to tells that involved clearing my throat and straightening the collar or cuffs of my shirt. Instead, I didn't move a muscle as I hoped that neither of them could see my face and ears heating up under the dim light of the streetlamp. Both of them studied me, waiting for me to give them something.

"Um," I cleared my throat once more, "She works at my company. Why?"

My sisters exchanged another look between themselves, one that made me almost groan with humiliation.

How did my sisters find out about Signe Lange?

More importantly, how in the *fuck* did my sisters find out about my wildly inappropriate attraction to the office manager?

"So you know, then?" Salma asked, pulling her phone out of her pocket, and leaning against my car. She didn't look comfortable, but I assumed it was difficult to find a comfortable position when you were seven months pregnant.

"Know what?" I asked. No way in hell was I giving anything away before they revealed their hand.

"About her book?"

I stared at them.

Raina blinked at me.

Salma started typing away on her phone.

"What book?" Maybe my sisters didn't know about my thoughts on Signe after all.

"Sig-nee's book. Well, I guess it's not a book yet." Salma looked up at me then, holding her phone a little closer to her chest as she appraised me.

I shook my head once before tossing my sister a bone by demonstrating the correct pronunciation, "Signe has a book?"

Raina narrowed her eyes at me, mirroring Salma's pose and leaning against my car, "So you *don't* know."

I shrugged my shoulders before shoving my fists in the pockets of my slacks, "Know what?"

Salma raised both of her eyebrows before tentatively stepping toward me and holding her phone out, "I want to discuss how to properly say her name in further detail, but that's not important at the moment. Did you know that she wrote a book about you?"

I felt my heart stop before it suddenly took off again.

"What?" I couldn't keep my mouth from falling open at her words.

"I'm actually kind of pissed at her," Salma explained, turning her phone screen towards me as she spoke, "I was so into this story. I loved the characters, but then she had to ruin it by revealing that *my baby brother* is the male lead."

I had no idea what she was talking about, so I took her phone and looked at the feed she had pulled up. It was a social media feed, and in the search bar was Signe's name as well as someone named Zayne.

There were dozens of images of Signe.

I tried not to focus on her picture too hard. It was the same reason I didn't stare at her too long at work. She took my breath away. She was a beautiful woman, with dark red hair, pale skin, and clear green eyes. Her smile was bright and wide and showed all her teeth, and her energy was contagious. I rubbed a hand over my mouth to stop myself from smiling at her picture in front of my sisters and instead tried to infer what they were talking about based on the images I was looking at.

After a few silent seconds, I gave them both a confused look.

"Here," Raina leaned over on my right, while Salma stood to my left, all three of us looking at Salma's phone, "This one." Raina tapped on an image, and a video started playing.

I huffed a laugh at the video, something my sisters gave me curious looks over as I realized that the scene looked familiar.

I was on my way to the break room when I heard Signe's voice echoing in the empty building. I had paused before I entered the break room because I wanted to make sure that I wasn't interrupting a private conversation before I refilled my coffee mug for the last time that day. After a few seconds of eavesdropping, I realized that Signe wasn't on a call with anyone, but instead, she was doing what must have been a livestream on the internet.

I didn't spend a lot of time on social media. I scrolled threads occasionally when I was curious about the topics that piqued my interest, but my own accounts were private and didn't have more than family members following me.

Filming or taking pictures of personal content at Sun Steer went against company policy, and while Signe didn't sound like she was posting anything problematic about the company, I still took the opportunity to mess with her by walking into the break room in the middle of her video.

I wondered if she would tell me what she was up to, but it looked like she ended the stream immediately after I had walked in. After playing a one-sided game of chicken with her, I decided to do my job and remind her of the company policy regarding social media.

I hadn't ever seen Signe stammer or struggle with words before, and I relished the feeling of seeing her tongue-tied in front of me, while also wanting to ease her concerns so she was back to her friendly, bubbly self.

It was immature of me to mess with her like that, but I'd had a long day, and it was entertaining. So no, I wasn't too surprised to see screenshots of myself waltzing through her video looking clueless. Technically, that was by design.

What I was surprised to see, however, were the comments that were left on the video and screenshots of the stream. The fact that this many people took screenshots and screen recordings of the stream wouldn't cross my mind until later. At the moment, I was just struggling to put pieces of a puzzle together.

> **WHO THE FUCK IS THAT?????!!!**
> **Is that THE ZAYNE I SAW?!**
> **Omg he's so hot.**
> **Doth my eyes deceive me, or did Zayne just**
> **casually walk through her stream?**
> **SIGNE IS THAT ZAYNE!!!!!**
> **Zayne is real?!**
> **I'd let that man step on me and thank him**
> **for it.**

"I..." I blinked a couple of times before adjusting my glasses and focusing back on the screen, "What is happening?"

"Signe wrote a novel about you," Raina explained, keeping her voice low so our family inside the house wouldn't hear, "A *romance* novel."

A blush immediately burned my face, my skin suddenly felt too tight and too hot. I lifted my free hand to cover my mouth in an attempt to look like I was mindlessly rubbing my jaw, but mostly because I didn't want my sisters to see the heat darkening the color of my cheeks and ears.

"Oh..." I couldn't gather any other words than that.

"*Oh,* is right," Raina kept showing me more pictures, comments, and tags, but everything was starting to blur while my mind spun.

"I was following this story so religiously," Salma whined, "When I heard that she got picked up by an agent, I screamed. You can ask Ben."

"Agent?" I asked. I don't know why that word stuck out to me the most, but it did.

"Yeah, for her books," Raina explained, "Sig-yuh is a romance author. She just recently got picked up by an agent and she's going to try to publish her story."

"And she will," Salma nodded, "I do not doubt it. The

fact that she has this many followers from this one storyline of hers is telling."

I felt the pinch in my brows deepen as I tapped on what looked to be Signe's account, @ReadHeadedWriter, and saw that she had almost twenty thousand followers. Twenty *thousand*. Her account was public, and when I scrolled through her feed, I realized that this account must have been relatively new.

And she already had *that* many followers.

"So...she writes romance..." I was struggling to form words still. Raina nodded her head encouragingly at me, reaching her hand over to tap on a cartoon illustration that Signe had been tagged in.

It was me.

I mean, it wasn't. It was a cartoon.

But it was me.

Glasses, hair, beard, button-down shirt, physique. When I noticed two specific veins on the cartoon's forearms, I resisted the urge to roll up my sleeve to see if it was truly the same as mine. The cartoon-woman that cartoon-me stood next to was seemingly random. Some small brunette woman who sparked no familiar faces in my memory.

"I hate that I didn't see it before," Raina spoke up, "I get the ick looking at the fan art now."

"This is fan art?" Why did my voice sound so raspy?

"Yeah, that's how big this story is in the online romance readers groups," Salma explained, "She started posting chapters online, as like a free fanfic kind of thing. Then, readers blew it up. That's how her agent found her and reached out to work with her. But now that she's signed, she's writing a full-on manuscript. It's going to be a physical book you can buy at bookstores and stuff."

I had no words.

Signe Lange, the woman who starred in an embarrassing number of my late-night fantasies, wrote a romance novel about *me*.

My brain felt like it was short-circuiting.

"...So..." I cleared my throat for what felt like the thousandth time, "How do we know for sure it's me?"

The imagery was telling, but it could all be a coincidence.

It could be any other Arab-looking man.

"All the comments during her live feed tonight, for one," Raina pointed out, tugging the phone from my hands, and handing it back to Salma. Her hazel eyes narrowed at me as one eyebrow of hers arched, "And the guilty look on her face as she read the comments."

The last image I saw on my sister's phone was of Signe's face near the end of the stream, which had a beautiful blush on it.

"She ended the livestream as soon as people started asking if *you* were Zayne," Salma explained, as she tucked her phone into the back pocket of her leggings, "Which makes her look guilty. Since then, everyone has been sharing screenshots of your blurry face and Zayne fan art, and *ugh*." Salma made a face that looked like she was about to throw up, "I have very mixed feelings reading a romance novel with a character whose looks are inspired by my brother."

I reached a hand up to rub my forehead.

Signe, the office manager, was currently writing a romance novel.

A romance novel that starred me, for some reason.

As far as I knew, Signe had never once shown a romantic interest in me. Not that there had been any opportunities for her to do so. I usually avoided her because of my inappropriate crush. That, and office relationships were generally frowned upon, and my status as CTO would make any hypothetical relationship dynamic problematic. Workplace attraction happened, so I had heard, and I figured the attraction between us had been one-sided. I had never considered, not even once, that Signe—

"This sucks," Raina spoke up, making me tune back into my sisters' discussion.

"I know, part of me hates that we won't get to read the rest of Zayne and Sydney's story." Salma sighed.

I shook my head in confusion at her words, "Why is that?"

They both gave me pointed looks before Salma explained, "Because you'll have to fire her. Then she will probably have to scrap the project because of how... unprofessional it is."

I snapped my mouth closed, thinking about that for half a second before blurting out, "Why?"

They both raised their eyebrows at me, making me feel ganged up on.

"Because your employee is writing a romance about you without your consent? Filming content for it on company property?" Raina asked, as if the question was rhetorical, "Because she's been posting about how she wants to quit her office job and be a writer full-time, and the one shot she had at achieving that dream, she decided to cross professional boundaries?"

All thoughts in my brain came to a halt.

"Wait," I held a hand up as I rubbed both of my temples with my fingertips, "Signe wants to quit?"

"That's the part that you—" Salma blinked, and even I could tell that something clicked in her brain at that moment before she asked, "You *are* going to fire her, right?"

I hesitated, before irritation with my sister's meddling took over, "Why do I need to do that?"

Signe wanted to quit. She didn't want to work at Sun Steer anymore. It made sense, it wasn't like her position offered a lot of room for growth. But she had been so happy and upbeat there. I had no idea that she wanted to quit. That she was looking for a reason to.

I ignored my sister's staring and thought about it some more.

If I had stumbled into Signe Lange on the street, outside of the office, would I have tried to talk to her? To get to know her?

Yes.

Absolutely, how could I not?

That question didn't require a lot of further thought.

Would I have wanted to ask her out after getting to know her?

Also, yes.

I wanted to ask her to dinner currently, and that was just based on professionally interacting with her at the office for the past year, but I couldn't. Because I was her superior, and the ethics of the situation made it obvious where that line was.

Raina started talking again, but I held a hand up as I stared at my car behind my two sisters. She stopped talking, and I could feel both of their stares impatiently waiting for me to gather my thoughts.

But...if Signe wanted to quit, then she would no longer be my employee...

"I could fire her..." I mumbled, making Raina's eyebrows shoot up with surprise.

"Or...?" She pressed, because, clearly, I was trying to think through some other options.

"...Or, I could just *wait* for her to quit." I felt my lips turn up a little at the thought and before my hand could block the movement, my sisters practically jumped on me.

"What?" Salma gasped.

"Why?" Raina grabbed one of my arms, and I quickly shrugged her off before gently walking around the two women and making my way towards my car.

"Thank you for the intel," I waved a hand dismissively at them as I opened the door and made my way into the car.

"Intel?" Salma asked, waddling over to the car, and placing a hand on the hood as I shut my door. I rolled the window down so that I could hear her talk because clearly, she wasn't ready to let me go yet, "Intel for what? This isn't a problem for you?"

Weirdly, no.

I knew it should. Logically, I knew that part of me should be disturbed that my employee was writing a romance novel with a man based on what I looked like. However, that wasn't what I focused on.

Instead, I felt flattered.

I guessed it was true what they said, how attraction really did determine if someone's actions were considered unsettling or endearing.

"I'll keep you posted." I waved to my sisters before rolling up my car window. Salma took the hint and released her hold on the hood, stepping back with Raina as the two stared at me with wide eyes as I drove off.

My blood was rushing in my veins.

It was an indescribable high I had, knowing that I was the inspiration for Signe's project. A *romance* novel.

I had originally intended to get as much sleep as possible that night, but now I had other plans. Plans that included scouring the internet for every word that Signe

Lange had typed. If this is what she did outside of work, I was desperate for every crumb. Every detail. What made her choose me? Was it entirely my physique? Was it the way I held myself in the office?

I felt my face heat again at the thought of her observing me in such a way.

I wasn't a prude by any means, but I did get a thrill knowing that *that* woman appreciated what she saw. I wasn't flashy like other men, though I liked to wear nice clothing, thanks to my sister's encouragement. I wasn't out every weekend trying to get laid. As far as I knew, I didn't have a natural charisma that drew women in. I was more reserved and dedicated to work as of late. Envious of the partnerships that my sisters had found and the family that Salma was creating.

But this knowledge my sisters gave me changed some things. Within the span of one evening, brushing off my attraction to the office manager as pointless was no longer necessary. Especially if Signe wanted to eventually quit her job at Sun Steer to pursue her own goals, anyway. Now, I felt like I just needed to be patient, spend this time getting to know her better, and maybe work on putting myself out there without making her suspicious that I knew her little secret.

I imagined what it would be like to have Signe truly reciprocate my attraction, to earn those flirty little looks she gave everyone who passed her desk at the office. To earn her wide smiles outside of work, to spend one-on-one time with her. To see little pieces of her glowing personality for myself.

To finally, possibly, know for myself what those tempting lips of hers taste like.

As I turned into my condominium and parked my car, I

sat in thought about my mother's pressing questions at dinner tonight. How I wanted to eventually settle down.

I was pretty sure that I wanted kids if my future wife happened to want the same.

What did Signe want?

It was too soon to know, or even ask, but I still wanted to find out one way or another. Even if she didn't seem like a kid person, I didn't think that mattered to me as much as just having a chance with her. This new perspective of Signe lit a fire under my ass, feeling motivated to try. To not try to distance myself from her as much as possible, but to even return the attention she was willing to give me.

Needless to say, I didn't sleep as much that night as I had originally planned.

SIGNE

I WANTED TO DIE.

That was a little dramatic, but the thought of walking into work the next day made nerves erupt in my stomach and the urge to vomit consumed me.

Deep breaths, Signe.

I kept reminding myself that I hadn't received any emails from work. I hadn't heard anything about this from Jaqueline or Mary or Jamie, which was promising. As far as I knew, no one at work knew about my novel. About my following. This was a good sign, and even though I finally revealed my face in my livestream yesterday, I was still entertaining the idea of scrapping the project entirely.

The bummer was, I had almost thirty thousand followers now.

That was a lot of people that I would disappoint if I scrapped the project. A project that was far enough along to already be under developmental edits at this very moment.

Perhaps I could alter Zayne's appearance in the newer manuscript? I still wasn't sure.

"Signe!" I jumped at the sound of my name. I had been

standing in front of our building debating even bothering to show my face today when Mary called from behind, "Whoa, are you alright?"

I pasted a smile on my face at the sight of my favorite engineer approaching with her studded laptop bag over her shoulder, "Sorry. I didn't sleep well last night."

"Oh, that sucks," Mary made it up to my side, "Is that why you zoned out on your way in?"

"...Yup." I followed Mary into the building without another word. I let her scan her badge to access the elevators first, and step onto the fourth floor of our building first, as she chatted about a new anime she had been watching. I nodded and smiled at her ramblings about her favorite scenes and action sequences, and when she finally waved goodbye after seeing me to the front desk, I settled into my chair with stiff limbs.

Feeling numb, I clicked the desktop to life.

Ignoring the stab of anxiety in my stomach, I opened my work email.

Preparing myself for the worst, I held my breath as I tapped on my unread emails and saw...nothing.

Well, not nothing. I already had a to-do list thanks to Brandon, but nothing that would hint at me losing my job.

The more I scanned my work email, as well as my personal, just to be sure, I realized that it hadn't hit the fan yet.

And then I thought about it some more.

I was part of a very specific, very niche online community. It wasn't a place that would create headlines, and even when things like my stories went viral within those circles, they never made it out to mainstream social media spaces.

Call me crazy, but I had a feeling that not a lot of people

in the office read romance novels. Let alone were subscribers, or friends with the subscribers to my accounts that still had my real name.

Perhaps accidentally revealing Zayne's inspiration wasn't as catastrophic as I originally thought. Maybe I panicked too soon, and none of this was really that deep.

I hesitated for a moment, my finger hovering over the email refresh button after clicking it again, wondering what to do with this information.

Did that mean that I just...kept marketing the story?

Maybe if I never acknowledged the resemblance between Zayne and Zaid, the internet would just forget about it. In fact, the more I thought about it, the more likely that everyone had moved on and was sharing a viral cat video or something.

Unfortunately, my anxiety was still there, lingering, the rest of the morning.

Even though everyone smiled and waved and even initiated small talk with me as they passed by the front desk, I was jumpy. I was nervous. I felt like any second, everything would come crashing down around me. Any second now, Jacqueline would pull me into her office to fire me for inappropriately writing about the CTO.

This is why when Nikhil snuck up in my blind spot and rapped his knuckles on my desk, I almost fell out of my seat, making his eyes widen and lean forward as if he was about to help me before I could tip over completely.

"Are you alright?"

"Yes!" I laughed at myself, both for startling Nikhil and for the chaos my nervous system was experiencing.

"I'm so sorry, I didn't mean to surprise you," Nikhil relaxed as I sat straighter in my chair and took a drink from my water bottle, "I was just wondering if you could do me a favor."

"Sure," I smiled as I capped my bottle and set it beside my computer.

"Can you call the restaurant to see if they can add another person to the reservation?" Nikhil asked with a twist of his fingers.

"I can," I sent him a small grimace, "But they might not let me."

"Yeah, I know it's last minute, but Padma decided to join me. She said she was fine dining by herself somewhere else that night, but..." Nikhil shrugged, and I was momentarily distracted by the love that shined in his eyes almost instinctually at the mention of his wife's name. I smiled and gave him a thumbs-up.

"I'll do my best," at that, he thanked me and sauntered off while I found the number for the restaurant where they would be dining, and called.

Every quarter, Brandon would gather a group of management employees to go on a work trip. It was only classified as a work trip because everyone still conducted work, and the company footed the bill. The reality was, that it was a group of employees who were all friends with each other and wanted a change of scenery from the office.

Last time Brandon asked me to book rooms at a resort near San Diego for three nights. This time, they were all going to the Ritz Carlton in Santa Barbara.

Did Brandon offer to do this for any of the lower-level employees?

No.

Did he ask me to keep the details of this trip quiet so the lower-level employees didn't get jealous?

Yes.

Did he bother to invite *me* on their fancy work trips? Also, no.

Nikhil's friendly demeanor aside, this was clearly a *man's* club—except for Mary, who had been invited by Nikhil to join them in Santa Barbara. I had a feeling that this was management's way of diversifying these weird outings, while also allowing everyone to get the vibe on each other before they promoted her to a higher managerial position.

Good for Mary.

If any other employee deserved an invite, it was her.

Don't worry, I was still secretly bitter about not being invited myself even though I scheduled and organized everything.

I hung up with the restaurant before messaging Nikhil that the reservation was updated with no problems. It was Friday, and I was already thinking about what my weekend was going to look like. Would I write a little for the second story like I had planned? Was it weird to keep writing at all even though Zaid's face had been exposed to my following?

"Signe," I heard a familiar deep voice speak, making my fingers freeze over my keyboard in the middle of a report I was filling out for Brandon.

"Mm?" I asked, pretending to be deep in thought as I forced my fingers to keep typing. The reality was, I didn't want to face him just yet. I also couldn't form words without my voice giving away my weirdness, so I took the opportunity I had to look the part of a "busy office manager" and calm my frantic nerves.

"Are you busy?" I both heard and felt his elbows rest on the front desk I sat at. It had a top ledge that concealed most of my computer screen, leaving just my head and shoulders available to whoever entered the floor. That being said, even though that should have provided a decent enough space to keep me separated from whoever was on the other side, the way that Zaid leaned his forearms on the ledge and hunched toward me made me think I was suddenly sitting at the smallest desk in the world.

"One sec," I flicked my eyes over at him, giving him what I hoped was a rueful smile and not a smile that said, "I have written dirty, dirty things about you and I am filled with anxiety about it." I quickly looked back at my report and deleted and retyped the same sentence a couple of times, because the one glance I gave myself happened to be direct eye contact with him. And I could feel the heat my body created in my face and neck knowing that I had his full attention. That he was peering at me intently with his lovely brown eyes, instead of looking away like he usually did.

Why wasn't he looking away this time?

Ohmygodheknows.

I froze at the thought, retyped the sentence one last time, and sat taller in my chair like I was finally ready to give him my full attention. Then I realized that was not normal of me and decided to casually slump against the back of my chair and sway side to side before I finally forced myself to face him again.

He didn't smile, he didn't smirk, but his dark eyes looked slightly amused, and I forced myself to keep eye contact as a way to prove to myself that I could be normal around him.

"What's up?" I asked, internally high-fiving myself at how cool and casual I sounded. As if this was just any other workday. As if he was just any other member of management. As if I didn't once picture him licking my neck —I mean my protagonist, Sydney's, neck—multiple times for the sake of authentic writing.

Zaid lifted one of his forearms off the ledge, holding a card in his hands, "Could you run out and grab some more coffee filters? We're out, and it's still morning." ...*Oh, maybe he doesn't know*. At his words, I glanced at the clock to see that it was barely after ten a.m. and that most people were still nursing their first coffees at this point. Then I remembered that he had refilled his coffee after six p.m. yesterday and wondered if it was just him who had used the last of the filters before the delivery of the new stock arrived today.

"We should be getting the case of new ones within an hour or two," I lifted a shoulder, "Is there any chance you could wait for it to arrive? I need to finish this for Brandon first, and I probably won't do that before the delivery comes anyway."

Zaid's lips turned down the slightest bit, his dark brow furrowing as if he wasn't expecting that answer. He lowered his hand with the card and released a sigh.

"I guess."

I scoffed. It was with a closed mouth and mostly through my nostrils. The noise made his eyes lift to meet mine again, and I felt inclined to tease him, just a little bit, "Do you think you'll make it?"

"Make it?" Zaid asked, his brow smoothing a little at my words.

"Without caffeine for an hour? Maybe two?" I explained. I had teased Zaid like this in the past. I teased everyone in the office like this. He had engaged with my riffs as little as he needed to, and usually turned away to make conversation with someone else or wait for me to finish before politely excusing himself.

Zaid's lips twitched a little, "It might be a close call."

"There are other beverages at your disposal here, in case you're curious about branching out," I adjusted myself in my seat, and I noticed how his eyes glanced down towards my waist as I did. It wasn't an inappropriate glance. It was just a reaction from movement taking place in front of him, but for some reason I found myself crossing my legs over each other as if he was undressing me with his eyes.

Simply because he was attractive, and my body responded accordingly.

His gaze quickly met mine again, unaware of the effect he had on me.

"Are there? I had no idea," He shook his head once, his expression serious and slightly confused as he confirmed his words, but my heart skipped a beat. I expected him to say something like, "I know" and then politely excuse himself and walk away. But he wasn't. He was playing along.

Oh my god, Zaid Ansara is playing along.

"Well, believe it," I nodded solemnly, "There's this thing called water." He wrinkled his nose at that, disgusted, and I snorted half a second before my hand came up to smother the sound, "I can't tell if that was you playing along or if that was your genuine reaction to water." I spoke through giggles behind my hand.

Zaid's lips twitched, and a hint of a smile ghosted his features as he observed my giggling, "It's just so...bland."

"What are you, seven?"

"How does that make me seven?"

I was grinning, so shocked and delighted because this was the longest conversation that I had ever had with Zaid that wasn't work-related, "You can't appreciate water for the hydration it provides?"

"I don't think that the fact that I like flavor outside of the taste of pipes and fluoride makes me seven." Zaid raised an eyebrow, and my heart fluttered. It wasn't flirtatious, but it was flirtatious. There was no way that Zaid was suddenly flirting with me at work, but my romance-loving brain and my body's reaction to his playfulness didn't care. My nervous system reacted as if he was eyeballing my chest.

He wasn't, unfortunately.

"I would argue that most children go through a phase where they only drink juice or milk because of the flavor, before they grow out of it and accept that drinking water is delicious too." I lifted an eyebrow back at him.

At this, his head tilted at me the slightest bit, "Do you have children?"

I blinked. Heat filled my chest and neck at his abrupt personal question, but I didn't let myself expose my surprise before I answered, "No, but I've been around a child or two."

"Nieces and nephews?" Zaid asked, his facial expression looked as if we hadn't been joking about his dislike of water before. Now we were onto a completely new subject matter.

"Um. Kind of? I have friends who have a cute little kiddo." I wouldn't say who because I didn't know if Zaid was into hockey. I wanted to lean towards no, but I didn't want to share who my friends were too openly just in case he was.

Zaid nodded once, blinking, and looked down the hallway as if he realized that this was a personal conversation in the workplace. Something he never engaged with. Well, that probably wasn't true. He was good friends with Nikhil, and they probably talked about not-work things all the time. But this was the first time he and I had ever asked questions about each other regarding anything outside of the company.

I could feel him retreating, and I didn't want him to.

"Do you?" I asked, resting my elbows on my desk, and settling in.

He stood up from resting his arms on the ledge and glanced back down at me, "Do I what?"

"Have kids?" I pressed, "Nieces? Nephews? Pets?"

Zaid huffed a laugh at that last one before leaning a hip against the front desk and pulling his phone out of his pocket to check it, "No pets, no kids. Just one nephew, and my sister is expecting another soon."

"That's exciting, tell her I said congrats!"

"For what?" Nikhil asked from a few feet away. His approach didn't startle me, but it did disappoint me. I wondered if Zaid would stop talking about himself with the three of us present.

"I was telling Signe that Salma's pregnant again," Zaid explained to Nikhil. His eyes brightened as he clapped Zaid on the shoulder once.

"Congrats! That's one Ansara kid down, two to go."

I blushed, not fully understanding Nikhil's comment, but suspecting what it meant.

To my utter amusement, Zaid blushed too. His ears turned redder than the rest of his face and neck, "Don't remind me."

"You're right, your mother is probably reminding you enough." Nikhil laughed, sliding his glance over to me and leaning in as if he were sharing a secret, "She is desperate for him to find a woman to bring home."

I widened my eyes and grinned at Zaid, "RIP you."

"Thanks," Zaid sighed as if it was the worst thing in the world. I couldn't relate. My mother didn't give two shits if I dated or not. She was absorbed in her pottery most of the time, and just wanted me to be happy and find joy in life. Whether or not that included a partner didn't matter either way.

I mean, I did want a partner. But I was also willing to be single forever if I didn't find anyone that I was willing to partner up with. I wasn't trying to settle for anything.

"Any progress in that area?" Nikhil asked, leaning a

casual elbow on my desk, and resting his cheek on his fist. I decided to play along and leaned both of my elbows on the surface and rested my chin on my fists, too. Zaid smirked at the two of us before rolling his eyes and directing his next question at Nikhil, "Did you find someone to monitor the deployment for tonight?"

Aaaand I'm out.

I straightened in my chair and returned to my report for Brandon.

I worked at a tech company. I understood enough to get by and do my job well, but the nitty-gritty details of coding and software development and deploying new features on the app? That was none of my business.

Until someone else made it my business.

Then I would just ask Mary questions so she could interpret what someone was asking me to help them with.

Nikhil also straightened as he responded to Zaid's question before the two of them turned away from my desk and started walking down the hall towards Zaid's office. I stared at their backs for a moment, giving myself time to admire Zaid's build without anyone noticing me, before getting absorbed in the mundane office work again.

That went...surprisingly well.

I doubted Zaid had any suspicions about my extracurricular activities.

Perhaps I should pursue acting or something.

It wasn't until I returned home that evening that guilt and anxiety seeped into my gut again, and I paced my small space for a while until I decided to think the situation through some more.

After scrolling on my social media content, I noticed that people were still asking about the whole Zayne/Zaid thing.

Frick.

I gnawed on my bottom lip in thought, my mind spiraling with the insane number of paths to take from this point forward, before my phone started vibrating in my hand with an incoming FaceTime call.

"Hellurr!" I heard Eloise St. James' cheerful voice as soon as her freckled face filled the screen.

"Hello to you, too!" I smiled as I plopped myself on my couch.

"I'm here too!" Iris, Eloise's daughter, squealed in the background before shoving her mom out of the image to grin at me.

"Hi, little Miss," I wiggled my fingers at her daughter, before she got distracted with something off to the side and immediately left to go do whatever it was four-year-olds did.

"I just wanted to call and see how the meeting with your agent went," Eloise turned the camera back to her, tucking her pale blonde hair behind her ears. In the background, her husband was chasing their four-year-old down the hallway of their home. Eloise easily tuned them out, pretending her husband wasn't riling their daughter up during her call.

"Oh my god," I was relieved to receive her excitement, because it made me put all my concerns about the Zaid clusterfuck on the back burner while I fangirled with my good friend about where my career was headed, "So good, Michelle is such a sweetheart and I really think she's going to help me get the story out there. Right now, we are working on developmental edits."

"Ooo," Eloise wiggled her pale eyebrows and winked, "I can't wait to read it."

"I'll be sure to send you an advanced copy if a publisher ends up wanting it." I had no idea if I could do that, and what I would hypothetically have control over, but whatever.

"Looking forward to it," She sighed, "I was actually calling to tell you something." Eloise looked a little excited but paused when her husband, Logan, and their daughter ran behind her again. Iris squealed maniacally as she barely escaped her dad's clutches.

Damn, I missed that little girl. It had been too long since I hung out with her.

"Are you ready?" Eloise focused back in, "Because...I'm pregnant!"

I gasped, my eyes bulged, and I immediately started squealing in excitement. I even went as far as to jump up off of my couch and run around my apartment for the theatrics of it all, "You're pregnant!"

"Yes!" Eloise giggled, matching my energy by getting up from her seat and doing a victory lap around her house with her husband and daughter, "I'm going to birth another one of his massive babies!"

I cackled, pausing my run to laugh at her first words after telling me she was expecting again. During my pause, Iris had reached up and yanked Eloise's phone down so her cute little dark ringlets could fill the screen and tell me, "I was a big, healthy, and strong baby!"

"Yes, you were!" Eloise nodded encouragingly at her daughter, her eyes softening when Logan finally scooped up little Iris and planted a chaste kiss at Eloise's temple.

Then the big guy turned to me and waved hello before walking away with a giggling Iris in his arms. It really looked like the man was enjoying retirement.

"Anyway, we need to get together again soon! We're going out of town for a few weeks with my parents, but maybe when we get back you and I can get breakfast or something together? Maybe a girl's night?" Eloise moved the phone so that her wide blue eyes took up the entirety of the screen. I could practically see the veins in the whites of her eyes with how comically close she put them to the camera.

"Of course!" I sighed as I slumped back on the couch again, "I doubt I'll have much going on unless the editing process ends up ruining my life."

Eloise rolled her eyes before pulling the camera away so I could see the rest of her gorgeous face, "Whatever, you're going to rock whatever it is you write. I'm so excited for you, you have no idea. I'm going to make Logan read whatever you end up publishing, too."

I widened my eyes, "I don't know how I feel about your husband reading smut that I wrote."

"We're all adults, it's fine," Eloise shook her head once before a loud crash sounded in the background, and her head jerked to the side, "Shoot, I should probably go."

"Sounds like it," I laughed, "Congratulations again!" I grinned, my cheeks hurting from the excitement I was feeling for my dear friend.

"Thank you! Talk to you soon!" Eloise pretended to kiss the camera before ending the call.

I laughed to myself, loving how chaotic her family life seemed to be.

Suddenly, my apartment felt empty, but that call with her really helped elevate my mood. My mood always elevated whenever I talked to Eloise, even more so when we actually got together, but I realized that unexpected call was probably what I needed to finally be able to take a deep breath and relax.

This allowed me to think more critically about how I needed to deal with my followers continually messaging me with screenshots of Zaid's blurred image from the livestream.

THANKFULLY, based on what I could see, nobody was able to snuff out Zaid's identity or real name, which made me breathe a sigh of relief. I didn't think he had any social media, which usually made me not trust a person. What could someone *possibly* be hiding if they actively chose not to have social media accounts? In this day and age, it was, in fact, an active choice to make.

This time, though, I realized that there were benefits to keeping your private life off of the internet. Like—and this is just an example—when your employee decides to write an open-door romance with a character who looks just like you, and the internet catches a glimpse of your face and realizes what she did.

I needed to say something. I had some readers privately messaging me begging for the details of the mystery man who walked through my live feed. Maybe if I just crafted some lame-sounding PR statement that wasn't necessarily a lie, but made it sound like Zaid wasn't the guy Zayne was based off of, the internet would calm down?

It was worth a shot.

I had worked too hard for this. I could see the light at the end of the tunnel. I didn't want it all to end.

I was desperate for success.

Chapter Five

ZAID

I DECIDED to consider that awkward interaction with Signe at her desk a success. We chatted, she flirted like she always does, and I did my best to reciprocate professionally, without looking too eager about it.

Regardless, I learned a lot after browsing the internet for anything Signe and her romance novel related, and I learned some things from my research.

Number one, her book was categorized as "open door" and she had already posted some explicit scenes on a free website that romance readers often used. I thought about reading it, but once I realized what I was reading, it almost felt like an invasion of her privacy. So, I decided to skip the more, well, intimate scenes of what she shared with readers.

She and I just weren't there yet.

Number two, the male lead in her story and I were very different people. Signe may have described Zayne for readers to picture me in their minds. However, our personalities were almost the opposite of each other. Zayne was confident. Flirty. Charismatic. He lit up a room with his presence.

That wasn't me.

That was more like Signe.

Zayne may have started off shy around the love interest, but he wasn't afraid of failure or rejection as he pursued Sydney. He was so confident that they were meant to be, that he had no problem respecting Sydney's boundaries until she was able to come to that conclusion herself.

And that was just what I found on the infuriatingly formatted website Signe had posted on. Who knew how much more developed her characters would be now that she was pursuing traditional publishing and had an agent in the industry supporting her?

After that, I realized that if I wanted to catch the attention of someone like Signe, I needed to take a step out of my comfort zone with her. Signe was social and approachable with everyone. I hadn't seen her *not* socialize with anyone in the office. It was partly why I never thought too much about gaining her attention, because she gave her attention to everyone who passed by her desk, and I didn't want to fill my head with delusions that I might have been special.

Now I know, at least, that there is something special about me, even if it just seemed to be my physique. But I couldn't blame Signe on that, because I hadn't gone out of my way to always reciprocate her attempts at casual conversation, so I figured I needed to extend a type of olive branch.

One thing I did notice after Nikhil and I started talking about that night's deployment, was how Signe immediately checked out of the conversation and focused back on her work.

I needed to get better at conversing with her, then.

Practice makes perfect, is what I told myself. I decided that while I was usually busy with meetings and putting out fires, it wouldn't take too much effort to greet Signe every day. I wanted to get to know her better, and I wanted her to get to know me better. I wanted to start to build a friendship with her so we could both see if a step in the romantic direction seemed possible.

If I was being honest, I was putting quite a bit of hope that Signe would be interested in me romantically as well, and not just as a pretty face to write about. We had our differences, like how she was clearly an extroverted woman who enjoyed trying new things (based on what I could sus out on her social media), whereas I sometimes found myself in a rut of familiarity and routine. I didn't mind the differences, in fact, I was in awe at how confident and social and simply *warm* she was. I couldn't think of a single person in the office who might not like Signe as a person.

Whereas, I had let my stress get the best of me at some points, making some sales reps and engineers tiptoe around me for a while.

From what I have heard, and learned on her social media accounts, Signe loved trying new restaurants. Perhaps taking her to my father's Italian restaurant for a first date wouldn't be a bad idea, because he only had great reviews for it.

No, then my father would just embarrass me with childhood stories the whole time. That option was out.

But I was getting ahead of myself. I wasn't sure Signe would even be willing to give me the time of day since she and I were so different.

Something that helped reassure me was that I also knew that Signe was an empathic person by nature. I had seen this empathetic side of her in action several times at the office. A while ago, Jacqueline was having a rough day because someone had unexpectedly quit without giving notice, and she was already someone everyone generally avoided interacting with because of her no-nonsense personality. Signe, however, had left her desk and went to Jacqueline's office to see how she was doing. I only knew this because as I was passing by Jacqueline's office on the way to Brandon's, I could hear Signe patiently listening to all of Jacqueline's complaints and woes, while also offering to help her out however she could. Even though Signe already had her hands full with her job.

Even though Jacqueline wasn't well-liked around the office, Signe didn't care.

Would she share that same attitude while seeking out romantic partners? I wasn't sure.

Considering this gave me a little bit of hope. A little bit of motivation to push myself and maybe take a tip or two from Zayne. To be a little more confident, a little more outgoing. It was the first time in my adult life I was willing to push myself in this way for the simple possibility of being with a woman like Signe. I was willing to accept how desperate this should have made me look, but I also didn't care.

"Knock, knock," I heard Salma's fake friendly voice from the doorway of my office, and I instinctively looked up at her to give her an annoyed look.

"How can I help—" My sarcastic remark died in my throat when Signe followed Salma in, holding little Zeki in her arms with the brightest grin on his face.

I had to clear my throat to control my emotions at the sight of Signe holding my nephew as if she had held him many times before. His bright blue eyes admiring her, and his cheeks that were slowly losing their baby chubbiness while rocking my sister's dimples made something tug in my chest.

"Mom wanted me to drop these off for you," Salma explained, holding up several small lunch-sized containers in her hands, "Mom overheard Ben say that you eat out for lunch most days, and she wanted to help you 'not waste money'."

I was torn between rolling my eyes at my mother's antics or grinning at the sight of Zeki playing with a lock of Signe's red hair.

"The company pays for my lunches, though," I found myself walking around the desk to take the containers of leftovers from Salma's hands, so she wouldn't have to balance them over her bump anymore. Once her hands were free, Salma gave me a smirk with raised eyebrows while she tucked her hair behind her ear, to let me know that she was *thrilled* to have officially met Signe like this.

"If you don't eat those, I will. It all smells amazing, and I won't snub a home-cooked meal," Signe spoke up, adjusting Zeki on her hip. The little boy instinctively tightened his little fists on her shirt, as if he was worried for a moment that she was going to set him down.

"Even though we just met Sig-nee out front, I think Zeki wants to keep her," Salma added, acting nonchalant about the fact that our office manager and her son were hitting it off. That didn't surprise me. Zeki was an excellent judge of character.

I saw Signe first, though.

I was more than willing to uphold dibs against a three-year-old.

"Does he?" I raised my eyebrows at the miniaturized version of Salma with blue eyes before speaking to Signe, "And feel free to eat as much as you want. I wouldn't want these to go bad." Half of the time, upper management used eating out as an excuse to have meetings that we didn't want other employees to interrupt or walk in on. Lunch was a loose term because even though food was present or we were at a nicer restaurant, work was still being conducted the entire time.

Because these lunch meetings wouldn't come to a sudden end, I didn't want my mother's food to go to waste. Plus, I liked the idea of Signe enjoying the Syrian and Lebanese food my mother prepared. I liked the idea of her enjoying part of my family's culture that way.

"I'm holding you to that," Signe smiled up at me, and quickly lowered her gaze to Zeki as he tugged a little roughly on the lock of red hair in his fingers, "Are you going to come back and visit me soon?" She then used her free hand to tickle his tummy, making him cackle with laughter and drop her hair from his grip.

"Zeki wanted to be held as soon as we walked in," Salma tilted her head towards me, before nodding at Signe and her son, "But I was struggling with holding the Tupperware and him, and when Sig-nee offered to hold him instead, he practically jumped in her arms." Salma smiled at me, another secretive look I couldn't quite understand flicking over her features.

"Ah," I nodded as if the pieces of the puzzle were all coming together, "He's wrapping her around his sticky little fingers." I tilted my head down towards Salma as if we were both observing this interaction in privacy instead of a foot away from Signe.

"Yes, he is," Signe crossed her eyes at Zeki, making him giggle as he put both of his hands on her cheeks to squish them together. Signe wasn't fazed by his touch, instead, she just laughed and uncrossed her eyes, squeezing him to her body as they both laughed at their silliness.

Zeki then grabbed a fistful of her shirt, accidentally tugging it down as he bounced happily in her arms while shouting, "Again!"

Signe quickly captured his hand and released his grip on her shirt, keeping her cleavage properly concealed for the workplace as she crossed her eyes at him again. I found my heart rate increased the slightest bit at the creamy skin my nephew almost revealed.

Don't obsess over a half second of the accidentally exposed cleavage, jackass.

I quickly glanced down at Salma, who gave me a suspicious look as she spoke up again, "Can I chat with you about something really quick? Are you busy?"

I was always busy, but I found myself much more agreeable in Signe's presence, so I nodded.

"Want to go see what snacks we can find in the break room?" Signe asked Zeki with a wiggle of her eyebrows. He nodded enthusiastically, so Signe lifted her head to address his mother, "Is there anything I shouldn't offer him?"

"Oh," Salma tilted her head, "Do you have anything back there not safe for kids?"

Signe explained, "I wasn't sure if there were any dietary restrictions he has, I didn't want to accidentally offer him something you wouldn't normally."

Salma and I both regarded Signe for a moment, touched at Signe's consideration. It made something in my chest ache.

Our family wasn't practicing Muslims and didn't uphold traditional practices like Halal. We weren't strict with religion beyond celebrating the holidays and weddings with our extended family who were. The fact that my mother married a non-Muslim, Italian man like my father, meant that we were raised less traditionally than our great-grandparents would have probably preferred.

The only thing that stuck with us from our Arabic heritage was our lack of interest in alcohol or pork, but our parents always made us feel safe to make those choices for ourselves.

"We don't eat pork, but I doubt any of the chips or cookies in the break room have that in them," Salma smiled as she studied Signe.

"I'll read the ingredients first anyway," Signe smiled and adjusted Zeki on her hip before turning around to leave, "Let's see who all we can say hi to on our way there."

Zeki giggled as they walked off and out of sight.

Salma closed the door behind them and followed me to my desk, before making herself comfortable in one of the seats that faced me.

"So...that's Sig-nee," Salma whispered, resting her hands on the edge of my desk as if we were planning something, "And I think I'm warming up to her."

I chuckled, shaking my head at her, and turned towards my desktop, "Is that what you wanted to talk about?" I asked, not reading any of the words on my screen.

"I really was just dropping off leftovers for you, but after meeting the woman who is actively writing fanfic about you, yes, I want to talk about Sig-nee."

"It's Signe."

"What?"

"Her name," I turned to look at her, still holding the edge of my desk and whispering like we were talking about a deep dark secret, "It's pronounced *Signe*. You keep saying it like 'Sig-nee'." I explained.

Salma blinked at me, "Pronounce it for me one more time?"

"Signe," I repeated, "Like see-nyuh."

"See-nyuh," Salma replied, "Signe."

"Right," I nodded with a sigh before clasping my fingers together on my side of the desk and facing her, "That's the French pronunciation, at least. I think the Norwegian pronunciation is more like 'sing-neh', but that's not how she has pronounced it in the past."

"I gotta be honest, I don't think I care about the history of her name's pronunciation that much," Salma tilted her head at me, "But it is fascinating that *you* do."

I lowered my brows at her, "She's an employee. It's not unrealistic for management to know how to correctly pronounce an employee's name."

"Especially if you plan on saying her name often," Salma raised an eyebrow at me.

"It's useful if I need to get her attention in an office with hundreds of employees, yes." I gave her a bland look.

"Or if you plan on calling out her name in the throes of passion."

"Sal—" I felt my ears and neck heat up, the situation my sister was hinting at both excited and humiliated me, which led me to gape at her.

"Oh my god, you *do*!" Salma gaped back at me in return, covering her mouth with both of her hands, "You want to sleep with Signe!" she whisper-hissed at me.

"I don't—" I rested my elbows on the desk while scrubbing a hand down my face in frustration, "I mean, yes. But that's not—"

"Is it just because she wrote smut about you? Because Zaid, you deserve better than that," Salma still kept her voice low, "There are plenty of other women out there who—"

I sliced a hand through the air, groaning in irritation and cutting her off, "Stop talking. You don't know what's going on."

"Then tell me," Salma held her hands up and out, clearly at a loss, "Because I don't understand why you're suddenly interested in one of your employees."

"I'm not *suddenly* interested," I glared at Salma, annoyed that she cornered me at work to have this conversation. My sister studied me before realization cleared her eyes and her lips parted in a small show of surprise.

"Oh," Salma's brow smoothed, "So...this isn't a new thing between you two."

"It's not anything between us, actually," I leaned to the side so that I could rub my forehead, struggling not to snap at my sister for not understanding what I hadn't told her yet, "But if she finishes the book, and it becomes as successful as you and Raina think it'll be, she can quit her job here." I paused, giving Salma a look of what I would assume to be exhaustion, based on how I was feeling in the moment.

She pressed her lips together, and I could almost hear the wheels in her head turning as she leaned forward and said, "And...if Signe quits working here...?"

I lifted a shoulder, feeling a little ridiculous saying it out loud, "...Maybe, if she seemed interested, I could ask her to dinner without risking a meeting with Human Resources."

My sister's eyebrows shot up again, and a playful smile spread across her cheeks as she leaned in again, "You think Signe's worried about HR? If that was the case, she wouldn't be staying up at night writing what she does about you." Then Salma's nose wrinkled, "Which reminds me, I need to get started on my neglected TBR to forget everything she has ever written about my baby brother."

I had no idea what a TBR was, but I rolled my eyes at her anyway.

"Maybe *I* worry about Human Resources," I retorted. I couldn't imagine someone like Jacqueline finding out about Signe's story. I could see Jacqueline's eye twitching already.

"Why don't you just fire her?" Salma asked with a tilt of her head, staring over my shoulder in thought, "I mean, then she wouldn't be your employee and you could ask her out."

"I feel like no woman would want to go out with a man who fired her for the sole purpose of being able to ask her out," I gave Salma a bored look. She nodded in agreement before I even finished my sentence, catching up with my train of thought.

"That makes sense. She has mentioned online wanting to quit her day job anyway. It should be her decision," Salma folded her arms on the edge of my desk again.

"Plus, this job works for her," I shrugged, "She has time to write. If she had to find another job, she may not be able to do that. I want to help her reach her goal...even if I have to pretend to not know about it for a while." I stared at my hands as I explained it to her. Silence filled the office for a moment, except for the ticking of a small clock on the shelving unit near the loveseat. After a few moments, I lifted my gaze to stare at my sister, who wasn't looking at me as if she was getting ready to tease me like I expected her to do.

"Zaid," Salma sighed as if just coming to some conclusion she already knew the answer to, "This...crush you have on Signe. You've had it for a while?"

I felt the heat of embarrassment coat my body upon hearing her question, even though I was a grown man, and it was normal for grown men to be interested in grown women. For some reason, the way my sister asked the question made me feel more self-conscious about it than I wanted to.

I didn't back down though.

I met her gaze and nodded my head once, confirming her theory.

"I see," Salma inhaled a deep breath, before blowing it out dramatically through flappy lips once. She studied something over my shoulder again, letting us sit in silence for a few moments before she nodded to herself and pulled out her phone.

"What are you doing?" I asked, narrowing my eyes on the sudden change of demeanor. She immediately went from relaxed and thoughtful, to sitting up straight and determined.

"I'm texting Raina," Salma explained, ignoring the groan of protest I made in my throat, "First, to let her know that there is more to this situation than she and I realized," Salma continued to thumb away on her phone, her eyes never leaving her screen as she spoke to me, "Second, to see if we can help you out."

"Help me out?" I asked, sitting back in my chair, and folding my arms, "I don't need your help."

"Yes, you do," Salma gave me a look of bored disbelief before returning to her message to our sister, "You have no game. Signe's probably used to men hitting on her left and right," those words made my stomach churn because she was probably right, "So you need to work very carefully here."

"I know that." In theory, though I was still fleshing out the plan regarding how this would all work. Before Salma had shown up in my office to give me the leftovers that were currently sitting forgotten on my desk, I was simply working myself up to approach Signe more. To just chat and get to know her better.

...Perhaps I didn't have "game" after all.

"First, she needs to see you as a friend." Salma glanced up at the ceiling as she quirked her lips to the side and pocketed her phone, "Actually, that part probably won't be hard. She just became best friends with my three-year-old in less than a minute. But you're also her superior here. So that's where we need to be careful."

"Salma, I'm serious," I used a tone I had used with my employees in the past, when I needed them to stop slacking, "I don't need your help. If anything happens with Signe and me, I want it to be because she and I made it happen, not because my sisters were bored and pried."

Salma quirked her lips to the side again in thought before replying, "Fine...but you do realize that eventually, you'll need to tell her that you know about her book, right?"

I gulped, anxiety started to fill my chest at the realization, "Why?"

"Are you kidding?" Salma asked, "You like her, right?"

"Yeah."

"And you want to date her? Not just casually, but like... *date* her?"

I frowned, "Yes." It was no secret to my sisters that I never got into the casual dating scene. I either wanted a connection with someone, or I didn't.

"Then eventually you need to tell her you know. One, because at some point it'll be her career, and this is a very foundational piece of her career. Two, because she will probably feel weird about it and want to tell you herself to clear the air, and if you wait for her to do that before you admit that you already knew about her romance novel, I don't know if she will appreciate that."

I blinked, because shit, Salma had a point.

But for some reason the thought of telling Signe that I knew about the book was distressing. It was something I would need to work myself up to.

"I'm just saying," Salma shrugged, "You don't need to tell her right away. In fact, I'd wait a little, in case for some reason, you pursue this and find out that you two aren't as compatible as you'd hoped. But don't wait until her dad is walking her down the aisle towards you to tell her, either."

I nodded and rubbed my chin in thought because that seemed reasonable. I didn't have to tell her right away, but if things started to get serious between us, that's when I would need to find the confidence to tell her that I knew about her side gig. Before we go on a first date, probably.

Just then, a knock sounded on my office door again, followed by Signe's muffled voice saying, "Quick! Now we gotta hide!" over the sound of my nephew's energetic cackle.

Salma smiled, chuckling to herself as we both stood from our desks to go answer the door. My heart was already speeding with the knowledge that I was interacting with Signe so much today. That perhaps stepping out of my comfort zone wouldn't be as big of a step as I thought it would be.

My sister opened the door and stepped to the side, putting a hand up to her brow as if searching far and wide for her son. We could both hear Zeki's giggles behind one of the large potted plants by my office. I also noticed how Jacqueline was peeking around her desktop to see what was going on out here with a small grin on her face.

"Come find us!" Zeki cried, followed by Signe shushing him through her own giggles.

"Where is Zeki?" Salma played along, hands on her hips as she stomped a little bit harder so her son could hear her approaching.

"Not here!" He called out, making Signe cackle at the hilarity of the toddler's logic.

"Not...here?" Salma jumped around the potted plant, making Zeki's laughter reach a shrill pitch as he ran out and threw himself into his mother's waiting arms. Signe stood to her full height, smiling wide at my sister and nephew as they embraced.

While Salma played with her son and tried to calm him down enough to leave, Signe stepped closer to where I was standing, crossing her arms over her chest as she addressed me, "Your nephew is the cutest."

"He is," I agreed, shoving my hands in my slacks attempting to look casual in her presence.

"I want to eat him."

I raised my eyebrows at her, a smirk tugging at the edges of my lips, "I think Salma might have an issue with that."

Signe turned back to my sister, who was currently munching on Zeki's chubby cheeks right where his dimple popped, and making him giggle, "...Would she?" Signe asked with a laugh and tilt of her head. I found myself staring at Signe's ample backside for a moment, because those jeans that she wore always drew my eye there, but I quickly lifted my gaze to my sister and scolded myself for being a jackass in the workplace.

"I'm willing to share," Salma laughed after nibbling on her son's cheeks one last time and settling him on her hip, "If you ever want to babysit, that wouldn't suck."

"I would love that," Signe responded, her eyes wide as if she genuinely would love nothing more than to babysit my nephew.

"Wait, really?" My sister got visibly excited, "That would be great! We never go out anymore because finding a babysitter is so tough."

"I'd really love to! Here, let me give you my number," Signe replied. Both women pulled their phones out while I frowned at my sister.

"I can babysit, too."

"You're too busy," Salma shook her head at me as she thumbed Signe's number into her device. Something darkened my mood a little at her words. She made it sound like I didn't have time for family, which wasn't exactly... wrong. How many times did I show up late to dinner? How many times did I blow off drinks with Ben and my father when they closed the restaurant because work got in the way?

I knew I was busy when I was a developer before I was promoted to CTO.

But I was never so busy that I couldn't make time for family.

Now that I thought about it, I hadn't heard anything from Brandon since I emailed him that list of possible replacements for me.

I studied Signe as she and my sister chatted some more about babysitting. Signe pocketed her phone and brushed her dark red hair behind her shoulders, going as far as to tuck some loose strands behind her ears. How confidently she became friends with both my sister and Zeki. I briefly pictured a future with Signe as part of the family, standing there in the middle of the office with them. How Signe would finish writing on her laptop at the end of the day and run over to my mother's house to help prepare family dinner. I could see Signe chasing little Zeki around my parent's island, giving my sister and her husband a break while they focused on fun adult tasks like cooking.

I thought about how in that scenario, I would still be arriving late to the dinner party as CTO.

I caught myself frowning and I corrected my expression before anybody noticed it.

I didn't want to keep being too busy. I wanted to show up on time. I wanted Salma to feel comfortable asking me to babysit whenever she needed. I wanted to show up at my dad's restaurant and grab lunch with him more often. I definitely wanted to be present at my parent's house when dinner was being made, not just when the food had gone cold. Maybe even watch a game with Ben or introduce little Zeki to the newest superhero movies coming out. I wanted to be part of the casual dinners, especially if I was considering bringing Signe home to meet my parents.

I...needed to really think about that.

"Say goodbye to Miss Signe!" Salma cooed, making me blink out of my spiraling thoughts as Signe leaned in to squeeze Zeki before saying goodbye.

"Bye!" Zeki shyly waved after his hug and snuggled into his mom's side before we all walked Salma and Zeki toward the elevators. Signe and I stopped next to her desk, and it wasn't until my sister and nephew disappeared behind the closing elevator doors that Signe turned and lifted a dark red eyebrow at me.

"What?" I asked.

"She called me Signe," she sounded accusatory, though the upturned curve of her lips let me know she wasn't upset about it.

I nodded once, not quite following.

"When she first got here, I introduced myself," Signe explained, tapping the employee badge she wore on her hip that had her company picture and name printed, "And even after I said my name, she called me Sig-nee." She lifted a shoulder and she casually walked around to her seat at her desk, "Which is normal. It didn't bother me at all, because that's what it's like living with a name like mine. I hardly ever correct people unless I think we are going to be seeing more of each other..." Signe sat down and grabbed the edge of her desk to pull her chair in, "But when she left your office, she called me Signe."

I shrugged my shoulders once, "I told her she was saying your name wrong."

"I figured," Signe smiled, a light pink color touching her cheeks, "...Thank you."

I attempted to look confidently casual, inspired by Zayne, "It's your name. It should be said correctly."

Signe stared at me, the light pink lingering on her cheeks before she gave me a shy smile and nodded, "You didn't have to correct her, but it feels nice to know that you did."

"Of course," I nodded, then awkwardly jerked my head back towards my office, "I gotta get back to work." I was nervous that, due to how rapidly my heart was beating from this one-on-one conversation I was having with her, and after being busted for teaching my sister how to say her name, that I would blurt out something else. Something like, "I love the sound of your name and it feels like a sin to let others say it incorrectly" or "Last night I had a dream that you sat on my face."

Both of those options were mortifying, so I opted for removing myself from the situation and ending on a high note.

"Don't forget to put your mom's leftovers in the breakroom fridge for me," Signe called out when I started my return. I glanced at her over my shoulder and threw her a grin, and I felt my heart thump heavy one time at the bright look in her eyes when she saw my smile.

"You got it," I gave her a thumbs up before continuing my retreat to my office. I didn't see anything as I made my way back, too lost in my thoughts about the realizations I had in the last few minutes since my sister let herself into my office.

Chapter Six

SIGNE

"ARE YOU READY?" Jacqueline asked, startling me out of my zone. I blinked up at her hovering over my desk before I quickly checked the time on my computer screen to confirm.

"Oh, yes, let me just save this really quick," I clicked out of the reports I was working on and locked my computer screen, before standing and pushing my chair in, "Do you have the list from Nikhil?" I asked her.

Jacqueline frowned, leaning her weight on one hip and tapping through her iPad. I took a moment to admire Jacqueline. I assumed that she was only a year or two older than me, but she was interesting because some days she looked a lot younger. I had already asked her about her skincare routine in the past, and she told me that she just washes her face with the same Head and Shoulders shampoo she uses for her hair.

I then asked her what it was like to be God's favorite, and she snorted before blushing and walking away.

Jacqueline was a tough nut to crack. Some days she would wear jeans and sneakers, making me feel like she was

101

a normal grown woman capable of silly friendships and teasing and joking. Other days, like today, she wore her pencil skirt with a button-up blouse. Her shiny brown hair pulled back into a tight bun, not a hair out of place. Glasses resting on her nose. This made her look older, I thought. Like a mature woman whose idea of fun was sipping wine and discussing finances and investments.

Like someone who played Monopoly because they actually enjoyed it and weren't bullied into it.

Other days, like when she wasn't interviewing potential new employees, she sometimes wore jeans and a button-up shirt, with sneakers. Her hair would be at least half down, her glasses only coming down from their perch on her head to read something in front of her.

During interview days, she was the epitome of professionalism.

I understood the need to dress a specific way, though. Women always struggled to be taken seriously in any male-dominated field. Our clothes sometimes became armor, designed to show authority. To make others take us seriously.

"Cute skirt," I smiled at her as I stood up and grabbed my own iPad and phone.

"Oh," Jacqueline looked down at herself as if remembering that she wore a skirt today, before giving me a shy smile and muttering, "Thanks." Then she blinked down at her iPad and said, "I don't have Nikhil's list, can you pull it up?"

I nodded and tapped away on my own iPad to the email he sent us, giving her a thumbs up and following her to the conference room. Most of the interviews were going to take place via video call, and neither of us had cameras hooked up to our work computers. So, using the conference room, and projecting the interviews on the screen, was what we opted to do.

Nikhil's interview schedule that he asked me to sit in on a couple of weeks ago, ended up conflicting with the managerial retreat to Santa Barbara. So, Jacqueline and I were stuck here, not sitting by the pool or on the beach, but instead going through first-round interviews for potential candidates for Nikhil to hire for his team.

Knowing that they were all living it up at the Ritz Carlton while Jacqueline and I covered interviews, I secretly hoped everyone there got a sunburn. Or at least didn't read any of the signs at the Santa Barbara beaches and got a bunch of tar stuck to the bottoms of their feet.

As we entered the conference room, waving hello to a passing intern who was watching over the front desk while I helped interview, I felt my phone buzz in my pocket.

I pulled my phone out to see a message from Mary.

> Mary: It's such a bros club here, but it's easy to ignore the insane testosterone levels when I'm sunbathing at eleven am.

> Me: I hope you forgot sunscreen.

I smirked as Jacqueline held the door to the conference room open for me to walk through.

> Mary: I wish you were here, I'd love to have another uterus to talk to.

> Me: Be sure to mention that to the bros next time they ask me to organize all that for you.

> Mary: I'm sorry!! ...Want me to make it up to you?"

I pocketed my phone to take a seat.

"Oh," Jacqueline blinked at something on her iPad, "Nikhil added another interview since the last time I looked at this."

"That's fine," I shrugged. We were only interviewing three, now four, people. At this point, I felt like these were just interviews to make sure these people were worth interviewing with Nikhil himself. That their resumes weren't just complete lies, and that they responded to meeting requests. That's where the bar was, apparently.

Truth be told, I thought it would be better to have someone from engineering here to help guide Jacqueline and me since neither of us coded or knew the languages the company used to develop software. However, I was excellent at picking up vibes and figured I could spot a liar easily enough.

Jacqueline tapped on her iPad, a small frown on her face as she thought about what she was reading. I felt my phone vibrate again, so I pulled it out and saw another message from Mary.

It was an image.

I lowered the brightness on my phone and held the phone closer to my chest. Mary had sent me some not-safe-for-work content before, usually some funny thirst trap or a funny meme. I had no idea what to expect, so better safe than sorry.

When I opened the image, I had to focus my eyes on it intently, because I couldn't wrap my head around what I was seeing.

It was an image of the resort Mary and the others were staying at. It looked like everyone was poolside, Mary's feet were at the bottom of the picture, propped up on a side table. Nikhil sat on the foot of one lounge chair, his elbows on his knees as he slouched with his head turned to talk to Zaid.

Zaid was shirtless and in short bright blue swim trunks.

I could feel the saliva start filling my mouth, and I internally chided myself for being a hussy—but first, I scanned every detail of the image Mary sent me.

Zaid had his hands behind his head, dark hair dusted his armpits and chest, and his biceps popped a little with the relaxed posture. He wasn't flexing, but his stomach was still flat with little dips where defined abdomen muscles showed themselves. His ankles were crossed, resting behind Nikhil based on the side view I had.

My phone buzzed with another text.

> Mary: Did you know the CTO was hiding all that?

I gulped because frankly, I suspected.

Because I was a pervert.

Another text from Mary came in.

> Mary: As someone who is a big fan of titties, I am a girls-girl first, so I figured I would share the view with one of my straight friends who would appreciate it.

I sent back a wide-eyed emoji, as well as a hot emoji and a melting emoji with the words:

> Me: You're doing the Lord's work, Mary.

> Mary: Just spreading the good word.

She replied with a thumbs-up emoji.

"They're here?" I heard Jacqueline speak, making me jump and quickly exit out of the chat thread before pocketing my device again. My heart was racing, as if I was busted, but when I glanced over at Jacqueline, she had her phone on speaker and was talking to someone.

"Yeah, she just logged in," the voice on Jacqueline's phone said.

"I'll set us up." Jacqueline nodded before ending the call, "Let's get the show on the road."

The brunette woman who showed up on the screen in front of our table was about my age, with a bright smile and friendly demeanor. She was surprised to see women in the interview, which made my heart break a little bit at her immediate visible relaxation.

She was friendly. The vibes were looking good with her, so I let Jacqueline ask most of the questions to determine her knowledge of the field. All her answers sounded like complete nonsense to me, which was probably a good indicator to prove that she knew the languages the company used well enough.

The next interviewee was a man, who was smaller in build and unprepared to talk to a woman in an interview. Though he seemed knowledgeable, it was his vague comment about sending the pretty girls in to scope out the candidates first that gave me the ick.

Even Jacqueline visibly frowned at him.

Next.

The third was also a man, who was friendly and said nothing weird about men or women. He was professional and spoke about coding and development and other stuff I had no knowledge of. He seemed just as qualified as the first interviewee, which...

"So, we're going with Alice, right?" I whispered to Jacqueline after the guy logged off, even though we were the only two in the conference room.

"That's up to Nikhil, I believe," Jacqueline was tapping on her iPad, going over notes, when suddenly she stiffened.

"Yeah, but she's just as qualified as what's his face, and she's a woman, so..." I raised my eyebrows at her expectantly, even though Jacqueline still wasn't looking at me.

"We don't hire anyone based on sex, gender, sexual orientation—" She started reciting her boring HR policies before I waved her off, even though she still wasn't looking at me. She seemed frozen; her eyes glued to her iPad as she bit her lip nervously.

"What's up?" I asked, leaning forward to glance at her iPad.

"N-nothing," Jacqueline blinked and sat up in her seat, clearing her throat and setting her iPad down on the table, "The last interviewee is here."

"In person? Not Zoom?" I asked, twisting around in my seat to see out the glass walls of the conference room and into the rest of the office. Sure enough, a man was waiting near my desk, talking to the intern covering for me as they pointed him in the direction of us.

I sat a little taller and waved my hand up, calling him over to let him know he was in the right place. He was far across the office, so I didn't get a good look at him, but I sat forward in my seat again and noticed that the usually stiff Jacqueline seemed a little stiffer than usual.

"Are you okay?" I asked her, lowering my voice.

"Yeah," Jacqueline finally turned to look at me. She lifted the corner of her lip, a smile that I didn't buy for a second, before tapping on her iPad back to her notes on the candidates, "Just wasn't expecting an in-person interview is all."

I shrugged, "At least it's the last one."

"Mhmm." Jacqueline hummed non-committedly right when a knock sounded on the door.

"Come in!" I twisted around in my chair and stood, walking towards the door right when the last interviewee opened it to enter the conference room.

Holy fucking hell this man was good-looking.

I blinked, pasting what I hoped was a professional smile on my face as my eyes did the quickest scan of his body I had ever done. I lied to myself and said it was to catalog his attire to make sure it was professional enough for an interview, but again, I'm pretty sure that I was just a pervert.

He had a tall and lean build, reminding me of a runner. His dark, almost black, hair was styled in that messy, relaxed way I never really understood but loved at the same time. He wore a leather jacket that looked broken in, but not cracked or damaged. Underneath it was a light grey button-down shirt, and his black trousers were form-fitting. On his feet were the type of sneakers that could either be dress shoes or casual wear. He was pale, like me, and his icy blue eyes pierced my soul as one corner of his pink lips tipped up in a grin. He took the hand that I held out to him to shake.

"Hi, I'm Signe," I started introductions, noting the scrape of his calloused fingertips against my hand.

"I'm Leo," He replied in a deep voice, making excitement light up inside me because *this* motherfucker had an *accent*.

"As in Leonardo?" I asked, enthusiasm evident on my face as we dropped hands, and I stepped back for Jacqueline to introduce herself.

"I'm not named after Da Vinci if that's what you're

wondering. It's just Leo," He replied with a grin that told me he had gotten grief for his name his entire life.

Also, this man was *British*.

"You and I both know I was thinking the Ninja Turtles, but okay," I looked to my side where Jacqueline had finally stood, and gestured to her as she held her hand out for him to shake, "This is our head of HR, Jacqueline. We're going to be interviewing you today."

Leo's eyes danced over to Jacqueline and narrowed the slightest fraction. I barely caught the movement before he smiled almost devilishly and held his hand out to her.

"Nice to meet you," Leo muttered before his lips pressed themselves together as if fighting a laugh.

"You as well," Jacqueline quickly ripped her hand out from his and turned on her heel back to her seat, "Let's get started."

Um. Okay.

I smiled at Leo, worried her cold attitude would throw him off, but his eyes stayed on Jacqueline as he rounded the conference table to take his seat across from us. He even opened his messenger bag and pulled out his own laptop before resting his elbows on the chair he sat in and grinned good-naturedly.

This was a man of confidence, though we would wait to see if it was false or not.

"So," Jacqueline cleared her throat again, and I did a double take when I realized that she was blushing. I fought my own smile, noting that Jacqueline could get rattled by an attractive man just like any other warm-blooded woman. It was good to know.

"So," Leo repeated, leaning forward on his seat, and resting his elbows on the table now, his hands folding over themselves as he made direct eye contact with the both of us. Jacqueline's eyes widened a little at the movement, and it took her a few moments to finally start the interview.

———

"So, how did my cousin do during his interview?" Mary asked me at the beginning of the following week. I was in the break room with Jamie, getting our coffee when Mary waltzed right in and skipped any pleasantries.

"Wait." I blinked at her, "Who is your cousin?"

"Leo," Mary shrugged past us, grabbing a mug of her own and filling it up as she continued, "Leo Turner."

"That man was your cousin?" I gasped, setting my coffee down so I could brace my hands on the edge of the countertop accordingly. I needed to properly display my shock.

"He currently *is* my cousin." Mary replied with a smirk, "How did he do with the interview?"

"Mary. He's so attractive." I placed a palm on my chest to emphasize what his face did to my loins.

Mary grimaced in response, "No he's not."

"I'm going to need you to trust me on this one," I nodded enthusiastically, "Your cousin is hot."

"Really?" Jamie asked, her eyes widening in curiosity.

"No," Mary snapped, a smirk on her lips as she shook her head, "He's not."

"Alright," I waved my hand over in a *cough-it-up* motion, "Show us a picture—a good one." Mary sighed in annoyance before pulling her phone out and scrolling a bit, and finally, we both huddled around her to see the social media account she had pulled up.

Dear god, the man was on a motorcycle.

"Oh," Jamie sighed, narrowing her eyes and leaning in.

"What does that mean?" Mary asked, her dark eyes fixated on Jamie's face.

"Well," Jamie shrugged, "He isn't hideous."

Mary's eyes widened at Jamie's words, making her look closer at her cousin's picture and zoom in, "...Is it the hair?" Mary asked, curiosity genuinely coating her question.

"And face," Jamie and I both replied at the same time, making Jamie giggle.

"The accent isn't horrible to listen to either," I shrugged, "Though I prefer my partners to be a little...sturdier."

"Sturdier?" Mary asked, frowning at the picture of her cousin, and pocketing the device, making Jamie's pink lips frown a little in disappointment.

"Yeah, or like...bigger?" I shrugged, "While men like your cousin are very nice to look at, when it comes down to it, I prefer to be tossed around a little."

Mary snickered while Jamie's eyebrows scrunched in confusion.

"Anyways!" I retrieved my mug from the countertop, lifting it in farewell as I stepped backward towards the exit of the break room, "It's a real bummer because I don't think Nikhil is going to hire—"

I smacked into someone behind me, a low grunt making my heart skip a beat as I struggled to regain my footing right as my coffee mug tipped towards me and spilled its contents right down the front of my dress.

"Frick!" I gasped from the pain of the hot coffee seeping through the clothing and burning my skin, while also turning around to an open-mouthed and wide-eyed Zaid.

"I apologize," Zaid immediately spoke, "Are you—"

"I'm fine!" I waved him off, embarrassment burning my cheeks as I set the mug back down on the counter and tugged the material of my dress away from my red skin, because fuck me for changing things up and wearing a dress to work for the first time in months. I had a feeling that if I wore my tried-and-true jeans and sweatshirt combo, this wouldn't have happened.

Additionally, would it really be so hard for Zaid to make some type of noise when he walked? Or for him to enter a room at a time when I wasn't inappropriately running my mouth?

"Are you burned?" Zaid asked, stepping further into the break room, ripping paper towels off of the roll to hand to me.

I glanced over at Mary and Jamie, who both stood there with their mugs in hand and staring wide-eyed at the spectacle before them. I grabbed the handful of paper towels from Zaid, hopelessly dabbing away at my cream-colored dress. I found myself jutting my bottom lip out in disappointment because this one was one of my favorites, and the stain was probably going to stick around.

"I'm so sorry about that," I glanced up from my dabbing to see Zaid raking his hand through his hair in stress, his eyes on my chest. He was staring at the coffee stain, but my body reacted as if he was taking his fill.

Because I was hopeless for this man.

Ever since Mary had sent me that picture of him shirtless and poolside, I couldn't get the image out of my head. It was like my brain had this override feature where whenever Zaid walked by my desk and gave me a shy smile in passing, my inner ho would scream *remember what his happy trail looked like*? And I'd become immediately flustered.

It was a problem, for a multitude of reasons.

Mostly because he didn't exactly consent to Mary sending me a shirtless picture of himself. Also, he didn't exactly consent to me writing about a guy who was the spitting image of him in my open-door romance novel.

I was disturbingly good at secretly crossing over some obvious boundaries when it came to Zaid Ansara.

In the couple of weeks after the horror that was my first livestream, I was still getting the occasional message or comment from readers asking who Zaid was, and if he was the real-life version of Zayne. It had been relatively easy to delete those comments from my posts without response, or to respond to direct messages with some sort of bull like, "Zayne is a fictional character who was made up in my big fat brain."

Unfortunately, I had a feeling that I needed to make a more formal approach to get my readers to drop it, especially if my plan really was to continue with my publishing plans. I didn't want to keep having a jump scare every time someone DM'd me about the CTO, and readers needed to not feel so comfortable prying into my—and also Zaid's—personal lives.

Maybe doing another livestream (in the safety of my apartment, and nowhere else) to talk about where I am in the publishing process would help move their attention elsewhere.

"Don't worry about it," I waved him off with my handful of damp towels, "It's my fault for not paying attention." Zaid frowned a little, his brows scrunching behind the black frame of his glasses as he met my gaze.

...Were his ears pink? Was he *blushing*?

Oh, dear lord, maybe he *was* staring at more than the coffee stain before catching himself.

"Do you have anything else you can wear today?" Zaid asked, rubbing the side of his neck nervously before handing me more paper towels. I tossed the soiled ones before reaching for his, my fingers brushing against his hand accidentally, but also not so accidentally, if you get my drift.

His dark eyes met mine in the briefest of glances before he cleared his throat and looked over at our co-workers watching us fumble through this social interaction.

"I don't, I guess I'll just smell like coffee today." I glanced behind me at Mary and Jamie, and I realized I was truly stuck with this. I was curvy, one of the larger women in the office. Even if the women in the room did have extra clothes, I wouldn't fit in them.

"I have gym clothes if you need them," Zaid shrugged.

Mary and Jamie weren't moving, but all three of us froze for a moment at our CTO's all-too-casual offer. He held a hand out after his question, his eyes flicking down to my chest before I handed him the newly soiled paper towels that he tossed in the bin for me.

"Gym clothes?" I asked, unsure if I heard or understood him correctly.

"Yeah," his eyes widened as they met mine, "They're not used or smelly. They're freshly washed. I was going to go to the gym after work." He shrugged a little, before rubbing his neck again, "I really am sorry about your dress."

"Oh, um," I shook my head once, "It's fine. I appreciate the offer, and your gym clothes probably are comfier, but I think I'll be okay."

"No," Zaid shook his head once, standing a little taller before he took a step towards the doorway, "I'll go grab them for you. You shouldn't have to wear wet clothes in the office all day." And then Zaid turned on his heel and was gone without another word.

The three of us stood in silence before I slowly turned

around to face my friends with an expression of disbelief on my face.

"Are you really going to wear Zaid's clothes all day today?" Mary asked with a raised eyebrow and a casual sip of her coffee mug. Jamie's mouth curved in a small smile at her question before taking a sip of her own.

"I think so?" I asked, blinking, "Am I allowed to do that?"

"Why wouldn't you be?" Mary asked with confusion in her expression.

"I don't know. Is that normal? What is the office etiquette for this situation?"

"Probably not to spill your coffee down the front of your dress in the first place, if I had to guess," Mary shrugged, "Nice bra by the way."

My jaw dropped before glancing down and yup, my white bra with red polka dots covering the cups was now officially visible, my dress now see-through even with the darker coffee stain wetting the material.

Oh, *this* is why Zaid insisted on me changing, and probably why his eyes kept dropping to my chest earlier.

"Oh god!" I wheezed, immediately cupping my breasts in shock.

That was also the moment Zaid decided to walk back into the break room with a stack of folded clothing, freezing the moment his eyes landed on where my hands were eagerly grabbing the ladies. *Jesus fucking Christ,* did he have some weird sixth sense about Sun Steer employees behaving inappropriately in the break room, that made the man come *running*?

"Thank you for the clothes," I spoke up attempting to distract the room from my hand placement. I casually released my grip on myself while trying to slide my arms over my chest, going for a more casual crossed-arms look instead of a self-groping one.

"It's no problem," Zaid cleared his throat again and lifted his hands to give me the clothing, before glancing at my crossed arms and deciding to set the stack on the breakroom table instead, "Hopefully they're comfortable enough."

And that, my friends, is how I ended up spending the day wearing basketball shorts and a slightly baggy t-shirt throughout the day. Mary teased me with a wiggle of her eyebrows every time she passed my desk, whereas Jamie simply grinned like she was in on a secret. An hour or two later, Jacqueline approached me at the desk to ask for my help with paperwork while she started the onboarding process for Alice, the newest software engineer.

But when she saw my all too casual getup, she paused in her stride and raised a dark eyebrow at me in question.

"It's fine," I casually waved my hands, "I spilled coffee on my work-appropriate clothes." Jacqueline nodded her head slowly, and I could see her struggling to determine if this was a problem for her or not. With a small shake of her head, she decided to move past the weirdness of my appearance and gave me instructions on what she needed help with. I gave her a thumbs up and a wide grin because I was *determined* to befriend Jacqueline in some way.

Zaid eventually came over to check in on me, and I found myself blushing uncontrollably because there was another detail to this situation that made me feel embarrassed, in addition to my list of secrets about him.

His clothes smelled *amazing*. I couldn't put my finger on it, but I guessed that he wore some type of expensive cologne or aftershave, because I swore on my life that no men's body wash or shampoo gave off this delicious of a smell. I was melting in my seat from it, and I found myself tugging the collar of his shirt up towards my nose randomly throughout the day to take a shameful whiff.

I was intoxicated. No smell had ever made me this aroused before. I partially wondered if it was some type of pheromone cologne that I saw advertised on my social media all the time. It wouldn't have surprised me, based on the visceral reaction my body had while being wrapped up in Zaid's scent throughout the entirety of the workday.

And when he came to check on me to make sure that the clothes were comfy enough? I melted on the inside.

"You're too nice," I grinned up at him from my seat, "You gave me the shirt off your back."

Zaid's lips turned up in the corners the slightest bit as he shook his head, "More accurately, I gave you the shirt out of my gym bag."

"You have a whole gym bag?" I raised my eyebrows, settling in with my elbows on the counter just to see how long I could keep a conversation with him going, "Like, a whole bag? You don't just show up already wearing gym clothes and call it?"

Zaid shrugged, shoving his hands in the pockets of his slacks, and leaning a hip against the higher ledge of my desk, "Not when I go straight to the gym after work, or if I go to the gym before coming into work."

"I am very unfamiliar with gym culture, I must admit," I said, shrugging one shoulder, "I go like once a year for the free week-long trial, and then decide walking around the beach is just as sufficient. And cheaper." One of those week-long trials was when I met Eloise, she was teaching a fun group cardio class. Even though I immediately bailed on the class, we still became fast friends.

"Exercise is exercise," Zaid shrugged again, "I need the formality of the gym, I think." His dark brows scrunched a little bit as he stared over my shoulder as if thinking about his answer a bit more, "It's nice having a routine I can do every time I go."

Oh my god, another fun fact about Zaid.

I was slowly becoming obsessed with him, and the little nuggets of personal information he would give me. I already felt like I won the lottery meeting his sister and adorable nephew a while back, but that didn't satiate my never-ending curiosity for this gorgeous man. I could feel my face lighting up with excitement from this conversation and tried so, so hard to school my expression so I didn't scare him off.

"What exactly constitutes a gym routine? Does it involve whatever else you take in your bag?" I sounded playful, but hopefully not sarcastic or patronizing. I could see Zaid lower his eyebrows a little at my expression, his lips quirking to the side as if he were onto me. Like he was waiting for me to tease him about something.

"It does, because hygiene is important, Signe," the way he lowered his head, as well as his voice, made my pulse jump in my veins, "I bring my own rags, lifting belt, and a change of socks and shoes. So that I don't bring in outside dirt and debris onto all the gym equipment and mats."

"Rags?" I asked, "For what?"

"My sweat," Zaid's eyebrow quirked the slightest bit, his dark eyes holding mine hostage as he let that hang between us. Exercise usually involved sweating, it wasn't an unusual thing to say.

But I immediately pictured him shirtless, like the image Mary sent me of him poolside, wiping his damp skin with a towel after benching or running or whatever it is men do at the gym. My mouth went dry a little bit, my cheeks heating as I made direct eye contact with upper management while simultaneously picturing him sweating in the most unprofessional context ever.

"Oh," was all I could say before I pasted a friendly smile back on my face, hopefully masking the horny thoughts I was desperately trying to shove into the back of my brain, "Duh." Zaid huffed a whisper of a laugh at that, his eyes crinkling in the corners as his smile accompanied the sound.

"But the clothes are comfortable?" Zaid asked, the subject change making me hesitate for half a second before I nodded my head enthusiastically.

"This is the comfiest I have ever been at the office," I grinned, but then I grabbed the edge of my desk and leaned forward, before checking over my shoulder and down either side of the hallway dramatically, "But unfortunately I have to ask you an uncomfortable question."

Zaid's brows pinched together the slightest bit, "You do?" *oh my god, was that genuine concern on his face?* I nodded my head solemnly as he leaned towards me, also glancing down the hall that I had just checked and matching my vibe completely. I almost felt bad for being theatrical about this, but it was also how I masked my own embarrassment over the question I just *had* to ask him.

"I do," I lifted a hand to my mouth as if I was going to whisper a secret to him, "What cologne do you wear, and where can I find some for myself?"

Zaid blinked, his eyes widening a fraction before the tips of his ears turned the slightest shade of red.

I loved it way too much when this man blushed.

"My cologne?" Zaid asked, confusion evident as he kept his hunched posture and leaned closer toward me.

"Yeah," I gently tugged at the collar of his t-shirt as if I needed to show him what I meant, "Your clothes smell amazing. I promise I'm not trying to be a creep, but I can't even focus on my reports for Jacqueline because I'm desperately trying to google what I'm smelling so I can buy it."

"You want to buy my cologne," Zaid's head tilted slightly as he rested his forearms on the higher ledge, encroaching on my space in a way that made my gaze immediately land on his mouth.

Oh god. I was staring at his lips. Making it very obvious what I thought about our proximity. I quickly averted my gaze and made direct eye contact as I desperately tried to continue the conversation so that he wouldn't pick up on my inappropriate brain, "Yeah. What am I smelling? Where do I get it? I want to wash my bedsheets in this stuff and snuggle in."

Whoops, too far, Signe. Based on how Zaid's lips parted after that particular comment, I realized there was no real innocent way to interpret that statement. Hopefully, he didn't think I was putting the moves on him. As much as I would love to do that, he was still upper management.

...But I was still telling the CTO that I wanted to sleep in his scent.

There was nothing appropriate about that.

Thankfully, Zaid being the sweet and chill guy that he was, let that comment pass, "I can send you the link. My sister gifted it to me a few years ago, and I have been ordering it for myself ever since." He lifted a shoulder as he stood to his full height, his eyes doing another glance over my casual work attire before he pulled out his buzzing phone from his pocket.

His lips turned down in a way that made me want to bite his bottom lip and tug, and I fought the urge to slap myself across the face to pull myself together.

"This is Zaid," he nodded his head at me with a quick smile before walking down the hallway, taking an important phone call, and abruptly ending our conversation that my libido was desperate to turn into more.

I sighed in both relief and disappointment from our ended conversation, before pinching my thigh and giving my woman parts a stern mental talking to. Jacqueline's reports needed to get done, and swooning over any word or movement from Zaid Ansara should not be my priority.

Chapter Seven

ZAID

I WAS A MAN BECOMING OBSESSED.

I prefer to be tossed around a little.

What else did Signe prefer?

How could I find as much detail about her sexual preferences as possible?

Late at night, I sat in my bed with my newly created social media account and mindlessly searched for Signe Lange's. My username was a random smattering of numbers and letters, and my profile picture was a picture of the ocean. It wasn't the most creative account to hide my identity, but I felt safer snooping through my employee's content with a fake account in case I accidentally liked anything.

Later that night, after taking myself in hand in the shower simply from the memory of Signe wearing my gym clothes, I still felt desperate for more of her. I figured seeing what she regularly posted and talked about seemed like a good way to get to know the beautiful redhead more.

I was scrolling through her pictures, which were a lot of aesthetic shots of writing and her laptop and coffee, in what looked like her bed, when a notification popped up at the top of the screen.

Signe was starting a live feed again.

Obviously, I immediately joined.

"...any questions you have. Nothing is into touch." I chuckled to myself at her *Ted Lasso* reference, while Signe winked her hazel eyes at the camera, and my heart stuttered in my chest because she was still wearing my clothes. It was almost nine o'clock at night, and Signe was sitting in her bed wearing *my* clothes. I guess she really meant what she said about wanting to sleep in my cologne. I made a mental note to send her the link tomorrow. I wanted to wait an appropriate amount of time to do so because part of me was afraid that I would look too desperate for her to smell like me if I sent the link right away.

Waiting a day or so to send her the link to my cologne felt more casual. Less desperate.

"Good news! I'm going to get the first round of edits back from my gorgeous, wonderful, genius of an editor soon," Signe grinned, her smile lighting up as she reached over and scrolled on her laptop, "Obviously, I can't say much about the content of the full manuscript yet, but you can bet your beautiful, luscious booties that I'll let you all know as soon as I have details to share."

I laughed to myself again. The number of adjectives Signe used to describe people was over the top, but also, I expected nothing less from her.

"...No, I'm single." Signe didn't shrug self-deprecatingly, or even wince or give any physical indication that her relationship status made her uncomfortable. Or something to be embarrassed about. Signe was confident, even declaring her relationship status online to strangers who asked.

"Oh, uh," Signe glanced down at herself, the questions were flooding the bottom of the screen at this point. Hearts took over the side of the display as her followers rapidly tapped the icon, "No, sometimes I like to wear men's clothes. These are just my jammies."

I scoffed to myself, loving the anonymity this fake account could give me so I could catch her in her silly lies. Those were *my* clothes that she still wore, not hers. Was she truly planning on sleeping in them tonight?

I ignored the twitch in my own plaid pajama bottoms at the thought.

"Nope." Signe shook her head as she answered another random question, "My characters are figments of my imagination."

I raised my eyebrows at her—

"Oh my god, you all are the worst!" She groaned and covered her face with both of her hands, hiding herself for a few moments before playfully glaring at the screen flooding with questions and hearts and laughing emojis, "Look. While there are physical similarities between Zayne's character and that man you saw on my feed weeks ago, Zayne is not based on that man at all. That man doesn't even know that I write romance. Everyone, this is what authors *do*," she shrugged, "Looking back, I shouldn't have been so on the nose with my physical description of Zayne. But my romance author brain just looked at him and thought, 'perfect candidate, it would be fun describing that appearance to the reader', which you all immediately proved me right about." She raised her eyebrows with an accusatory stare at the camera, making my lips twitch.

I knew Zayne's character was different than my personality, but I still felt a little jab of disappointment at her answer for some reason. She was acting so nonchalant about it, making me second guess myself. Was she simply using my appearance for her writing and nothing more? Was she not interested in me in any sort of romantic capacity?

Before I could stop myself, I typed a question into the mess of others right when she paused to read them.

> Avytk890: Who is the man you based
> Zayne on?

Thankfully, dozens of other people had the same question ready to go. Suddenly, different variations of that same question took over, and Signe's nervous expression as she bit her bottom lip with her teeth made anticipation rise.

Was she going to ignore the question until someone asked something else?

Signe released a heavy sigh, before tucking a strand of red hair back behind her ear, "Full disclosure, he is a coworker. I am not going say where I work full-time because I don't trust any of you to not invade my or his privacy," she smiled, though her tone was firm, "He's a really great guy, and it would mean a lot to me if everyone could leave him alone."

I was clutching my phone with my hands, desperate for her to say *anything* more about me.

Was I truly a mature man? A grown adult?

I doubted it as I typed my next question.

> Avytk890: Are you two friends?

My question was immediately lost in the mess of other questions readers were asking, but I could see Signe reach forward and scroll through the mess.

I was a trendsetter. Other people started asking

variations of my question as well, and I caught myself holding my breath as I waited to see what question she would answer next.

"You know me, I try to be friends with everyone," Signe shrugged her shoulder this time, "Though half the time I can't tell if we're friends or if he just tolerates me because we work together," Signe replied, her shoulders shaking as she controlled her laughter and narrowed her eyes to comb through questions again.

> Avytk890: But you based Zayne off of him because you're attracted to him?

Signe's lips were moving as she mumbled through questions, and I felt my heart lump itself in my throat as her lips murmured my latest question to herself.

"Okay," Signe laughed again after reading my question, "Obviously my coworker is good-looking. You all saw him, and you all left thirsty comments about him. You all thought he was attractive when you drew fan art of Zayne and Sydney. Don't be silly."

That made my heart thump heavy in my chest, my breathing shaky as I watched Signe Lange tell thousands of followers that she was attracted to me to some degree. I breathed a sigh of relief, especially when I saw her cheeks turn the slightest bit pink after her declaration.

"I'm not answering any more questions about the inspiration behind Zayne," Signe shook her head once, "Again, you all need to be mindful of my and my coworker's privacy. If you have any questions for me about writing or the querying process, I'm ready to answer what I can at this point."

Probably should have thought of that before creating a

fictional character based entirely on my appearance, I thought to myself.

I knew how to keep my privacy; the fake account I was using to stalk her was evidence of that. I closed out of her live feed, wanting to do more research, instead of watching her answer other questions from those who were more interested in her work itself than I was. I scrolled through her page, opening up the three pictures she's posted of herself so far.

Signe was stunning. There was no other way to describe it. I found myself even liking the images, feeling a little better that there were already thousands of likes and comments left by her following.

A following that grew to nearly fifty thousand.

I grinned, a feeling of pride that I didn't deserve flooding my chest. I scrolled, skimmed captions, and learned a few more details about Signe that I didn't know before.

How she preferred peppermint lattes over pumpkin spice lattes and was desperate for fall to come and go so she could finally enjoy her drink of choice.

Or how she was allergic to flowers, something she announced by posting a selfie of her with swollen watery eyes after walking through a park where the flowers were blooming everywhere.

I found myself chuckling at that, loving the confidence she had to post a picture most people would consider unflattering. Not Signe, she posted whatever she wanted even if she wasn't wearing makeup or didn't have her hair done. She wasn't even dressed up in her posts, just wearing leggings or loose-fit jeans with casual t-shirts.

A desperate, lonely part of me truly hoped that one day, I would be able to see her casual loungewear in person.

At that embarrassing thought, I decided I had done

enough internet stalking for the night and decided to finally plug in my phone and go to sleep, but it took a while for my mind to calm down enough to do so. I needed to find out what Sun Steer's official policy on fraternizing in the office was. My romantic feelings towards Signe were only growing each passing day, and I needed to make sure I wasn't being unethical by constantly entertaining the idea of her and me, together.

I made a mental note to work up the courage to glean the information from Jacqueline, who would definitely know the answers to my questions. Deciding that was my next step, I was finally able to embrace the dreams of the woman who took up all the free space in my mind.

IN THE DAYS that passed after Salma dropped off my mother's leftovers for me in the office, Signe would give me a thumbs up every time I walked past her desk. She eventually ended up eating everything, and I took all the dishes home to wash them and return them to my mother.

I reminded my mother that whenever I did eat out for lunch, it was on the company's dime. And usually some sort of formal business meeting. This dissuaded her from giving me another mountain of leftovers the next time my family and I got together for dinner.

Though a few days ago, Signe happened to ask me one morning if I could send her the recipes of the leftovers she had eaten, so she could try recreating the meals herself.

I shrugged and said I'd ask my mother for it because I was running late that day already and couldn't stay at her desk to chat, but the reality was that I was thrilled over the fact that Signe loved the homemade Syrian dishes my mother prepared so often. Sometimes the flavors could be strong for those who weren't Arab, but Signe had downed each one.

However, my thoughts about Signe enjoying my mother's leftovers were quickly put in the back of my mind, because just a couple of days after watching her latest live stream, the universe gave me a wonderful opportunity to ask Jacqueline the question that would have immediately given me away otherwise.

I had walked in on two employees romantically intertwined in the break room.

Thankfully, Mary and the small blonde woman didn't notice me, so I forced myself to ignore my surprise and promptly walked right back out. I ended up shutting myself in my office for a couple of hours afterward.

I had seen the two women with Signe before, and I had walked in (eavesdropped) on several, not entirely work-appropriate, conversations with the group. I hadn't expected them to go as far as to try to swallow each other's mouths in the office, an action that *definitely* wasn't appropriate in the workplace.

I was a little embarrassed, feeling like I had walked in on a private moment between the women, but also pulled myself together enough to remember that we were in the office and that, weirdly, I could use this to my advantage.

I knocked on Jacqueline's office a couple of hours later, allowing myself entry when she nodded at me and waved me in while she finished typing something on her laptop.

I closed the door most of the way, leaving a small sliver of space open before sitting myself down in one of the chairs across from her desk. Even though there was a large window right next to Jacqueline's office door, I still understood that there was rarely a reason for a man like me to shut himself completely in a woman's office.

"How can I help you?" Jacqueline asked, clicking out of her tabs before sitting straighter in her chair and giving me a blank but professional expression.

"I just had a question about, um," I cleared my throat and tried my best not to rub my neck or give any more nervous cues than necessary, "Our office's fraternization or relationship policies."

Jacqueline's eyes widened at me for a moment, before she masked her expression again and gave me a stiff nod, "What would you like to know?" She followed up her question by reaching for her mouse and clicking on something on her desktop, probably pulling up the policies in question.

"Let's say, hypothetically speaking," I cleared my throat again and tried to sit straighter. I was upper management after all, and I wanted to put on a professional front as easily as Jacqueline did, "That two employees wanted to start a romantic relationship," Jacqueline's eyebrow twitched upward ever so slightly, making me want to continue forward before she could start scrutinizing me, "First, is that frowned upon? Second, what is the proper procedure for those two employees to establish that relationship while protecting themselves in the workplace?"

Jacqueline's lips pressed together in a thin line, and she leaned forward on her elbows with a somehow still straight back before tilting her head towards me, "Is there someone you are romantically involved with here, Zaid?"

I could feel the blush hit my face immediately at her forward question, and I gave myself a self-deprecating smile before a nervous chuckle left my mouth and I shook my head, "No, this isn't about me." I hesitated for a second before deciding to be as honest as I could with her, "I just happened to notice some, um, romantic behavior occurring between two employees in the break room."

Her eyebrows immediately pulled down, "Who? What were they doing?" She reached down under her desk and pulled out her iPad, unlocking the device and pulling up the notes app she loved to use.

"I don't feel comfortable sharing," I shook my head at her once, "Nothing outwardly inappropriate occurred," I lied, "But it was obvious to me that the two employees were romantically involved to some degree. I just wanted to make sure there were policies in place where two consenting adults could explore a romantic relationship with each other without the fear of being fired for doing so."

Jacqueline's eyes narrowed at me ever so slightly as the corners of her lips turned down, before shaking her head once and setting her iPad on her desk, "If two employees want to start a romantic relationship, I would encourage them to visit me and document it. That protects both of them as the employees, as well as us as a company," I nodded at her explanation, "There would only be a problem if one of them was in a superior position over the other."

I felt something sink in my gut at her words, "I don't think that's the case, because they're on different teams." I lifted a shoulder.

"That's good to know," Jacqueline nodded, "However, let's say we had an intern on one of the sales teams who was fraternizing with a manager in engineering. That still consists of a complex power dynamic, because even though they're on different teams, one employee is clearly in a position of power over the other. Does that make sense?"

I felt the thing that sunk in my gut settle hard, reminding me just how inappropriate my feelings for Signe were.

"I think so," I nodded, and because I hated myself, I played along with her scenario just to let her know I understood her loud and clear, "So, someone like me in an upper management position would still be in a position of power over someone like Frank," I lifted a shoulder at the mention of one of the sales reps that often reminded me of Jacqueline's twin, personality-wise, "Which would create an unfair power dynamic, even though we're two different departments."

"Exactly," Jacqueline nodded, "If you and Frank ever started a romantic relationship, of course, I would want you both to come to me and document it. However, even though I couldn't stop two consenting adults, I would also strongly encourage the two of you to not cross that boundary in the first place."

I nodded, "That makes sense."

"There are seven point five billion people in the world," Jacqueline lifted a shoulder, looking more casual than I had ever seen her be, "Therefore, there is almost no reason to get involved with someone at work."

I smiled at her, "I understand. However, in the case of the two employees I mentioned earlier, I don't think there will be any problem with power dynamics." Unless of course, Nikhil promotes Mary like he planned to. I knew Jacqueline had already started the formal paperwork for the offer.

"I still think you should tell me who it is," Jacqueline gave me a pointed look, "It won't do any good to keep them a secret. If I know who it is, I can call them both in for a meeting and have this discussion privately and directly. Also, I can remind them not to do anything inappropriate while in the office."

Logically, I knew that she was right. It was the

responsible, professional way to go about it after all. However, I also knew that these were Signe's friends. I didn't even know if one of the women was officially out yet, and my gut prioritized their right to privacy over the company's official policies.

"Maybe I'll approach them myself and send them your way," I lied again as I braced my hands on my knees and stood, "Thanks for letting me interrupt your workday."

"Anytime, Zaid," Jacqueline smiled at me as she turned back to her computer, hopefully moving on from our conversation, even though there was little to no chance that I could move on myself.

I was distracted the rest of the day, constantly spiraling about how my position wasn't just a position I wanted to step down from for personal reasons, but also a position that made my intentions with Signe significantly more problematic.

———

I FOUND myself staring at Brandon's image on the screen as he spoke, all of us in the office, but taking this meeting with a potential collaboration over video call. Brandon was in his element, excited and charismatic about the technology we were building as a company, and how we were feeling more confident about incorporating our code with hardware.

Yes, Brandon was working hard to ensure the company took off as we had envisioned all these years ago, but I was realizing that at some point our focuses had changed. While Brandon had stayed focused on Sun Steer for the past decade or so, keeping the motivations for success high, I had started to concern myself with other things.

Things like, what type of work I enjoy spending forty-hours a week on.

Or gorgeous red heads that I couldn't keep my eyes off of.

He still hadn't responded to the email I sent him weeks ago, and part of me felt like I was nagging if I brought it up again with him so soon.

But, if I had managed to find the courage to approach Jacqueline, then I needed to find the same courage to approach my old friend.

Chapter Eight

SIGNE

I WAS WALKING BACK from refilling my coffee in the breakroom, jotting notes down on my phone for ways to fix the major plot hole that my editor pointed out to me a few days ago, when I heard Zaid laugh.

I stopped in my tracks and immediately lifted my head up and to the side, spotting him leaning against the wall with Nikhil. Both of them were staring at me with grins on their faces, and I glanced behind myself to see what they were smiling at. After seeing nothing and nobody behind me, I met their gaze again.

"Nice sweatshirt," Nikhil explained.

I glanced down at the black sweatshirt that had the words, "My Body Hurts And I'm Mad At The Government" in white letters and returned their smiles.

"It's a fan favorite." I smiled.

"Fans?" Zaid asked, "You have fans?"

I opened my mouth before shutting it, realizing that bragging about my fanbase who was currently still obsessing over a fictional character inspired by a very non-fictional man probably wasn't the smartest thing to do.

"One day," I winked, recovering.

Nikhil grinned and started chatting with Zaid again.

And that was when my day went to hell because I suddenly felt a warm wet gush in my underwear.

Shit.

I stayed standing in my spot, glancing at my phone again to check my health app to see if I had gotten my days mixed up.

I didn't.

My period just decided to come six days early. Ugh.

I quickly walked over to my desk to grab my purse, opening the hidden zipper pocket to grab a tampon, but feeling my chest tighten in panic when I realized that there weren't any in there.

I started opening the small bank of desk drawers underneath my desk, desperately searching for a tampon or pad or *something*.

I had recently lost my period cup and hadn't gotten my newest one delivered yet. I couldn't remember the last time I needed an actual tampon or pad, which probably explained why I couldn't find any in the places I would normally stash them.

"Everything alright?" I heard Zaid ask. The two men were now watching me frantically search my desk for feminine hygiene products.

"Fine," I smiled at them as I double-checked my desk area. Purse. Drawer. Drawer number two. Drawer number three. Drawer number four, which I already knew for a fact only had Hostess pastries stashed in there away from Mary's grabby hands.

I tried to hide my panic by smiling at Nikhil and Zaid again, who gave me curious looks in return, and made my way over to Mary at her desk cluster where the software engineers worked.

"Hey," I smiled, before leaning on her desk casually with my elbows as if I was just saying hello, "Do you happen to have a spare tampon?"

Mary's mouth opened a little and her eyes widened before she ignored whatever code she was working on and started opening her desk drawers. They were all empty, save for a spare pen or empty energy drink can rolling around.

She came up with nothing, even after padding the pockets of her cargo pants, "I'm so sorry," Mary whispered back to me, "I use a cup, I haven't needed one of those myself for a while."

"Damn," I smiled at her good-naturedly, "I'm in your same position, except I don't have my cup on me."

"Oh no," Mary's eyes widened, pulling her phone out and thumbing away at it, "I'll ask Jamie." I nodded and leaned against her desk. Mary was the only uterus owner on this side of the building. All the other software engineers, except for Alice who hadn't started yet, were men. Men, with their useless penises that didn't bleed once a month.

Mary's phone vibrated in her hand and a second later a frown pulled at her red-painted lips, "Shit," Mary's dark eyes lifted to meet mine, "She just used the last of her stock today."

"Frick," I sighed, "Maybe I'll ask Jaqueline."

Mary nodded and wished me luck as I departed, wondering if I would have to run to the nearest convenience store, or maybe even just call it a day and go home early.

Nikhil and Zaid weren't near my desk anymore, but now they were standing in the middle of the open-concept area between all the upper management's personal office spaces. Brandon was with them, and it didn't look like a particularly fun or happy discussion that the men were having, so I didn't draw too much attention to myself as I walked past them toward Jacqueline's office.

Thankfully, her door was open, and I peeked my head inside while I gently knocked my knuckles on the doorframe.

Her head jerked up from her computer screen, and she reached up to remove her earbuds as she said, "Hey."

"Hey," I stopped in the threshold of her office and lifted my hand to the side of my mouth to keep our conversation from echoing into the open space behind me, "Do you have a tampon?"

Jacqueline's lips made an O shape before she reached down into her purse and started rummaging around.

I crossed my fingers in anticipation as she searched.

"I'm so sorry," Jacqueline winced as she set her purse on her desk, "but there is a box in the lady's room."

"Oh," I nodded and gave her a thumbs up, so she wouldn't feel too bad at not having a spare tampon for me to use. Heading in the direction of the restrooms, I awkwardly nodded at the men still standing together in the open-concept area, chatting about a Python or something, and made it to the restroom. I didn't remember seeing a box of feminine hygiene products in the past, but to be fair, I usually avoided using public restrooms at all costs and never lingered. Because gross.

There was no box of pads or tampons to be found, and my whine of frustration was met with another small but unpleasant gush in my underwear.

Fuck this.

I turned around, ready to go home, when I saw what Jacqueline must have been talking about.

Of course! Most ladies' rooms had a box mounted to the

wall. Older ones were usually coin-operated, but surely Sun Steer wouldn't expect women to pay for hygiene products in their office, right?

I jumped over to the feminine hygiene product dispenser and turned the little knob, but it stopped halfway.

I cursed and tried again.

Nothing.

"Are you fucking kidding me," I grumbled through clenched teeth before trying a third time.

A quarter was really required for this shit?

In *this* economy?

I was on the verge of boiling over with female rage.

I stomped my way towards the bathroom door, throwing it open, ready to tear the office apart for a fucking quarter when Zaid suddenly appeared in front of me.

I was momentarily surprised to see him, but not enough to cool my temper.

"Are you alright?" Zaid asked, shoving his hands in the pocket of his slacks and glancing nervously over my shoulder towards the women's restroom, where I had just stormed out. I couldn't even take the time to admire how the man made a polo shirt look attractive and athletic because I was so stressed out over my situation.

"Do you have a quarter?" I asked, holding my palm out.

Zaid's dark eyebrows jumped as he glanced at my outreached hand and gave me a confused expression, "A quarter?" I had to give the man credit because he immediately started patting his pants with his hands, before pulling his wallet out of his back pocket.

"Yes," I had no idea what facial expression I was making, but I was positive I was weirding Zaid out. At the same time, I continued, "Because, for some reason, Sun Steer thinks it's appropriate to *charge* their employees who own uteruses for feminine hygiene products."

Zaid froze as he opened his wallet, and his lips parted the slightest bit before he pressed them together again and cleared his throat, "Oh. Um—"

"Which is insane to me, considering Sun Steer has an entire mother's lounge in case anyone is breastfeeding and needs a place to nurse or pump. It *almost* feels like women aren't worth supporting until *after* we pop a baby out." I interrupted him, stepping forward and eyeballing his open wallet. He took the hint and continued to pull out three quarters, before dropping them in the palm of my hand, "Tell me, Mr. Ansara," I glared up at the CTO of Sun Steer, the rage of all my female ancestors filling my veins, "Does Sun Steer make you pay for toilet paper so that you can wipe your own ass?"

Zaid was silent, and visibly stunned at my abrupt and crude question.

"N-no," He managed to choke out, shaking his head once in the negative.

"So why the hell am I expected to insert a quarter into a dispensing machine to get a tampon?"

"Signe!" I heard Jacqueline's voice down the hall, which made both Zaid and I turn our heads to see her stalking towards us, "This isn't appropriate—"

"No," I shook my head in agreement, "It isn't. I shouldn't have to ask someone for a quarter so that I can avoid bleeding through my pants at work."

"*Signe!*" Jacqueline gasped as she finally reached us, sending an apologetic look to Zaid.

"It's okay," Zaid stepped towards me, his large hand resting on my shoulder as he addressed the head of HR, "She's allowed to be upset."

"Damn straight." I nodded.

"Go," Zaid used his warm grip on my shoulder to turn me back towards the restrooms, "I'll make sure to disengage the coin mechanism later."

Jacqueline and I both hesitated our steps to stare at Zaid for a moment, who in response simply pushed me toward the bathroom again.

"Go ahead, Signe," Zaid encouraged, before turning to Jacqueline, "Can you help me find who installed those dispensers?"

"Y-yeah," Jacqueline nodded, pulling her phone out of the pocket of her jeans, and tapping away. I left them in my dust as I ran back into the bathroom. My simmering rage was starting to die down at the relief of inserting the quarter into the machine and having a tampon fall into my hand.

I then decided to use the two extra quarters Zaid gave me to grab two more. I probably wouldn't need these two tampons for the rest of the workday, so I set them on top of the stupid coin-operated dispenser in case one of the other people who had periods in the office ended up in the same pickle I was.

I was still grumpy the rest of the day.

Maybe it was because I was on my period, (but I was the only one allowed to say such a thing) or maybe I was stressed about all the work ahead of me now that I received edits back.

I decided to send Eloise a text about it after work, knowing she would validate my anger.

Me: I had to pay 25 cents to use a tampon at work today.

Eloise: Pardon my French, but what the fuck? Did you ask your job to comp you for that?

Me: Actually, I yelled at someone from upper management to give me a quarter. So, technically, I guess Sun Steer did comp me for it.

Eloise: Good for you. Fucking men. Fucking patriarchy. Fucking fuck.

Me: PREACH.

I inhaled a heavy breath through my nose, before releasing the air through my mouth. I could always count on her to let me vent and validate me for doing so in these random moments like this.

Eloise: Not to change the subject too soon, but didn't you post recently about getting edits back? How is that going?

I slumped, realizing that Eloise still had no idea that the book she was so excited about was technically fanfic of a very real person that I worked with. The person who was kind enough to give me his quarters so that I could rectify the tampon situation at work.

Regardless, only a small part of me was currently anxious about the CTO-inspired romance I was still editing. I figured I'd let my anger fuel the excuse of doing such a thing, that Zaid could deal with the fact that I secretly wrote a character inspired by him, if I have to live in a world where it was expected of women to pay more for the mere fact that we were born with uteruses.

It wasn't logical, but that didn't stop me from feeling my feelings about it.

This is also why I responded to Eloise with a thumbs up and sobbing face emojis, and nothing else.

THE NEXT MORNING, I wasn't as upset as I was the day before. Which, if I was being honest, may have solidified my theory that my period actually does influence my emotional response to things on occasion. I was walking to my desk that morning, my mind scrambling for ways to apologize to Zaid for chewing him out for no real reason, and also to Jacqueline, for being an employee who felt comfortable yelling at the CTO for simply being a man.

As I rounded my desk to set my purse down, though, I came to a halt.

There was a snake plant on my desk, right next to my computer.

It had a little red bow tied around the terracotta pot, and a note neatly tucked into the band of the bow.

I glanced around to see if whoever left this on my desk was still around, but the halls were empty.

So, I plopped myself into my chair and admired the cute little snake plant.

Though I loved flowers and thought that they were pretty, my sinuses did not. I was allergic to anything that pollinated, which meant I was always one step away from dragging around a Zyrtec or a Benadryl IV stand during the spring and summertime. If anyone was going to get me some sort of plant for any special occasion, an indoor plant like this was a better way to go for me.

But did anyone I worked with actually know that?

Instead of wondering what special occasion justified the plant on my desk, I plucked the note out of the bow to see if that provided answers.

Sincerest apologies, Zaid
Sun Steer Technologies

I felt my mouth gape open in surprise.

He was *apologizing*.

Even though I was the one who snapped at him.

This is how Mary ended up finding me, trotting over to my desk with raised eyebrows and a smirk on her lips, "Are you the reason I have a new plant on my desk this morning?"

"Huh?" I asked, blinking at Mary in an attempt to focus on her.

"I would assume so," Mary continued, slamming her elbows on the elevated ledge of my desk, and nodding towards the snake plant, "Is Zaid apologizing to all the women in the office? Because Jamie has a snake plant on her desk too. And so does Jacqueline."

I sat there, slack-jawed at Mary's words.

"Did you get an apology note too?" I asked.

"Sure did, in the cleanest handwriting I had ever seen from an engineer," Mary smiled at my plant and trailed one of her fingertips up the leaf.

"I mean, it's cool, but I'm also wondering why we didn't get flowers. That's what men normally give women to apologize, right?" Mary and I sat in silence for a beat before she shook her head once and continued, "Well, it doesn't matter. The plant will last longer, and it's still beautiful. I'm happy with it. I'm off to enjoy my cute little plant that doesn't smell as good as flowers." Mary smirked before tapping her knuckles on the high ledge of my desk and sauntering back toward hers.

I smiled at her antics before quirking my lips to the side and studying the snake plant some more.

I loved it, I never even thought about having a desk plant here. I never thought about doing much to personalize my desk space because I always mentally had one foot out the door. I wanted to be a writer, not an office manager.

But I appreciated the lift it brought to my job. The place where I spent at least forty hours of my week.

However, Mary had a point. Why not flowers? Why a desk plant? I decided to go ask the man himself, standing from my desk and doing my best not to physically skip over to his office.

I had just turned the corner to the wing where upper management's offices were, when I spotted the CTO exiting his office with an empty coffee mug.

"Mister Ansara," I spoke, gaining his attention as he lifted his eyes away from the phone in his hand.

"Miss Lange," I felt my heart skip a beat at how easily he played with me now. How he was more willing to meet my energy. I wondered if I was too harsh, too judgmental of the man when I first started here. How I wrote him off as shy and never expected much from him. Just because he was shy, didn't mean he didn't have a personality. A personality I was slowly, dangerously becoming obsessed with as time marched on.

"I got your note," I lifted the folded paper in between my index and middle fingers as evidence as I started walking with him towards the break room.

"Good," Zaid nodded his head once with seriousness, "I'm afraid it won't undo the systemic sexism that is plaguing corporate America," he lifted his shoulder, "But I figured it was a step in the right direction."

"So," I released a surprised laugh, loving how dry his humor was, "You're apologizing to all the women in the office on behalf of—"

"All the men in the office, yes," we reached the break room and he stepped to the side, gesturing with the empty mug in his hand that I should go inside first.

I laughed again before crossing the threshold "I feel like I should be the one apologizing."

Zaid hesitated as he placed his mug underneath the dispenser, lifting one eyebrow in question as he turned his head to look at me, "For what?"

"For snapping at you yesterday," I shrugged, "Not for taking your quarters, but for my attitude when you were just, I don't know, going about your day?"

"On the contrary," Zaid turned back to his coffee as he pressed the buttons to start the brew, before folding his massive arms and leaning a hip against the countertop, "I appreciate you pointing out the issue to me. I don't know who decided to install dispensers that made women pay for products, but I have someone coming today to rectify the situation."

"Really?" I asked, unable to hide my smile.

Zaid nodded, "If I don't have to pay for toilet paper to wipe my own ass," I groaned in embarrassment as I tugged the collar of my t-shirt over half of my face to hide my flaming cheeks, "Then women shouldn't have to pay for products so that they don't, um…" he waved his hand in the air, the tips of his ears turning the slightest shade of pink in embarrassment.

"Bleed through their pants?" I whispered underneath the hem of my shirt.

"Yes," Zaid chuckled as we settled into silence again, nothing but the sound of the coffee maker pouring liquid energy into his mug.

"Can I ask," I cleared my throat and lowered my shirt back into place, "Why a desk plant? Why not flowers?"

Zaid had just been reaching into his pocket to pull his phone out again when he froze with my question.

For a moment, he looked like a kid who got caught with his hand in the cookie jar. Like a kid who got caught in a lie or busted for something. The reaction surprised me, but the way he immediately cleared his throat and schooled his features made me wonder if I had imagined that reaction.

"I wasn't sure if anyone had allergies," a small pinch in his brow formed with his words.

"Huh," I tilted my head to the side, "That's very considerate of you."

"My younger sister can't handle certain flowers," Zaid replied as he thumbed away at his phone, "Star-gazer lilies specifically, because of how potent they are."

I blinked at him, surprised that his sister and I happened to have that in common.

"I see," I fidgeted with the bottom hem of my t-shirt, "Anyway, thank you again. The snake plants really go with the vibe of the office. With the other office plants around the building, I mean."

"That's good," Zaid nodded as I started making my way out of the break room, "Signe?"

"Yeah?" I asked, glancing over my shoulder in the doorway to look at him.

He seemed so relaxed leaning against the countertop, the presence of business casual in his slacks and his tried-and-true black t-shirt, waiting for what I assumed was his third cup of coffee that morning already, "Don't forget to water the plant."

I rolled my eyes at him and smiled, "It's a snake plant, it's low maintenance."

"But will still require some water on occasion."

"You're one to talk," I stared pointedly at his coffee cup before meeting his teasing expression, "You also require some water on occasion."

"Nah," he retrieved his mug with the freshly brewed coffee and took a loud slurp to emphasize his point. I just shook my head and laughed before leaving him in the breakroom to die of dehydration.

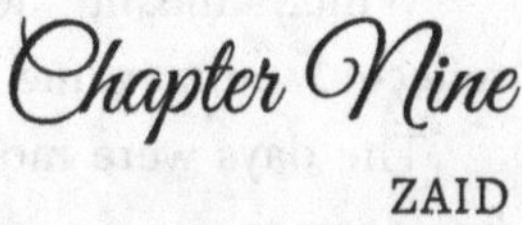

Chapter Nine

ZAID

Weeks had passed since the tampon/desk plant debacle where I almost blew it with Signe and exposed the fact that I had recently stalked her social media accounts, which would prove that I knew about her allergies and secret book.

Thankfully, my blatant lie that one of my sisters was allergic to flowers happened to pay off.

Things changed a little between Signe and I since then, in a good way. We said hello to each other almost every single time we passed one another. Sometimes if she was walking past my office to go talk to Jacqueline or Brandon or someone else, she would just knock on the door frame without even looking in to see what I was doing.

The first time she did this I startled in my seat, though now I recognized Signe's two-knock pass every time it happened. She never waited for me to respond with a hello or a knock on my desk. Instead, she would knock and just keep walking.

It was very intentional of her, and it made my chest heat with something every time it happened. It reminded me that she was thinking of me, even if it was just as a platonic friend. For the moment. Hopefully not forever.

———

FALL HAD COME to Orange County.

Which meant nothing, because the weather still reflected summertime.

The days were mostly clear skies and eighty to eighty-five-degrees.

In a few weeks, the Santa Ana winds would start up, making fire season a risk, but again, fall didn't exist here. Some trees would shed their leaves, but the desert-like climate usually still looked the same. People still went to the beach. Flip flops and shorts and t-shirts were still everyday wear.

Sun Steer's holiday party in December would probably be at the beach again this year.

The Halloween party that Signe and Jacqueline worked on together was in our office, in the AC. It started right at the end of the workday so that families with kids could bring children to trick-or-treat desk to desk, or office-to-office in my case.

It also meant that I had to cut myself off to be present at the party. Meetings didn't linger today, and the timer on my phone had just startled me out of a work-induced trance. I removed my glasses to rub my eyes after staring at my computer screen all day.

I silenced the alarm, only then hearing the noise coming from outside of my secluded workspace.

The office was loud and busy, two things I generally didn't care for in a workplace setting because it became incredibly hard to focus on my tasks. However, I was happy to make an exception for today, because somehow the blanket of noise and adults and children happening outside my office made me feel a little bit like I was invisible in here. That being said, I was also aware that I should be going out of my way to not appear invisible to one woman in particular.

My phone vibrated in my pocket, so I shifted in my seat and pulled it out to see that Raina had texted me. Even though she was already here with Ben and Salma, who brought Zeki for the trick-or-treating thing.

> Raina: Just curious, did Signe happen to see your costume yet?

> Me: I haven't worn it yet.

I hesitated before putting my phone down again, wondering why my sister was randomly texting me this. They had already brought Zeki to my office to trick-or-treat, and I wasn't dressed up then. Why she was curious made me suspicious.

> Raina: !!! DO IT! She's going to lose her mind.

> Me: ...Is there a reason you suggested this costume that I should know about?

Last week at family dinner, Zeki was showing me his Spider-Man costume that he wore proudly until his parents forced him to change out of it for bedtime. When my sisters asked me what I was dressing up as for the company party, I told them that I probably wouldn't. I planned to just wear my work clothes that day since I had meetings scheduled and needed to look professional.

Raina casually suggested I at least buy something simple like a scream mask, so that I wouldn't be a party pooper and accidentally hinder company morale by not properly participating, but also so that I could still look professional throughout the day.

Raina: Do you want me to lie?

Me: Didn't Salma tell you that I don't want you two meddling in this?

Raina: I'd argue that it's not so much meddling, as it is seizing an opportunity.

I rolled my eyes and pocketed my phone again. I wasn't quite sure that my little sister wasn't pranking me.

I set my phone down and tried focusing on my screen at the last email I'd received and decided that it could, in fact, wait until tomorrow. I eventually needed to join the party outside of my office, take a few photos with employees, and ensure everyone was happy and safe. The usual.

Just then, Nikhil pinged me with a message as I went to stand up from my desk, and concurrently a knock sounded on my office door.

"Yeah?" I called, quickly reading his message.

"Can I come in?" Signe's voice rang in the space. I glanced up at her, torturing myself as I adjusted my rolled sleeves to see where her eyes landed. As soon as Signe stepped into the office, leaving the door partially open and letting the noise from the party fill the room, her eyes followed the movement of my hands.

My heart thumped in my chest, both from her gaze and from her presence. After following her on my secret account, and therefore seeing additional romance reader content, I recently learned that there was a very large number of women who enjoyed the look of men's forearms in a dress shirt with the sleeves rolled up. Based on the glance Signe gave mine, I was inclined to think she was one of those women.

I had no idea what Signe dressed up as, but my guess was some sort of fictional princess.

But she was beautiful, nonetheless.

She had curled her red hair in tons of tight ringlets, and she wore a dark navy dress with sleeves to her wrists and a skirt to the floor. The dress reminded me of something you'd see at a Renaissance fair. She had a fake bow and arrow on her back, but the bust of her dress was what made me swallow a dry lump in my throat and glance back at my computer to Nikhil's message.

"Nikhil was going to come to talk to you, but he got pulled away by his kids and asked me to come to check to see if you got his message," Signe explained. She had both a company iPad and her cell phone in her hands.

"Yeah, I'm reading it now," my brow scrunched as I placed my hands on my hips. I was still standing behind my desk, getting ready to come join the party, but I figured I could take a moment to check this for Nikhil first, "Can I see your phone? I need to look at this from an employee with fewer credentials and access to certain features on the app."

"Wow, tell me how you really feel." Signe quipped, scrolling on her iPad once before she tapped her password without looking, and handed me her unlocked phone in her palm. She must have still been working on that checklist Jacqueline made for her to ensure everything for the party was going to run smoothly.

I reached for her phone and gave her a look that let her know that I wasn't buying into her self-pity, my fingers gently brushing against hers. Signe's head popped up as she locked eyes with me for a moment before I looked away first.

I was once again pleased at how affected she seemed to be by casual touches from me.

"The password to get into the app is SL9469," Signe said as she tapped on her iPad.

"Wow, that's a specific set of numbers and letters."

Signe hummed, "It's the same set I use for everything."

I hesitated before looking at her phone, "What do you mean?"

"I used the same password for everything, so it's easy for me to remember." Signe glanced up at me and smiled.

"Signe," I shook my head at her, "That's unsafe. If someone finds the password to one of your accounts, they suddenly have access to *all* of your accounts."

"Yeah, I'm willing to take the risk for convenience's sake," Signe shrugged before glancing back at her iPad.

"You shouldn't though." I was feeling anxious about this, perhaps I could just log into all of her accounts and change her passwords myself to something more secure. Both proving my point and ensuring she was being responsible with her information.

"Oh my god, it'll be fine. I have nothing valuable for people to steal anyway," I was about to protest when she waved her hand at me to cut me off and ask, "Why didn't you dress up?"

"I will," I glanced down at her phone in my hand to see that the screen had locked, so I tapped her one and only password in to unlock it again. It displayed a white background with plain black text filling the screen. I was going to try to swipe out of whatever this was to get to the company app to test Nikhil's concern, but the words on the screen caught my eye and made me pause.

"I need you to be a good girl and stay quiet while I lick your cunt," he growled.

My heart sped up in my chest, every muscle in my body locked, and I could feel the heat rising to my neck and face before I could even think about trying to stop it. It was like a train wreck. My thumb was positioned to swipe out of the screen, there was no reason for me to *not* continue to swipe out of this screen. And yet, I couldn't stop my eyes from reading the text.

"Good, because I need to take pictures of everyone's costumes for the company newsletter...What's wrong?" I vaguely heard Signe ask as my eyes read faster than they had ever read anything.

...The first swipe of his tongue made me feel as if sparks were lighting up inside me, I had to fist my hands in his thick hair as I bit my lip, each pass of his hot mouth on my center made me...

Jesus fucking Christ, was this Signe's book?

"...Is everything alright?" Signe's voice made me jump a little, my heart lodging itself in my throat as I realized that I had been standing there dumbstruck as I scanned her phone. My brain scrambled, I was pretty sure I was staring at her phone with a slack jaw and everything. By the time Signe stepped closer to me, her flowery scent filling my nostrils, I had taken too long to try to conceal what exactly I was reading before she stood on tiptoes to see what I was gaping at.

Then Signe's eyes widened, and her mouth dropped open before she gasped, "Oh god!" and reached for it.

I immediately pulled my hand back, and I could not tell

you why that was my first reaction to her trying to rip her phone out of my hands, but it was.

I raised it higher above my head, my eyes still scanning the text in a frenzy, as if my life depended on it.

"Please, I-I'm going to come!" I panted, earning another growl from Zayne as he feasted on me.

"Oh my god! It's not what you think it is!" Signe squealed, reaching her hand up and hopping up and down attempting to get her phone back. I choked on an inhale as I read that last line because, holy shit, it *was* Signe's book.

I felt her grip on the skin of my forearm, desperately trying to get my hand back down to her level, but I resisted. I was grinning now, going as far as to adjust my glasses on my nose against her grabby hands so that I could focus better on the phone that was above both of our eye levels. I even let my thumb scroll to see the rest of the text after I finished reading that scene, making Signe release a screech that evidenced how mortified she was.

"What do we have here, Signe?" Was that really my voice? I tried to clear it, making it sound less gravelly and dry. I wanted to go for friendly teasing, but my words came out in a lower tone. She immediately froze, her hands gripping my arm that held her phone out of reach tightened.

"Oh my god, oh my god," she finally let go of my arm and covered her face with her hands, her shoulders hunching in on herself. I could see through her hands that her ears were as red as her hair, and part of me reveled in the fact that she was just as embarrassed and shocked as I was.

Even though these were *her* words.

Signe wrote this, using a character loosely based on *me*.

Not that I was supposed to know this.

Then, someone outside the office laughed very loudly. The laugh of someone who was probably drinking alcohol, and I felt my heart sink into my gut. I snapped out of it.

This was so wildly inappropriate.

"I-I'm sorry," I stammered, quickly swiping out of whatever app that story was saved in, and pulled one of her hands back from her face to place her phone in her palm, "That was—I didn't mean to make you—I—" I sighed, stepping back from Signe until my back hit the wall of my office, and pinched the bridge of my nose, "I did not mean to make you feel uncomfortable. That was unprofessional of me."

Signe was silent, and like the coward I was, I kept my eyes closed as I silently counted in my head attempting to control my body's visceral reaction to Signe's writing.

Nothing but the laughter and voices from the party taking place outside of my office echoed between us in my office, which suddenly felt way too small.

I decided to inhale and be the bigger person, my hand now scraping itself down my face as I turned my head to the side, where my office window was, and spoke, "If you want to reach out to Jaqueline to file a report, I completely—"

"What?" Signe asked.

I ground my jaw, before repeating, "If I made you uncomfortable, you could reach out to HR to protect—"

"Wait, wait," Out of my peripheral vision, I saw Signe's hands rise, palms out as her arms held her iPad to her chest, "Are you sure *you* shouldn't be the one filing a report right now?"

I felt my brow scrunch before I turned to look at her,

pushing my glasses up the bridge of my nose to make sure I was both seeing and hearing her right, "Me?"

"Yeah," Signe blinked, before something clicked behind her expression, "I mean...I'm the one who gave you my phone with..." she waved her hand vaguely, "I didn't mean to, like, scandalize you with smut."

"Scandalize me?" I asked, my heart racing a little at how calm she was acting about all of this.

"Well, yeah," Signe lifted a shoulder again, "I mean, you didn't ask to see—well—what I read." I decided to ignore that Signe was choosing to make me believe that this was a random book she happened to be reading and not her very own manuscript.

I shook my head, "I should have closed out of it as soon as I started reading. I shouldn't have held it out of your reach, or—"

"Oh my god," Signe rolled her eyes, her cheeks still deliciously red, "You were teasing me. It's fine. Friends tease each other."

I ground my teeth together before trying again, "But as your superior, I shouldn't put you in a position where—"

"Zaid, it's fine," Signe sliced her hand through the air, as if that was the end of the discussion, "Let's just agree that neither one of us felt like we were sexually harassing the other and move on. Yes, you're my superior, but we're also friends. Let's pretend that I didn't just hand you my phone with explicit smut on the screen."

I blinked, before staring at her to see if she was serious.

She stared at me in return, her red brows rising a little bit as if challenging me.

"If you change your mind and decide to speak with Jacqueline, I understand."

"The same goes for you." Signe countered, "Anyway,"

She carelessly waved her hand in the air, shooing the problem away, "Do you still need to look that thing up for Nikhil?"

She held her phone up in an offer, and I shook my head before replying, "I'll figure it out later."

"Sounds good," She smirked, "Now, what are you dressing up as?" I felt my lips twitch, relief mixing with a new type of anxiety at the thought of revealing my costume to Signe after that whole situation.

A costume that Raina was very invested in.

"It's not that cool of a costume," I admitted, standing away from the wall I leaned against and walking around to the back of my desk, feeling a little more professional with the furniture separating us, "You're going to think I'm lazy."

"Probably," Signe smiled.

I huffed a laugh and shook my head, opening my desk drawer to find the mask I had bought yesterday.

"Close your eyes," I instructed.

"That's what little effort you put in?" Signe seemed shocked, animated. Like how we usually were. I was suddenly so grateful that she was able to put the whole *the CTO of Sun Steer just accidentally read smut on her phone mere seconds ago* debacle behind us so casually, "I just have to close my eyes for a moment for you to change?"

"I could just not dress up at all," I lifted an eyebrow at her, a look that I was learning made her smile every time. Her lips pulled back, showing her white teeth, and making her eyes crinkle in delight.

"I guess I should be happy with what little effort you're willing to put in," Signe sighed as if exhausted with me. She set the iPad down on my desk before she closed her eyes and folded her arms across her chest. I held my breath as I pulled the scream mask out of my desk drawer and slipped it on, glancing at my reflection on my dark computer screen to make sure it sat right and that I could see out of it just fine.

I then glanced around my desk space, realizing that I couldn't do the type of casual doorframe lean that I also read about online. I could use the back of my chair, but that had wheels, and knowing me I would likely slip and land on my ass. I decided I would simply stand tall with my arms crossed casually as if I was truly put out by dressing up for the Halloween party. Plus, this brought attention to my exposed forearms again. I glanced down and flexed them a little, hoping that they looked as good as women on the internet claimed about good forearms.

"Open your eyes at your own risk," I replied, my voice partially muffled by the scream mask.

Signe opened her eyes, her expression already one of disappointment, before she looked at me and her gaze widened, and her lips parted. I stayed still and silent, waiting to see if this worked. Was she scared of the mask? Was she disappointed that I just wore a basic scream mask and regular work clothes? Was she weirded out?

My face felt hot underneath, but I was pretty sure that was due to her scrutiny.

I saw her tuck her bottom lip into her teeth, before popping it out again and clearing her throat. I took a good look at her face again, and I realized that her flushed cheeks and chest were darker, indicating that she was blushing a *second* time in my presence. Seeing me in this mask with my arms crossed made her do so.

Was it a *good* blush, though?

Hopefully, a blush that didn't make her want to call HR.

"Good lord," Signe wheezed. *Wheezed.* I chuckled under

my mask, my heart racing erratically in my chest, and my palms even started to get a little sweaty.

"Does this count?" I asked, my voice lower and gravelly again. It was like I was in tune with her on a biological level. If there was any indication that Signe was feeling a fraction of what I felt for her daily, my temperature, pulse, and voice responded accordingly.

"Um," Signe cleared her throat, "That'll work."

"Are you sure? I don't want to disappoint you," I made a show of placing my hands on my waist. Signe's eyes traveled down my form, appreciative, before she tore her gaze away and stared at my masked-covered face again. Like she couldn't look away.

I inhaled, my chest rising with the movement and earning Signe's attention, before I stepped around my desk as casually as I possibly could.

"I know it's not as thorough as your costume," I made a show of tilting my head and dragging my gaze down and up at her outfit, exaggerating the movement so she could see where my eyes went even behind the mask.

I saw her hands ball into fists from my perusal, tucked tightly under her folded arms.

"It works." Signe's voice was strained, and I thought I saw her breathing tremble a little bit under my stare. Was this working? Did she like this? Perhaps it was insanity. Perhaps it was the fact that Signe had already brushed off the previous inappropriate behavior I exhibited in her presence that made me more confident. That made me want to push this just a *little* bit more.

"You aren't lying to me, are you Signe?" Funny, because I was lying to myself at that moment, telling myself that I was lowering my voice for the mask and the act of the costume, and not because it sounded like we were in the privacy of a bedroom. I took another step towards her, thrilled that she held her ground, and tilted her head up just enough to meet my masked eyes.

"N-No," Signe stammered, shaking her head once as her gaze became hooded. Her flush was still painted on her pretty face. Her chest was heaving like mine, and her eyes watched my hand as I trailed my fingers on the edge of my desk as I approached her. This would be the second time we were in each other's personal space within minutes, and my pulse hummed in my veins at the thrill of it. How I was pushing the boundary here, and how Signe was clearly into whatever this was rapidly developing between us.

"...You promise?" I asked, "This works?" I left maybe an inch in between us.

"Yup," Signe whispered, "That works, ahem, pretty well."

I released a low laugh again, and her eyes fluttered a little bit at the sound. My heart was beating, and I knew what I wanted. What I had wanted for way too long now. It took every fragment of my willpower to stand there, feeling her body heat radiating towards mine, and do nothing else. To not cross that line. To steer clear of that boundary between us. If my mask hadn't been covering the entirety of my face, I was confident I would have already closed the distance between us and claimed her mouth. Invaded her lips with my hungry tongue, desperate to taste her and see if she would make the sounds I had only dreamed about until now. Every muscle in my body was pulled taut, desperate to feel her under my hands.

But I just stood there.

I could see emotion dance across her expression, how her surprise and obvious interest turned almost hungry. How she licked her lips and kept gazing at my chest and arms and face. How she was having an internal battle of her own to some degree.

I hated myself for it, but I knew I needed to pull us out of it before we did something we regretted. Before we did something the people who stood outside my office with the partially open door would see and report us for.

I gave myself one last moment, for purely selfish reasons, by leaning down near the side of her head. As if my masked face was whispering in her ear, "You're not going to give me grief for my costume, Signe?"

I felt and heard her shiver a little bit before she spoke, "No, I—"

"Good girl," I stood straight after I cut her off, and thank god the mask was covering my expression because I had the widest grin after I heard Signe release a quiet whimper from the sound of my praise, and then collect herself as if she had just realized where she was, who she was talking to, and what I had just said.

I turned on my heel and started walking towards my office door, keeping my mask on my face simply to hide the fact that I was wrecked for this woman. That this employee plagued every thought. I paused at the doorway and glanced at her over my shoulder, thrilled to see her standing where I left her with one hand on her chest, as if she was feeling her heartbeat, and another on her forehead, as if she was checking for a fever. Her eyes were wide as she stared at me, her mouth hung open before the corner of her lips pulled up in a surprised smile as she saw me turn around to check on her.

"Goddamn," Signe laughed, "I guess I deserved that one."

Chapter Ten

SIGNE

"I HAVE to tell you both something," I glanced through the aisles of secondhand clothing we were all rummaging through, after putting back a bright orange jumpsuit that I unfortunately didn't have the complexion to pull off. We had finally, after months, been able to sync our weekend schedules and go shopping together on Saturday morning.

"Is it bad?" Jamie asked holding a pair of jeans up to herself.

"No," I winced a little as I considered it some more, "Well, maybe?"

"Tell me everything," Mary demanded, ignoring her own search and facing me.

"It's not necessarily bad," I inhaled a deep breath as I lowered my voice, in case anyone from work happened to be browsing this thrift store too, "It's just a little...icky?"

"Icky?" Jamie repeated.

I inhaled through my nose, staring at these two ladies whom I have been lucky enough to call friends ever since I started working at Sun Steer. I didn't want to talk to my mom about this, and Eloise was busy with what I liked to refer to as "grown-up stuff". Eloise's pregnancy was really taking a toll on her body, and even though Logan was recently retired and available to take care of her and their daughter, my own drama seemed very trivial in comparison to growing another person.

If I was going to talk to someone about this, Mary and Jamie were my best options.

Even if I was still deeply worried about what their reactions would be.

"I have been keeping a secret from you both," I decided to start, hesitating for no other reason than because I wanted to, "And I need someone to talk to about it and I'm hoping you two can be those people for me."

Jamie's eyes widened while Mary's narrowed with suspicion, but both women made gestures to encourage me to keep going.

"What is it?" Mary asked, stepping closer to us.

"I may or may not be at risk of getting fired?" by the way both of their expressions morphed into a mixture of horrified, I decided to just keep talking, "That is, if anyone important finds out about what I did."

"What did you do?" Jamie asked in a low whisper.

"I…" I dropped my face in my hands, unable to look at them as I admitted my crime, "May have stolen Zaid's identity?"

"What the hell?" Mary asked, "Why? How?"

"I wrote him into my book."

Silence.

You could hear a pin drop in the silence the three of us sat in after I finally admitted it. I kept my face in my hands for a few extra moments, telling myself that I needed to put on my big girl socks and face my friends, so after a few more painfully quiet seconds, I lifted my gaze to meet theirs.

Their expressions were mostly confused.

"You...what?" Mary was the most confused.

"You wrote a book?" Jamie asked.

"So, here's the thing," I folded my fingers together under my chin, "I'm writing a romance novel and it's a super big deal. I am in the middle of the first round of edits. I have a literary agent who is helping me with my end goal of signing a three-book deal with a publisher of my dreams, and I might be able to make writing my full-time job. The problem, however, is that when I first started writing this book, I used Zaid as inspiration for the romantic interest."

Mary was nodding along a bit as I explained, and to my complete and utter relief, she seemed to take in all the details of my secret hobby just fine. She wasn't offended that she didn't know about it already, she just accepted the new information.

"So, not actually stealing his identity. You just wrote a character based on him?" Mary asked, earning a nod from me in answer, "I don't see a problem. I'm pretty sure authors write other people they know into their stories all the time."

"Yeah," Jamie added, "I assume his character has a different name?"

"Right now it's Zayne Abdul."

"Wow," Mary deadpanned, "You're so creative."

"That's not even the bad part." I winced.

"What's the bad part?" Jamie asked.

"My followers, which isn't a small amount," at that, Mary pulled her phone out and started thumbing away, probably looking for my author accounts I previously blocked her from, "Um, may have figured out that Zayne is based on a real person."

"How?" Mary asked without lifting her gaze from her phone.

"Zaid walked through my live-stream one time and my followers put two and two together."

The two women stared at me, Jamie added a little thoughtful nod while Mary glanced back down at her phone and started scrolling, before her eyes widened in shock, "Oh, damn. You're not kidding." Based on how she lifted the phone closer to her face and her fingers dragged on the screen to expand an image, I guessed what she was looking at.

"Is that a drawing of him?" Jamie gasped in a whisper. She reached forward and pulled Mary's phone out of her hands so that she could take a better look. As if she had done so before and it was a familiar gesture. To my surprise, Mary didn't fight to keep her phone or look surprised by Jamie's reach. She let Jamie grab it right out of her hands.

Odd.

Jamie was usually so passive.

"Yeah," I scrunched my shoulders and leaned against a rack of clothing, tugging the collar of my t-shirt up over my nose in embarrassment, "It's bad, isn't it?"

"I mean," Mary's lips quirked to the side as she and Jamie huddled over her phone to scroll through my feed, "It's not...great. Do your followers know his real name or where he works?" I shook my head in the negative as I groaned into my shirt, the heat of embarrassment flooding my cheeks and neck.

"What do I do?"

"You can change your character's name, for one," Mary gave me a contemplative look, "But you said you already wrote the book?"

"Yeah, but my followers have been in love with this character from day one. It's why I even have an agent and potential publisher in the first place. My followers fell in love with Zayne and blew this story up."

"Well...shoot," Jamie handed the phone back to Mary, "I'm guessing Zaid doesn't know you did this?"

"No," I shook my head as I released my face from the collar of my t-shirt, "I was hoping that I could just get away with it. I'm already so far deep into this that it would be suspicious for me to change details like the male lead's name and how he looks, and I have a hard time believing that the CTO is someone who explores romance readers' spaces on the internet," I bit into my bottom lip as I made myself share this next portion of the situation, "The problem is that he and I are friends now."

"And you weren't before you did this?" Mary asked with the rise of a dark eyebrow.

"No, I mean, well," I released a heavy sigh, "We were cordial. I said hi in passing and stuff, but he never went out of his way to befriend me. The past few weeks though, we've become friends. We tease each other. He let me wear his clothes. He got me a desk plant to apologize for the lack of accessible feminine hygiene products. I befriended his sister and am probably going to babysit his nephew soon. He's read smut on my phone, and—"

"Hold up," Mary held her hands up to stop my rambling the same time Jamie released a short, loud cackle that she quickly smothered with her hand, "He read *what* on your phone?"

"Oh my god, it was horrifying," I placed another sweatshirt into the shopping cart we were sharing before we all started walking towards the dressing rooms, "I was going over edits the morning of the Halloween party. Well, I forgot I had that up on my phone, and so later when Zaid asked to use my phone to troubleshoot something for Nikhil, he saw the smutty scene that I had left open." I still felt my stomach tumble into knots at the memory.

"How smutty was it?" Mary asked, surprising me with her question.

"Um...pretty smutty."

"On a scale of one to five," Mary pressed.

"I don't know," I threw my hands up in the air, "The guy was going down on the woman and calling her a good girl. Rate that how you wish."

Jamie cackled behind her hand over her mouth, her shoulders shaking as her face turned the brightest red I had ever seen. Mary just smirked at me and wiggled her eyebrows, "Damn, Signe. What else goes on in that pretty little head of yours?"

"It's a filthy, filthy place," I admitted, "And Zaid read a glimpse of it."

"Did he realize the scene was inspired by him?" Jamie asked with her own eyebrow wiggle. What the hell, that was a Mary move. What was going on?

"No," I rubbed my forehead because a headache was starting to slowly make itself known, "He actually ended up apologizing for even reading it."

"What? Really?" Mary asked.

"Yeah," I grinned a little at the memory, "He knew I was embarrassed about it as I tried to get my phone back, but he held it up out of reach and used his arm to keep me away so he could continue to read it and mortify me. I don't think he realized it was *my* book, just a book that I was reading earlier."

Another few seconds of quiet passed between us while my friends absorbed this new piece of information about the clusterfuck that was my life. Jamie ended up being the first one to clear her throat and break the silence while we waited our turn for the one single dressing room stall in the store.

"...It sounds like he was trying to take some mental notes about women's pleasure."

"That's exactly what I was about to say." Mary agreed with an aggressive head nod.

"Are you serious?" a horrified and amused giggle erupted out of my throat with the words.

"Anyways, you two must be close if he's able to tease you about the smut he thinks you're reading," Mary gave me a look that almost felt accusatory, "I mean...you got lucky. Imagine if Jacqueline saw smut on your phone in the office."

I felt all the blood drain from my face at the thought, "Oh god."

"Yeah," Mary nodded along, "But he was cool with it. Cool enough to keep reading just to tease you, which, if we think about it, is an insane thing to tease an employee about."

I sat with her words for a moment, realizing she was right.

"But he's the sweetest guy," I added, "He must be too laid back to get worked up about things like that. I mean, I yelled at him over tampons, and he took it like a champ. I don't imagine Zaid being the kind of guy to get upset very easily. I don't think he gets upset at all, actually."

Mary and Jamie both exchanged a look before staring back at me.

"As a software engineer, who works with a team of very annoying software engineers, I can tell you that Zaid does, in fact, get upset about things."

I tilted my head at Mary in surprise, "He does? I've never seen him truly upset."

"You've never seen him upset with *you*," Jamie defended

Mary, "I've seen him get annoyed with the sales and product teams quite a few times. He never yells or raises his voice or anything inappropriate, but his words are stern and leave no room for misinterpretation."

I just sat there, tapping my foot as I thought about it, "I... haven't seen that side of him...actually, that's a lie. He was short with me once before."

When I first started at the company, but it was obvious to me then that he was just a guy who had a lot on his plate and didn't have time to shoot the shit.

I empathized, Zaid's job didn't exactly sound easy breezy.

"Probably because he doesn't get upset with you—oh my god," Mary gasped and turned to look at Jamie so quickly that her dark hair whipped me in the face. She even startled Jamie who looked back at Mary with alarm at the sudden shift of demeanor, "What if Zaid is into Signe?"

"Oh my god, I can see it," Jamie nodded enthusiastically a second after she processed Mary's hypothesis, excitement pulling a wide smile on her cheeks, "Can you imagine?"

"I can *totally* see it," Mary whipped her head back around to me, "What if—"

"Stop," I reached forward and slapped my hands over Mary's mouth, muffling whatever else she was about to say, "I can't...I just can't..."

I shook my head and released Mary's face to drop my hands in front of me, letting my gaze fall there too as Mary asked, "What do you mean?"

"I—" My heart raced in my chest with the words, "Obviously I have a very...confusing crush on the man. I can't get my hopes up that it might be reciprocated on his end. That makes what I did with my book that much more inappropriate."

There was only a beat of silence between us before Jamie asked, "What if he reciprocates, *and* won't be offended at the thought of starring in your romance novel?"

But it was Mary who responded, an analytical tone to her words, "The thought of Zaid not being even remotely interested in you is highly unlikely, Signe. You're beautiful and smart and funny. Why wouldn't he be?" Mary released a heavy breath before resting her weight on one hip and crossing her arms over her chest, "While I agree that writing a man into your romance novel that you have a real crush on is inappropriate on paper, I don't think Zaid is the kind of person to not hear you out if you talked to him about it. Especially if he knew you did this before you two started being friendly with each other."

I released a heavy sigh, rubbing my cheek with my palm in thought, "While it's an exciting thought, it's a huge gamble. The thought of him reacting poorly and me having to tank the story is too big of a risk. This is my *dream*..." I glanced at my two friends, who gave me sympathetic looks.

Jamie rubbed her forehead, "This is a messy situation."

I nodded in agreement, "I'm meeting with my agent and editor later today, to discuss how to fix a plot hole I'm stuck on...maybe I'll bring up the possibility of just changing the character's name. Just to sever an additional link to Zayne and Zaid."

I felt a wobbly smile tug at my lips as I stared at my two friends. Even though I wasn't quite sure what to do to make any of this better, I did feel a little bit of relief that I had opened up to them about this. That they were trying to help me, instead of judging me.

"Thank you for listening," I added, "I'm sorry I kept my secret from you."

Mary and Jamie both exchanged a look so quickly, that I would have missed it if I blinked.

"Of course," Jamie replied, "Thanks for trusting us."

"I still don't exactly know what to do, but I feel a little bit better with the two of you in the loop," I smiled at both of them, surprised to see Jamie start gnawing on her lip before quickly darting into the changing stall. Someone else had finally vacated it and almost stumbled over from Jamie's enthusiasm to finally have her turn.

Mary and I giggled at Jamie's antics, glad that she seemed so excited to try on the jeans that she had picked out.

LATER THAT NIGHT, I inhaled a deep breath of encouragement, stretched my shoulders as if I was getting ready to run a marathon, and shook my hands out before finally accepting the incoming video call.

"There you are!" Michelle greeted me when my image was finally displayed on the screen.

"The one and only," I grinned with my fingers flat under my chin, "Sorry for the delay, I just needed to finish up some stuff first." Which really meant I needed to sit on my bed and spiral about every decision I had ever made up to this point in my life.

"Should we get started?" Layla, my editor spoke up. She had jet-black hair that fell in loose waves past her shoulders. You could tell by the way she sat with one leg propped up against her chest on her chair, that she was wearing pajama bottoms with her black tank top. Flowery tattoos teased her collarbones.

"Yes, but before we do, I wanted to run something by you

both," I held a finger up and took a sip of my tea, waiting for their response.

"The floor is yours," Layla nodded, folding her hands on her knees and resting her chin on top of them, dark eyes locked on her screen.

"What if we changed Zayne's name to something else?" I tried so, so hard to balance that line between casual and serious. Like I wasn't desperate for this change to happen, but also, I had thought about it a lot and thought this suggestion was important.

"Oh," like I had surprised her, "Um. What else did you have in mind?"

I froze.

Frick.

I should have thought about this more instead of actively trying not to think about it in case I talked myself out of bringing this up.

"I don't know, what if we named him something like... Zander...or maybe even something that isn't a Z name?" I tilted my head in thought, "What about Sam? Or Connor?"

Michelle's eyebrows scrunched in confusion, "Connor?"

"Yeah," I lifted a shoulder, "I'm just not sure if Zayne is a good fit."

Layla blinked at me, before speaking up, "I'm not sure Connor is a good name for someone with the character's Arab background."

I shrugged again, "What if he wasn't Arab? We could change that too." Damn, I was sounding over-eager here.

"...But then everything about his family, like when he brings Sydney home to meet his brothers, changes." Layla shook her head, "I just feel like these details are already too ingrained in the story."

"Plus," Michelle chimed in, "Readers are obsessed with

Zayne and already have character art circulating of him. Changing both his name and ethnicity would throw everyone off. You might even lose interest in the story."

I frowned, "You think so?" I had thought about it myself off and on, but hearing my agent confirm why I had pushed through with Zayne made nerves simmer in my gut.

There was no way out of this.

"I know changing the background might seem like a good way to deal with the one plot hole I mentioned in my edits," Layla shrugged, "But I think we can get creative and find a better way to address it."

I blinked because I hadn't considered using that as the reason I wanted to change his name, but I wasn't going to correct her. I'd made my bed. I needed to lie in it and allow Zayne to be Zayne.

"Speaking of that..." Michelle started talking about the ideas she had regarding the plot hole, and although I was able to keep up with the conversation just fine, and add my two cents, I kept thinking about how there was no way out of this.

Either I continued with the story with the love interest exactly as I had written him, or I had to pull the plug on the entire project and lose the progress I had made.

...But I wasn't willing to do that yet, so instead, I took extensive notes during the meeting with these ladies on how to troubleshoot the plot.

I WAS ALREADY SETTLED in at my desk that following Monday morning when Jamie and Mary walked off the elevator together. Mary looked casually confident as she always did, but I could immediately tell by the way Jamie forced herself to stand a little taller, and with a determined downturn to her lips, that something was up.

"Morning," I greeted my friends.

"Good morning," Mary replied as she leaned her arms on the ledge of my desk, before checking our surroundings. I immediately leaned toward them too, "How did your meeting go?" Mary whispered, ensuring our conversation wouldn't echo down the halls.

I slumped a little, "Not...great..." I kept my voice in a whisper too, making both women stand closer together and lean their heads towards me. Jamie almost pressed firmly against Mary's side, and I was surprised she went to such an extent to make our conversation feel more private.

"Your character's name is staying the same?" Jamie asked.

"It looks like it...I couldn't push for the change without revealing what I did. I didn't want to give my agent and editor the ick and potentially make them drop me and my story." I mindfully traced a leaf from the snake plant that Zaid gave me in thought.

"That's a bummer," Mary added, before turning to Jamie and giving her a look I couldn't quite decipher, "But I still think telling Zaid would be fine. I thought about it more over the weekend, and not that I claim to understand men, but I feel like he would be the kind of guy who is flattered to star in your story." I rolled my eyes, loving the idea in theory, but not daring to get my hopes up.

"Plus, Zaid isn't really friends with anyone else in the office besides Nikhil and Brandon," Jamie added, "You're the only other one who he seems to be friendly with...maybe he has a little crush too?"

I tucked my lips into my mouth, "As exciting as that theory is, think about the logistics. Let's pretend that my crush is possibly reciprocated, is that even allowed? He's upper management, I'm a glorified receptionist. Doesn't Sun Steer have a no-fraternization policy or something?"

Jamie kept her eyes on her fidgeting fingers as she recited, as if from memory, "Sun Steer employees are discouraged from starting any romantic relationships in the workplace, however, if any fraternization occurs, it is expected of the employees to disclose the relationship to human resources to ensure the protection of all parties involved."

I blinked at her, "Wow. Were you looking that up recently or something?"

"Actually, yes," Jamie nodded.

We all let the silence hang after Jamie's words, but the energy between the two women was thick. I easily picked up on it and kept staring between the two of them to see what they were being so weird about. Why they were suddenly fidgeting and having a silent conversation with each other.

"I don't like keeping secrets," Jamie finally said, meeting my eyes.

"What? You have a secret, too?" I asked, leaning my elbow on the desk after checking over my shoulder to ensure nobody else was entering the hallway.

"Are you sure?" Mary asked.

"Wait," I lifted both of my palms up, "Does Mary know your secret and I don't? Jamie, what the hell?" I was mostly joking around, but a small part of me was a little hurt at being left out. I guess I couldn't be too upset though since I only just opened up to both of them about my book and the chaos around it.

"Mary and I are..." Jamie paused, visible nerves making her swallow something a couple of times before a shy smirk tugged at her lips. At that, Mary turned to me and beamed.

"Jamie and I have been in a situationship for a while now," I felt my mouth drop open when I saw Jamie reach forward and rest her hand on Mary's arm as if she had done it a dozen times before, "And we are thinking we want to make things official."

I was slack jawed.

I released a gasp of laughter right when Jamie's cheeks started to heat under my reaction to their news.

"You sneaky motherfu—" I cut myself off because I was, in fact, at work, "That's amazing! Oh my god!" I stood up from my chair and ran around my desk to the two women. They were grinning and prepared themselves for the group hug I initiated, squishing them together while I wrapped my arms around each of them. The bonus of being the tallest one in the group, "I'm so happy for you two. Oh my god, I had no idea."

"That was by design," Jamie's voice was muffled against my shoulder before I finally released them, "I wasn't quite ready to, well, come out yet..."

I pressed my hands to my cheeks, "I'm so honored, thank you so much for trusting me."

Jamie grinned while Mary rubbed her back, pride beaming from her, "Jamie was really touched by you trusting us with your secret, so we talked about it, and she thought it was time."

Jamie nodded, "And now we need to tell..." her voice trailed off when her eyes landed on something over my shoulder. I turned to see Jacqueline walking towards us, wearing a cream-colored pantsuit with her dark hair slicked back in a perfect bun on her head. She was tapping away on her iPad, but when she stepped closer to my desk she finally looked up and saw all of us staring at her.

Jacqueline gave us a small friendly smile, before

scooting her glasses up the bridge of her nose some more and asking, "Am I interrupting?"

"No," All three of us answered, making me giggle.

"Actually," Jamie forced her shoulders back, the same posture she had when she stepped off the elevator a few minutes ago, "Do you have time to meet with the two of us today?"

Jacqueline immediately tapped on her iPad to pull up her schedule for the day, "I have some time before lunch, about thirty minutes or so. Can I ask what for?" Jacqueline lifted her gaze to my two friends, and I beamed when Jamie nodded to herself and replied.

"Mary and I want to disclose our relationship."

I immediately started walking back towards my desk, wanting to make the situation feel more casual and less like a formal gathering as Jamie came out to a second person today.

"Ah," Jacqueline nodded, a smile tugging on her lips, "I can help you with that. I'll have the document ready for you both before you show up." I had to hand it to her, she didn't seem surprised at all that Mary and Jamie were dating. I wondered if there had been some sort of sign or body language that Jacqueline had picked up on that I didn't.

I thought I was an observant person, but apparently not.

"Just as a reminder," Jacqueline added their meeting to her schedule and gave the two women a look that reminded me of one my mom would give, "You both are still at work and while it's none of my business what you both do on your own time, it's important to keep in mind that passionate displays of affection shouldn't happen on company property. More importantly, the breakroom," Jacqueline raised a dark eyebrow right when both Mary and

Jamie stiffened in surprise at her words, "You two haven't been exhibiting *that* kind of behavior, right?"

I had never seen Mary speechless before, but I loved seeing the woman blush in clear embarrassment for the first time.

"N-no," Mary shook her head as she stammered her reply. "We wouldn't think of doing that, right?"

"Not at all," Jamie added.

Both women used tones that heavily implied that they both, did in fact, do that.

Ah, *that's* why Jacqueline wasn't surprised.

"Glad to hear it. I also want you to know that I am forbidden from disclosing relationships between employees to others. If the only people you want to know are standing at Signe's desk right now, it'll stay that way until either of you decide otherwise." Jacqueline nodded to them, before turning to me, "Can you help me with this?" She airdropped a document to my iPad, and I opened it up for her to walk me through what she needed that morning while Jamie and Mary continued to their own desks, finally starting the workday.

I was so, so proud of Jamie and Mary. Mary for being patient with someone like Jamie, and Jamie for not only being brave enough to come out, but to come out to me and her company within the span of minutes. Huge steps were being made, and I made a mental note to squeeze her again the next time I saw her.

Chapter Eleven

SIGNE

I POCKETED my cell phone before walking into the office the following Monday, exhausted from finally ironing out a solution to that stupid plot hole I never wanted to think about again. At this point I was almost done reworking the manuscript with Layla's first round of feedback, and I was getting the manuscript for what Layla described as line edits.

After opening up to Mary and Jamie about my life choices, I decided to reach out to Eloise again. I knew it was difficult for her to do much at the moment, because pregnancy wasn't an easy experience on her. I remembered her having constant nausea and exhaustion with her first pregnancy, so I assumed that this second one was just as bad.

I ended up sending over some chicken noodle soup from

a favorite diner of ours, texting her husband to let him know I was feeding the two of them that evening.

Logan just texted back a thumbs-up emoji, because men.

Eloise was older than me, in her late thirties or so, but I considered Eloise St. James my only close friend outside of the workplace. We could go months without hanging out in person, but as soon as we did, things picked back up again just like they did last time we got together.

Eloise and I were also at very different points in our lives. She was married, and had a cute little girl with a second kiddo on the way.

Whereas I researched how difficult it would be to take care of a goldfish over the weekend. Then I decided I didn't want the responsibility of taking care of a goldfish.

Regardless, I loved her daughter and was excited for her second kiddo to be born so I could soak up all the baby snuggles I wanted.

As I finally made it to my desk, pondering on whether my life would ever turn out like Eloise's has in the next ten years or so, I heard the elevators ding.

In walked Jacqueline, with her earbuds in her ears as she gently bobbed her head from side to side. She was typing something on her iPad, completely focused as she mouthed something that looked a lot like lyrics to a song.

"Good morning," I grinned, my eyes widening when Jacqueline startled at my greeting as if she wasn't aware that I was already here and watching her vibe to her music.

"Oh," Jacqueline placed a hand on her chest, a nervous smile on her lips as she replied, "Good morning."

"What are you listening to?" I asked as I clicked my monitor to life.

"Huh? Oh. Um," Jacqueline lifted a shoulder as she continued to march towards her office, "Just a podcast."

I hesitated, before nodding and letting her continue with a wave of my fingers.

She was listening to music just then.

Why Jacqueline felt embarrassed by the music she listened to piqued my curiosity. What music could she possibly feel embarrassed about? I thought everyone was openly admitting how much we all lied and secretly loved Nickelback in the early two thousands and I wasn't sure what other well-known disliked bands there were.

I was going to figure this out, one way or another.

Then the elevators dinged again, and in walked the man of my dreams.

Zaid.

"Nice sweater," the CTO nodded his chin towards me as he shouldered his laptop bag and stopped at my desk. I glanced down at my cream-colored long-sleeved sweater that said "I'm a delight" in a black serif font.

"Thank you," I posed with my hand under my chin in a cutesy anime way I had seen Mary do many times. Zaid chuckled at my antics, "I saw on your schedule that you're going to have a meeting at a fancy Italian restaurant today, so feel free to order me some pasta to-go."

Zaid raised his dark eyebrows at my request, "Are you a fan of Italian food?"

"I'm a fan of food," I corrected before nodding, "But yes, Italian food is like, a comfort food for me."

"Then you'll probably like the food from this place," Zaid smirked, "I know the chef, and I can personally confirm that all the dishes are excellent."

I widened my eyes, "Say less, but I'll need to taste test myself just to be sure." I thought about the restaurant some more, turning to my computer and typing in the name of the restaurant in the shared calendar, and noticing that there had only been one time Zaid had taken a lunch meeting there. Today.

"What is it?" Zaid asked, lingering at my desk.

"You know the chef, but you haven't taken a meeting here before," I pointed to my laptop, "I mean, I usually schedule the reservations for these fancy business meetings, but I haven't scheduled one for this restaurant before today."

Zaid nodded once, before lifting a self-deprecating shoulder, "I actually have taken meetings there before, if I know the person is partial to Italian cuisine. But I don't normally need to make a formal reservation to go. Brandon just asked that I make a formal reservation for this one so it would align with the company books."

I widened my eyes, "Wow, you and the chef must be real homies to be able to just walk in."

"Yeah," Zaid smirked, "I'd consider my dad and I to be homies."

I stared at him for a moment, having already tasted his mother's delicious cooking. Zaid must have grown up with the fanciest, tastiest home-cooked meals if his mother's food was already that delicious, and his father was a professional Italian chef as well.

"What?" Zaid asked after a moment of my stunned silence.

"I'm just picturing what your childhood was like," I said, resting my chin on my fists and forming a dreamy expression on my face, "You probably never had to heat up a hot pocket once."

Zaid rolled his eyes before something stuck out in our conversation.

"Wait, can I ask you a question?" I held up a finger right

when Zaid stood taller, getting ready to walk toward his office.

"Min oyoni?" He replied, adjusting his shoulder bag.

"What?" I furrowed my brows in confusion. He blinked at me once, as if startled, but then shook his head, before translating for me.

"I meant, yes?"

"Oh. Well, excuse my caucasity," I started, "But I thought that Ansara was an Arabic last name?"

"It is," Zaid nodded distractedly, checking his phone.

"But...your dad is an Italian chef—which, sounds like he might be an Italian man," I reminded him.

"You're correct, he is," Zaid smirked, still not looking at me as he tapped away on his phone, but I felt relief at seeing how he was visibly enjoying my confusion. I felt a little more justified in it.

"So why does your Italian father have an Arabic last name?"

"He doesn't," Zaid finally pocketed his phone and lifted his dark gaze to meet mine, his smirk twitching in amusement, "My mother wanted her kids to have her last name."

"Oh," I sat back in my chair, understanding, "Why did she do that?"

"Because, and I quote," Zaid lifted his fingers to produce quotation marks with his words, "my mother 'did all the work, so why should her husband take all the credit?'" Zaid smiled as I felt my own smile spread across my cheeks.

"Your mom is my hero," I rested my hands over my heart in respect for the woman.

"She's an only child, and she wasn't about to let her heritage be completely washed away with my father's last name, and thankfully, my father didn't feel nearly as passionate about the subject," Zaid shrugged before taking another sip of his coffee, "He's the laid back one in their relationship."

"Doesn't that sound like the perfect relationship dynamic, though?" I asked, sitting up in my chair and resting my elbows on the desk near my keyboard, "One person is a little more headstrong and passionate, and the other is more laid back and chill?"

Zaid gave me a look I had no hope of deciphering before he nodded once and murmured, "Yeah, it does."

Butterflies erupted in my stomach.

It was obvious that even though we were just friends, that was the dynamic Zaid and I had with each other. I wore goofy-looking sweatshirts into the office regularly, while he always wore his plain professional t-shirts and polos, or sometimes a button-up.

"What about your name?" Zaid asked, surprising me a little at how he continued the conversation.

"What about my name?" *Besides the fact that you say it perfectly every time.*

"Where does Signe come from? Is it a family name?" Zaid asked, pushing his glasses farther up his nose.

"It's a name my mom found on a list of popular European baby names," I grinned, "It's not that deep. When my mom was pregnant with me, she got really into researching her own family history, seeing where her ancestors immigrated from and stuff. She loved learning about her Scandinavian roots. So, when I was born, she named me Signe, but then quickly focused back on kickstarting her pottery career."

Zaid's eyebrows raised, "Your mom makes pottery?"

"She does," I nodded, "She has a business making custom dinnerware for the one percent of the US. She charges enough to live off of." I was proud of her, I also had a few of her homemade mugs at my condo. I loved the imperfections of handmade pottery, even though at this point my mom had to really try to make sure all her cups, plates, and bowls weren't perfect duplicates of each other.

"What about your dad? What does he do?" Zaid asked.

"I don't know, never met the guy. I wasn't exactly a planned pregnancy," I saw Zaid's eyes widen, and I could see he was getting ready to apologize for bringing up the fact that I didn't have a father figure, but I raised my hand and stopped him before he could start, "Don't worry, I'm not broken up about it. I never needed, or really wanted, more than my mother."

Zaid nodded, a thoughtful expression crossing his face, "I'm glad to hear you both had each other."

"Thanks," I glanced back at the open calendar on my desktop, "But don't forget to bring me your dad's food when you're back. I meant it, Mr. Ansara."

At that, Zaid grinned and rapped his knuckles on the top of my desk twice, similarly to how I knocked my knuckles on his office door whenever I passed by it, before focusing back on his phone and sauntering towards his office.

God dammit, my silly crush on Zaid was becoming dangerous.

ZAID

"This was delicious," Mr. Martin said as he rubbed his round belly with a grin on his face, "I'll have to come back here again sometime."

"Of course, we'd love to talk more," Brandon nodded

enthusiastically at the potential investor. I spent the entire meal watching Brandon be at ease in his element. He loved the formality of this meeting. He loved being able to flaunt my family connection to this high-end restaurant. He loved looking like he had a lot of money to show off, so Mr. Martin felt comfortable giving him even more.

All of us were standing, pushing our chairs in while the two of them started talking about the next steps when I took the opportunity to shake Mr. Martin's hand in farewell as I made my way to the kitchen.

I stayed to the side to let a waiter pass, nodding at them, and allowing myself through the kitchen doors.

"This pasta is overcooked," my dad called over his shoulder to his staff, "We need a fresh batch!"

"On it," Ben called out his reply as he made his way toward the pantry, "Oh, hey, Zaid!"

"Hey, man," I nodded at my brother-in-law while he ran past me, only to meet my father's eyes as he turned to see who his sous chef was greeting.

"Zaid!" My dad greeted me before addressing the rest of the busy kitchen, "I'm taking five, everything should be how I left it when I'm back."

"Yes, chef!" The rest of the staff replied in unison.

I grinned while I followed my dad out to the bar, taking a seat at leather barstools. The bartender nodded their head at me in greeting, setting a wine glass in front of my father and a carbonated water in front of me.

"I haven't seen you here in a while," my dad hummed as he took a sip, "I knew you had another investor meeting, but I didn't think you'd have time to say hi."

"I'm making time," I lifted a shoulder, "Brandon seemed to have things covered, the guy seemed very amicable."

"That's nice," my dad nodded, "...Have you talked to him about stepping down again?"

I froze, realizing that no, I hadn't. I had been too focused on Signe. It was easy to be distracted by her when she was the first and last person I saw in my work day. I had completely forgotten about bringing up the fact that I sent Brandon that email, well, a while ago now.

But then I realized he hadn't ever brought it up with me either, which concerned me. Maybe I never hit send? Maybe it got sent to his junk folder? Or didn't go through at all? Brandon not letting me know he got my email for potential replacements was very unsettling, to say the least.

"Not yet, but I think I will soon since today went so smoothly," I nodded to him as I sipped my water, "I'm very ready to step down." Mostly so that was one less thing keeping me from asking out the woman of my dreams.

"That'll be good, I hope it happens for you soon," my dad nodded to himself before glancing over his shoulder, "I'm going to tell you something, but your mother is going to be upset at me for telling you."

I quirked a brow at him, "Okay."

"She's talking about setting you up," my dad leveled me with his dark hazel eyes, "Several times now. I've discouraged her from doing so, but you know your mama."

I groaned and scraped a hand over my face, "Yeah, you can only do so much."

"Unfortunately," my dad chuckled, "She just wants to see you happy, even if she entertains the idea of overstepping from time to time."

"I get it," I sat there with him at the bar, wondering if I could take the moment we had where it was just my dad and me, to tell him about one woman in particular I wouldn't exactly hate being set up with.

But Signe and I weren't anything.

We were coworkers who got along and joked around, and that was it.

I knew what my father would say, too, about how I shouldn't put one of my employees in a position like that. He once ripped into two of his employees because he caught them making out in the freezer, so I had a general idea of where he stood on workplace relationships.

"I'll try to stop by here more often, though," I added, setting my glass down and checking the time on my phone. I needed to get back to the office.

"I'll never say no to that," my father stood with me, wrapping me up in a tight hug and patting my back with his palm, before kissing my cheek and saying, "I love you."

"I love you, too," I replied, returning his kiss with one of my own, "I'll see you at the next dinner."

"I look forward to it." With that, my dad stole another sip of his wine and headed back into the kitchen, the double doors swinging behind him as he disappeared. I felt better about going out of my way to spend time with my dad when I hadn't made a lot of effort to do so the last few years.

I double-checked that Signe's to-go meal was right where I left it, on the end of the bar top next to the kitchen doors and made my way to my car. I liked the idea of spending more time with my dad at his restaurant again, but I needed to approach Brandon more seriously about my stepping down for that to happen.

I also just needed to be better at not becoming immediately distracted as soon as I saw the gorgeous red-haired woman every time I walked in and out of work.

Chapter Twelve

ZAID

GETTING a text from Salma two hours before I stood on her doorstep, letting me know that Signe had to bail on babysitting was just what I needed tonight. Instead of sitting at home, spiraling about what Signe was up to while she played with my nephew, I got the chance to go play with the little guy myself. That, and I would be too busy playing with Zeki to let myself wonder too much if Signe was okay. If she canceled on Salma because she was sick, or had an emergency, or anything else that was none of my business.

However, when I knocked on Salma's door to a sheepish but stylish-looking Ben, I immediately grew suspicious.

"What is it?" I asked, narrowing my eyes at my brother-in-law.

"Salma being Salma," Ben wouldn't meet my eyes as he waved me through the threshold, giving me space to toe off my sneakers before I heard squeals of laughter from Zeki himself.

"You're so fast!"

That voice, however, made me halt my steps and shoot a wide-eyed look at Ben. He tried his hardest not to smile, but he patted my shoulder as he continued our walk to the living room.

"My love," Ben called to his wife when we entered the space. Signe was chasing little Zeki around the couch, making him cackle almost maniacally while my sister stood off to the side, bending over to slip on her heels for date night.

"Yeah?" She turned towards her husband and gave us her wide-eyed surprised look. The way she dropped her mouth and froze her movements for a bit was so convincing, that I almost believed the act she was putting on for Signe's benefit. Signe, who had picked up Zeki after successfully catching him, also stiffened a little bit at my unexpected presence.

"Ayre," Salma murmured, standing straight, and pressing her palm to her forehead in false distress, "I forgot to let you know that we didn't need you."

"Oh," I nodded, narrowing my eyes at her the slightest bit before shoving my hands in the pockets of my sweatpants and shrugging. Sweatpants, I was wearing fucking *sweatpants* in front of this woman.

She was wearing casual clothing too, leggings and a baggy shirt that—wait—was that *my* shirt?

"Hi Zaid," Signe smiled, setting a wiggling Zeki back down on the ground when he struggled out of her hold to run straight towards me.

"Hey Z," I grinned, bending low and wrapping my nephew up in a hug before spinning him once. His peals of laughter were contagious, and I found myself chuckling a little bit as he kept patting my arm to encourage me to toss him up in the air.

"I'm so sorry," Salma was rubbing the back of her neck, and her expression was a perfectly practiced one of remorse.

She was such a good liar, "I didn't mean to schedule you both."

"Oh, it's no worries," Signe played with her fingers nervously, before nodding and smiling at my nephew in my hands, "I can take off if Zaid wants to babysit tonight."

"No, it's okay. I can leave," I shook my head as I set Zeki back down, only for him to shake his head and wrap his arms around my legs desperately.

"No!" Zeki whined, digging his forehead into my shins as if I was seconds from disappearing on him.

Signe's expression warmed at the sight of Zeki clutching to me so desperately, and I felt immediately uncomfortable at the situation my sister had put us in.

"It's alright," Signe, grinned, waving at Salma and Ben as they continued to get their coats and Salma's purse, "Maybe I can come play with you another time, yeah?" Signe brushed her fingers through Zeki's hair as she made her way to pass by us, making him lift his head from my shins and reach out to grab her—actually my—t-shirt.

"No!" Zeki cried, now holding both of us captive in his tiny little fists. He tugged and Signe stumbled into my side a bit at the movement, grabbing onto my bicep to catch herself before tripping over my nephew.

"You can both stay, if you want," Salma casually spoke over her shoulder as Ben helped her into her coat. I lifted my head to glare at my sister because this was very much overstepping, except Signe had already turned to look at me with a casual shrug of her shoulder and a friendly smile.

"Would you be okay with me staying here too?"

Her hand had just released itself from my bicep, and the loss of heat from her touch made me instinctively lean closer to her. Hopefully, the movement could be written off by Zeki's death grip on the both of us, but I hardly ever got this physically close to Signe, and now my body was humming with energy at the reality of this situation.

"Of course," I glanced down at my nephew with a grin, wondering if Salma had somehow put her three-year-old up to this, "I don't think Z's giving us a choice anyway."

"I wouldn't disappoint the toddler if I were you two," Salma nodded, patting Ben on the ass once and loud enough to make him blush, "We're planning on being out late, but make yourselves at home." Without letting either of us respond, she grabbed Ben's hand and rushed for the front door, "Have fun, and thanks again!" Ben managed to wave goodbye to us before he and my sister were gone, the sound of the front door closing behind them echoing in the space as Zeki finally released his grip on Signe and me and reached his arms up to be held.

"So," Signe bent down to oblige him, "What do you want to do first?" she asked as she sauntered back towards the play area of the living room they were in before, "Watch TV? Play?"

"Play!" Zeki squealed, pointing to a rubber ball near his shelf of toys. Signe smiled at me over her shoulder as she let the little man down so he could retrieve his toy. I gave myself a silent pep talk, determined not to spiral about how unprepared I felt for co-babysitting with Signe.

I pulled my phone out to send a quick text to my sister while Signe and Zeki got started on rolling the ball back and forth to each other.

Me: You aren't clever. Did you put your son up to this, too?

Salma: Believe it or not, that was all him.

> Me: This is messed up. You're really
> overstepping, Sal.

> Salma: Unrelated, there are condoms in
> Ben's nightstand drawer.

Then I immediately closed the text thread and pocketed my phone before I vomited in my mouth at the thought of Salma and Ben ever needing condoms.

"You want to get in on this?" Signe's voice pulled me back into the room. Zeki started slapping the ground next to him, attempting to get me to join.

"Of course," I grinned, tickling my nephew on his tummy once as I settled in on the ground with my legs crossed.

SIGNE

Sweatpants.

The man was wearing *sweatpants*.

They were black, not light grey, so it wasn't like they were super scandalous. Logically, I knew that Zaid's sweatpants probably weren't scandalous at all, but my filthy smut-loving brain couldn't handle the sight of him casually walking into his sister's house, completely surprised at my presence there.

As I picked up all the toys around the living room, while Zaid laid his nephew down for bedtime, my mind kept replaying specific moments throughout the night that I knew would stick with me forever.

Moments like Zaid sitting cross-legged on the floor in his sweatpants.

Like Zaid bending over to grab his nephew, his sweatpants showing off those glorious glutes I admired way more than I should.

Or when Zaid carried Zeki in his hands and allowed the kiddo to kick off of the various walls and reachable ceiling, letting him pretend to be Spider-Man, showing off the muscles in his arms and shoulders through the long-sleeved Henley shirt that he wore.

It was as if this night was specifically designed to make me think the most inappropriate thoughts about Zaid possible. There was no posture or position that Zaid could be in that didn't show off how beautiful the man was. He didn't even have a double chin when he laid on his back as his nephew sat on his chest and pretended to beat him up.

And the fact that Zaid was probably the sweetest and most involved uncle I had ever seen? I was a goner. It was hopeless. My crush on Zaid was rapidly developing, even though that wasn't supposed to happen.

Zaid's face lit up whenever Zeki did the most mundane, unimpressive things, as if his three-year-old nephew was the light of his life, and it made my heart feel like it was going to fall out of my vagina.

How could it not?

Here I was, no better than the average man who sexualized a woman simply because she was attractive and existed.

Zaid wore sweatpants, and if he stepped a certain way, I could probably see a perfect outline of everything the man was packing. Because of this, I adamantly averted my gaze whenever the opportunity to see said hypothetical outline arose. I knew myself; I knew that if I saw anything, I would gape at it, and that he would undoubtedly notice my gaping, and then he would probably cover himself up and kindly ask that I leave.

And then we would both go to work on Monday and things would be weird for the rest of our days. Anytime we passed each other, we would probably pretend we hadn't been 'kind of' friends the last couple of months. Instead, he'd probably tell himself, *don't make eye contact with the groin starer*, and I wouldn't blame him one bit.

"He's down," Zaid's deep voice startled me out of my panicking thoughts, making me drop a few blocks and gasp as I spun around to face him. His dark brows rose over the black rim of his glasses a moment before he quickly dropped back to the floor with me to help pick up the toys, "Sorry, didn't mean to scare you."

"I'm fine," I giggled nervously as we both deposited the blocks back in their bin. I was blushing, *blushing*. He was close enough to remind me that his cologne was mouthwatering.

"Did you have too much caffeine?" Zaid asked, and I could hear the smirk on his lips even though I was standing and making my way over to the couch, desperate for space.

"Why?"

"You're...twitchy." Zaid's brows furrowed as he slowly followed me to the couch to sit on the opposite side, "Are you okay?"

"I'm fine," I grinned a little too wide but knew I couldn't come back from it, "What are we going to watch?" I grabbed the remote and immediately hit the power button, but the TV screen remained black.

"That's the sound system remote," Zaid stepped forward and gently removed the controller from my hands, his warm fingers brushing over mine casually even though my heart jumped as if he tried to cop a feel.

"Oh," I settled back onto the couch, tucking my legs underneath myself and leaning against the throw pillows on the armrest, "What's your favorite movie?"

Zaid hesitated for half a second before he shrugged and asked me, "What's yours?"

"I'm easy to please," *whoa, there, Signe*, "I'll watch almost anything."

"Almost?" Zaid asked, his eyes glancing over at me as he continued to scroll through the options on the TV screen.

"I have to be in the right headspace for things like *Game of Thrones*," I admitted, "Violence and gore isn't fun to watch when you aren't ready for it."

"That's fair," Zaid nodded, glancing over at me again, and raising his eyebrows as he asked, "What about *Bluey*?"

"Sure, what's that?" I asked, grabbing the throw blanket that was resting on the arm of the couch and throwing it over my legs. It wasn't until I had adjusted my seat to fit the blanket over the entire lower half of my body that I realized Zaid didn't answer my question, and I glanced up from my fidgeting to see him staring at me wide-eyed and open-mouthed, "What?"

"Did you just ask me what *Bluey* is?" Zaid asked as a shocked chuckle escaped his lips, "Is this your first day on planet Earth?"

I cackled, before slapping my hand over my lips because I remembered that little Zeki was supposed to be sleeping.

"Geez," I laughed behind my hand, "Zaid, that was so mean!"

He rolled his eyes as he lifted the remote and pressed play on the movie he was talking about. I settled in and was surprised to see a blue screen with cartoon dogs dancing.

As soon as each member of the cartoon dog family was

introduced (Mom, Dad, Bingo, and Bluey) I slowly turned my head to look at Zaid.

He was watching the TV intently. One of his arms was stretched out on the back of the couch while the other rested on the armrest. He had one ankle resting on his knee, and I could see his lips twitch as he noticed my slow head turn in his peripheral vision.

"Zaid?"

"Hmm?"

"Is this a kids show?"

"I think it's a show for all ages." He countered, leveling me with an annoyed expression I didn't buy for one second.

"So, it's a kids show," I laughed, "Why are we watching a kids show? The kid is in bed."

"I think you need to watch a couple of episodes to understand, shush." He nodded his head towards the TV, desperately trying to hold back his grin of amusement.

"A *couple* of episodes?" I asked, sitting up a little in mock outrage.

"They're like eight minutes long, shush!" Zaid lifted his hand off the arm of the couch to point at the TV, raising his eyebrows at me like a parent waiting for their child to comply. I laughed as I snuggled up with my throw blanket and settled in.

The first episode was cute because it was, in fact, a children's show, but there was a one-liner that the mom delivered that made me laugh out loud.

The second episode had some comedic moments from the youngest sibling that I also really enjoyed.

The third episode got me. It was insane to me that this was for kids, because the entire episode was a flashback of the mom when Bluey was a baby, and how easy it is to assume the worst of your abilities as a mother. I found myself getting emotional, and by the end of the episode when the mom realizes that she doesn't need to compare herself to all the other mothers, I turned my head and gaped at Zaid.

He was watching me with a knowing smirk on his face, noting the tears I was desperately trying to keep contained in my eyeballs.

"How dare they do that to me," I breathed, "This is a *kids* show?" I asked.

"I told you," Zaid shook his head once as the next episode started playing. The theme song would surely be stuck in my head for a while. "I'm just grateful that my sister has a kid now," Zaid lifted a shoulder, "So I can at least try to justify the chokehold this show has on me."

I laid my head back on the couch and laughed, smothering the sound with my hand again so I didn't wake up little Zeki. I heard Zaid rumble his laughter next to me on the couch before we both settled into silence, giving this Australian cartoon our undivided attention.

Until I asked Zaid a question that popped into my mind, "Do you want kids?"

Zaid's dark eyes darted to me quickly, and I immediately lifted my hands up defensively, "I know it's a personal question," I added, "But I'm not going to lie to you, you're giving off a lot of strong dad energy tonight."

"Strong dad energy?" Zaid asked.

"Yeah," I nodded, "Like a man who has baby fever."

I could see the tips of his ears redden, and I desperately wanted to know why, "I wouldn't call it 'baby fever' exactly." Zaid shrugged a shoulder before rubbing his hand on the back of his neck, "I always liked the idea of kids, though."

"Huh," I nodded my head toward him, "I can see that for you."

We sat in comfortable silence again for a few moments, and it wasn't until I laughed at another one-liner delivered by Bluey's parents that Zaid spoke up again, "What about you?"

I knew what he was asking, so I took a moment to think about my answer, "I mean, I'm not going out of my way to watch kids' shows," I gave him a pointed look and he narrowed his eyes at me, before smiling, "But I'm not against them."

"Not against them," Zaid replied with a nod of his head.

"It's just," I chewed on the inside of my cheek, wondering how best to explain my complex feelings about it, "I feel like too often women who have baby fever focus on the baby fever part, and spend less time considering if their partner is someone who should be a parent. But the thing is, I don't believe everyone should be a parent," I could feel Zaid's eyes on the side of my face, but I continued, "I can find someone I love, someone I can see myself spending the rest of my life with, while also understanding that that person may not ever want kids. Or, that they possibly shouldn't have kids depending on their specific circumstances. So, while I think that it's fun to romanticize the idea of having kids now and then, I'm not making it a goal I want to check off quite yet. I want to find out who my forever partner is, first. If that person ends up being someone who also wants kids, then I'll consider the option more seriously."

There was a silence hanging between us after I finished my ramblings, and I glanced over at Zaid to see him studying me with a thoughtful expression.

"That's very...mindful," the corner of his lips tipped up, "So, eventually, you'd like to settle down with someone?"

"Sure," I lifted my shoulder, "But I don't think that's a

box I'm trying to check immediately either. I know that I don't need anyone else to complete me. I'm already whole and fulfilled as is. That being said, if I stumble upon someone who I can see myself spending the rest of my life with, I won't fight it either."

Zaid was silent again, so I raised my eyebrows at him before adding, "Sorry, that was a lot of rambling."

"Don't apologize," Zaid smiled, "I was just wondering if you could have a word with my mother. Her entire focus lately has been finding me a wife."

"Didn't Nikhil say something about that?" I tilted my head to the side as I remembered the conversation in front of my desk, "Is it hard? Having your mom on your ass like that?"

Zaid huffed a laugh before lifting his hand, splaying his fingers, and tilting his hand side to side, "Yes and no. On the one hand, it is something I want because I do think I would be happy with a partner. I'm just not thrilled at how involved my mother wants to be in the process."

"Ah," I adjusted my seat on the couch, my cheeks heating a little bit at the thought of Zaid finding a person he loves, and being excited about starting a life with them, "Can't relate. My mom doesn't care if I'm in a relationship or not. She just wants me happy, however that looks."

"Must be nice," Zaid released a heavy sigh with the words as he focused back on the cartoon dogs on the TV screen. I gave myself a few more moments to admire Zaid. Seeing him casually sprawled out on the couch, happily watching a children's cartoon was doing things to me. I was serious when I informed Zaid of my stance on kids and romantic relationships, but I also couldn't deny the flutter my heart made throughout our conversation.

How I discovered that this introverted, work-focused man longed for a family of some kind.

Sure, he said that he liked "the idea" of kids but show me one grown man who enjoys children's cartoons like this. Who happily babysits his nephew after what I assumed was a long day at work? I had a feeling that whoever Zaid ended up with, they were going to have the most loving man in the world fawning over them.

Inside of me, a little green monster of jealousy growled at the thought.

But...I was the one sitting on his sister's couch watching cartoons with him.

I was the one at work he was becoming more and more friendly with.

Perhaps Mary was onto something a few weeks ago when I told her about the book, perhaps something was happening between the two of us. Something that we both weren't ready to acknowledge quite yet.

Chapter Thirteen

SIGNE

IF THIS GUY referred to me as "kid" one more time, I was going to throw up in my mouth.

Jake, the date that I swiped right on this morning, who had immediately messaged me asking if I wanted to meet up for lunch, was a little older than the men I usually went out with. He was forty-two, twelve years older than I was. He was handsome. He had dark brown hair with a touch of grey over the ears. Jake had blue eyes, a kind smile, and no pictures of dead fish or animals anywhere on his profile.

Most importantly, he wasn't Zaid Ansara.

I was determined to squash any romantic hopes or interests on my part. The progress I was making on my manuscript didn't allow me to explore whether Zaid returned my feelings. The ethics were still very grey.

I had just said something to make Jake laugh, which made me wince as his laughter boomed loudly and a little obnoxiously across the little café we sat in. Whatever I said probably justified a small chuckle or a scoff, not...whatever that was.

"You're funny, kid," Jake wiped a tear from his eye as his shoulders shook, another laugh escaping him.

I couldn't stop my grimace this time, an expression he noticed but pretended not to as he finally pulled himself together enough to clear his throat and rest his forearms on the table.

I made a show of checking the time on my phone, "I should probably get back to work soon," I turned my wince into one of disappointment, even though I was desperate to get out of there and block the guy. The date wasn't the worst date I had ever been on, but it wasn't a good time either. He never asked me questions and was already in the habit of cutting me off mid-sentence to add his own two cents. The only time I could get a word in was when I interrupted him, which is probably why he was so startled by my last sarcastic remark to whatever story he was telling, and I laughed as obnoxiously as he did.

"Oh, wow, I didn't realize it's already been an hour," his eyes widened as he gave me a sheepish expression, darting to my chest quickly while pulling his wallet out and laying some money down on the table.

I thanked Jake for covering the bill as we both gathered our things and stood, walking awkwardly next to each other out of the cafe. He placed his hand on my lower back to guide me out of the door first, so I took a larger, dramatic step away from him to get him to drop his hand as soon as we were both outside.

"I had a great time, kid," part of me was convinced he couldn't pronounce my name and was too prideful to ask me how to again, "Are you free this weekend?" He stood in front of me, blocking my path and lowering his head to meet my eyes. His body was a little too close to mine again, so I stepped back once more to create distance.

"I'll have to double-check," I smiled, mentally checking the list of how to turn down a man and not become a skin suit afterward, "I'm getting together with some friends." Vague, believable, and gives enough reason to not commit to anything at this very moment. I finished it off with a friendly smile and shouldered my purse, checking the time on my phone one more time to emphasize the importance of me returning to work at this moment.

"You're not going to ghost me, are you?" His words were a joke, and his tone was a joke, but the look in his eyes let me know this wasn't the first time a woman was not interested in making plans with him after one date. I felt my body tense at his words, and my smile became a little wobblier than I would have liked.

"Does that happen to you often?" I countered, wondering if I had just blown everything.

He rolled his eyes, his friendly smile fading to something more bitter, before shoving his hands in his pockets and saying, "I've been doing this longer than you have. I know when a woman is trying to shake me, I'm not stupid."

I blinked at him, my mouth hanging open in shock before I caught myself and snapped it closed, "Okay."

Jake gave me a once over, longing clearly in his eyes before he replied, "You're not even going to try denying it?"

I lifted my shoulder, "I don't really see why I should."

He frowned, looking down at the ground, "Is it something I did?"

I tilted my head, shifting my weight on one hip before crossing my arms across my chest and assessing him, "Do you really want to know, or do you want me to soothe your ego?" I tried to ask the question as gently as I could, but he still flinched. He still pressed his lips together in a firm line before giving me a hurt expression. After the longest couple of seconds of my life, he finally lifted both of his shoulders and grumbled to the ground.

"I keep striking out," his hand lifted, and he rubbed his neck as he continued, "If there is something I'm doing that's off-putting, I'd like to know."

I sighed, checking the time on my phone once more before I saw a text message from Zaid.

My heart skipped a beat at the notification, but I ignored it while I addressed Jake.

"Look," I relaxed my body language, my tense shoulders loosening, in an attempt to get him to relax as well, "You're a really nice guy. You're chivalrous and kind and handsome," his head lifted a little as hope coated his expression, right before I added, "But you didn't let me get a word in."

His brows furrowed the slightest bit, "I didn't?"

"No," I shook my head once, "I know all about you. I know what you do for work, what your hobbies are, and why your cat got his name. I know about your friends and their partners and a couple of fun memories you have with them," he was nodding slightly as I listed off all the things he spoke about during our date, "And yet, you don't know any of those things about me in return."

His ears started to turn a little pink, his lips tucking into his mouth before releasing a clearly embarrassed sigh.

Right when he opened his mouth to reply, I quickly cut him off, "And you interrupted me six times within one hour."

Jake's eyes widened a little before he slumped his shoulders, "I'm sorry. I didn't realize."

"Thank you," I gave him what I hoped was an encouraging smile, "But now you know."

He gave me another sheepish expression, his gaze

dropping to my chest once more before he leaned forward the slightest bit and asked, "Is there any way I can get a second chance?"

I felt my smile falter, my eyes tightening as I struggled to keep a polite expression without hurting his feelings, "I... don't think so."

Jake nodded, stepping back away from me, "Then, well, thank you for letting me know what I can work on going forward."

"Of course," I smiled, exhausted from this short but stressful conversation. *How was I the one teaching a forty-two-year-old man how to act on a first date?* We bid each other goodbye, me awkwardly shoving my hand out for a shake at the same moment he opened his arms for a hug, and then I speed-walked back to the office.

I also kept checking my surroundings to ensure that he hadn't started following me back to work because even though he seemed to understand my rejection, I hadn't been so lucky in the past. Men could be persistent.

As soon as I entered the building, I pulled my phone out to read Zaid's text, which was really just a meme about how most meetings could be emails instead. I had seen the meme plenty of times because I had been an active member of the internet for years. However, the fact that Zaid had stumbled upon this meme and felt the need to send it to me made something warm bloom in my chest.

It's just a stupid meme, Signe.

I was grinning as I stepped off the elevators towards my desk, almost stumbling into Nikhil.

"Eyes up, Signe," Nikhil nodded before stepping around me and entering the elevator I had just vacated. *See? I* thought to myself, *Nikhil could say my name right, so why couldn't Jake?*

"My bad," I waved goodbye to him as I stepped backward toward my desk, "I was just—" warm, large hands grabbed my shoulders and halted my retreat. I yelped in surprise, freezing at the same moment a low voice spoke into my ear.

"You are O for two, Signe," Zaid teased before quickly releasing my shoulders, allowing me to spin around and see that I was a step away from colliding with him.

I narrowed my eyes at Zaid playfully, ignoring the heat coursing through my veins at the sound of this man saying my name right every single time, "Maybe you both were just in my way."

Nikhil's laughter was cut off by the elevator door's closing, so Zaid raised a dark eyebrow as he watched me round my desk and set my purse down, "Sure, blame the victims you were bulldozing into. Not the fact that you were glued to your phone." His dark eyes dropped to said phone in my hands.

"I was looking at the meme you sent me, for your information," I raised my eyebrows, showing him my screen that still had the meme displayed as evidence. Zaid grinned, making me get lost for just a moment as I contemplated what it would be like if Zaid had been my lunch date instead. How easily the conversation would have flowed between both of us. How I wouldn't have been eager to step out of his touch if his hand rested on my lower back.

Hell, I was frazzled by the feeling of his hands on my shoulders a moment ago, and that was simply in self-preservation on his part.

My phone buzzed in my hand, and Zaid's eyebrows lowered as his eyes focused on whatever notification popped up on my phone. I turned the device around to see and frowned at the message I had just received from Jake on the dating app.

Jake: If you ever want to get together again, just say the word.

I grimaced, before blocking his account and closing out of the app.

"Whose Jake?" Zaid asked, resting his forearms on my desk.

Damn, those were nice forearms.

Those two veins always did things to me.

"Hmm?" I asked, as I wondered if he brushed his arm hair in a certain direction, or if his arm hair naturally fell perfectly like that.

"Jake?" He pressed, making me tear my gaze from the free forearm porn I was admiring, to stare the CTO in the eye.

"Oh," I waved a hand dismissively in the air, "Just a lunch date that I won't be seeing again." I gave Zaid a look that showed just how unimpressed I was with Jake.

Zaid was silent for a moment, his lips pressed together as a myriad of expressions flickered over his face before I had the chance to recognize them, "A lunch date? Do you do those often?"

"Sometimes," I shrugged before plopping down in my desk chair, "Though today reminded me why I took such a long break from them," I pulled myself closer to my computer, before rethinking and pushing away to turn to face Zaid directly, "He didn't even comment on my sweater!" which was astonishing, considering the number of times his eyes dropped to my chest.

I tugged the bottom of my sweater away from my body,

showing off the lettering to Zaid while also concealing the shape of my breasts underneath so it wouldn't be weird.

Zaid's dark eyes dropped, and the corner of his lips tipped up before he made eye contact with me again, "He didn't?"

"He *didn't!*" I slapped my palms down on the desk, loving how Zaid was validating me on this one, "Do you have any idea how easy it could have been? This sweatshirt is an icebreaker itself. It can start lots of interesting conversations. Instead, he just talked at me the entire time."

Zaid frowned, "What a loser."

"I know," I glanced down at my sweater, reading the text out loud, "'Hot Girls Read Books'. He could have asked me what I liked to read, what I read most recently, what the worst book I ever read was. The more I think about it, the more insane it is that I wasted this sweater on him."

"What do you like to read?" Zaid asked, startling me from my rant and making me snap my head up.

"Huh?"

"What do you like to read?" Zaid repeated himself, nodding towards my sweatshirt once before adjusting one of the rolled-up sleeves of his shirt. I narrowed my eyes at him, my lips quirked to the side as I wondered how this conversation could go. How I ended up in a conversation with the very man whose appearance I was plagiarizing every single day.

"Romance, mostly."

"Why are you looking at me like that?"

"Like what?"

"Like you're challenging me."

"Maybe I am," I shrugged, pulling my chair forward so my torso could lean over my desk as I narrowed my eyes even more at the CTO. I had a feeling that he and I both remembered the smut-tastrophy in his office during the Halloween party, so I was preparing myself for some sort of eye roll or scoff or any other sort of dismissive remark, "Got anything to say about what I read?"

"Um," Zaid blinked, yet held my stare without moving a muscle, "No?" He was playing a weird game of chicken with me. I leaned into his space, my hands gripping the edge of my desk while I narrowed one of my eyes. I was studying his expression for tells of a lie of some sort. He just stayed put, leaning his forearms on my desk and waiting for me to finish my inspection.

"Interesting." That was what I said before I pulled away and turned my body back toward my computer.

"Why is that interesting?" Zaid asked, removing his forearms from my desk to stand taller.

"Most men hate the genre; it makes them uncomfortable." I turned to give him another stink eye, letting my eyes trail his body up and down as if I was suspicious of him and not just taking the opportunity to ogle his form in the workplace.

"I don't know enough about the genre to hate on it," Zaid shrugged, pulling his phone out of his pocket and frowning at something, "Besides that snippet you showed me on Halloween, of course." I smothered a giggle; glad he was willing to still joke about the time I accidentally gave him smut.

Zaid's eyes stayed glued to his phone, though. His job always seemed way more demanding than mine.

While thumbing away on his phone, Zaid nodded his head goodbye, heading towards his office, and I made myself inhale a deep breath to get back into the workflow mindset. I rested my hand over my heart, begging it to calm down, desperately reminding it that Zaid was not someone we needed to develop feelings for. That the CTO of the company I currently worked for was not someone I should crush on this hard.

Stealing his looks for a fictional character in my novel?

Sure, whatever.

Becoming more and more attached to him, desperately clinging to every word he speaks and every smirk he gives?

Fun, but not the end goal.

While it was easy for me to lose myself in his dark eyes, admire his always perfectly trimmed beard, and every other part of his playful personality, I needed to keep my head in the game.

Even though a year ago he never would have put both of his hands on my shoulders in the office.

And the fact that he was comfortable putting his hands on me in any form, self-protection or not, made something flutter in my stomach.

No, I scolded myself, *even if he is attracted to you in that way, it's not okay.*

I replayed those words in my mind over and over again the rest of the day, even though I knew I had little hope of truly convincing myself.

Chapter Fourteen

ZAID

THE THING with playing the long game like I was, is that the woman you're romantically interested in has no idea that you are, in fact, romantically interested in her. I have been enjoying the friendship I have been developing over time with Signe, and I love spending casual time with her throughout my workday. However, because of professional boundaries and my bending over backward to keep my attraction toward her a secret, I am now seeing the downside of my plan.

Like when Signe came back from her lunch date.

Sure, it was a bad date. She made it very clear she wasn't interested in seeing the guy again.

But when was she going to feel the need to go on another one?

Was I delusional for thinking that we had both been working towards something together? There were multiple moments in the past few months where I could have sworn she was feeling for me just as I was feeling for her, and yet the fact that she went on a sudden lunch date implies otherwise.

How much longer would it be for her to quit work here, or me to wait the appropriate amount of time to ask her out after she quits so I don't seem over eager, and then have us going on a first date?

She needed to wait for me, for us, but I had no way of communicating that to her without crossing several ethical boundaries in the workplace. That, and there was still a very real possibility that when I eventually asked Signe on a date, she would be uninterested in doing so. So, there I was, standing awkwardly at Signe's desk while she vented to me about the loser she went to lunch with. Focusing way too hard on settling my facial expression into a relaxed one. Keeping my hands loose, instead of tight fists, hopefully coming off as friendly and listening, and not a man thinking, *I want to grab your phone and delete every dating app you have downloaded until I can make my intentions clear* like an overbearing psychopath.

It wouldn't be until later that night, when I visited my mother's house again for our weekly dinner, that an idea came to mind. A purely selfish idea, that I refused to feel guilty about. I was watching my sisters load up my mother's Tupperware with the many leftovers that would surely last a week and a half when I asked if I could take a few containers off of their hands.

My sisters, somehow, gave me looks that implied that they knew exactly why I was suddenly going out of my way to take enough leftovers for two people.

I ignored them.

The next day when I approached Signe at her desk, holding two Tupperware containers filled with my mother's homemade cooking, I wondered if I was being too obvious.

"Do you have plans for lunch?" I asked her, lifting the second container as evidence to back up my entirely false claim, "My mom doesn't seem to understand that I am one person, and can't eat all of this on my own."

Signe's eyes lit up as a grin spread across her face, making me want to kiss her so badly that the muscles in my arms tightened with restraint. I was thankful that my hands were already busy holding the containers.

"I'll never say no to Mama Ansara's cooking," Signe typed a couple of things on her computer before standing from her chair and making grabby-hands at the Tupperware I offered her.

"Thank you," I smiled as I handed it over and we both started walking towards the break room, "Now it won't all risk going bad."

And that was how, a couple of times a week, Signe Lange and I started having lunch together. At first, I was nervous about this new routine because I usually ate lunch at my desk, or at whatever restaurant during another meeting. However, in my head, it was more important to rearrange my schedule for the foreseeable future, so that I could spend lunch with Signe. Perhaps, by spending half of the week's lunches with her under the guise of having too many leftovers to eat myself, she wouldn't feel the need to log back onto her stupid dating app and waste time with a man who probably wouldn't be worthy of her attention anyway.

It was during the second week of this routine that Signe's work friends joined us for the first time. As I watched Mary, Signe, and Jamie laugh and chat about their days, I wondered if I was holding Signe back with my plan. Perhaps I was keeping her from finding someone who she would be happy with.

I then decided that I didn't care.

I wasn't allowed to tell her how I truly felt due to my employment status, so I was settling for being possessive of her time just this once. Realistically, Signe could still go out with other men after work. Or on the weekends. Or whenever she felt the need to take time off.

I found myself frowning at my meal at the thought, wondering if maybe I could find a way to keep her busy during the evenings as well.

"Are you not feeling it today?" Signe asked as she nudged my bicep with her elbow.

"What?" I snapped my gaze in her direction, feeling the touch of her elbow on my arm long after she removed it.

"You're frowning at your food," Signe raised her dark red eyebrows at me, "If you're not feeling salad today, I'll eat yours." She reached forward to grab my food, and I reacted by grabbing the bowl with both of my hands and dramatically leaning away from her with a look of concern.

"Back off," I grumbled at her with a teasing smile, "I like to savor my food, unlike some." I gave a pointed look at the empty bowl in front of her, before setting my bowl down and reaching for my water bottle to take a sip.

"Huh," Signe shrugged, "If I enjoy it, I swallow."

I immediately started choking on the water I just drank at her words, taking a fist, and pounding at my chest while Mary cackled at Signe's innuendo.

You're still at work.

She's just messing around.

She would have made the same joke whether I was here or not.

She's your employee.

"The sad thing is," Signe giggled with her friend, a blush coating her cheeks, "I didn't even mean it that way. My brain just thought, 'Yeah, that's a normal thing to say to your boss'."

"I'm not your *boss*," I countered after clearing my throat, desperate for any pitiful excuse to justify my infatuation with her, "But don't let other employees hear you make jokes like that."

Mary suddenly, loudly, cleared her throat and nodded her chin towards the breakroom door, and Signe and I both looked over our shoulders to see Jacqueline walking into the room holding a takeout container in her hands.

"Be cool!" Signe hissed before gently kicking my leg underneath the table. I grinned at her before taking another drink from my water bottle, and I focused on Signe's gaze which had dropped to my throat to watch me drink. Her eyes glazed over just the slightest bit, in a way that made me wonder if she liked what she was seeing.

Then I remembered I was just taking a drink of water, and realized there was probably nothing attractive about that for her to admire.

"Can I join you all?" Jacqueline asked, stepping towards the table with a takeout container in her hands. It looked like she had entered the room to grab something, but then pivoted when she saw all of us there.

"Of course," Signe kicked the chair next to her out for Jacqueline to take.

I had never seen Jacqueline eat with these women.

Or eat anywhere other than her desk.

"What's that?" Jacqueline asked, looking at the food in front of me.

"Salad," I replied.

"No," Signe gave me a dramatic look of annoyance before sitting straighter in her chair and holding her pinched fingers up as if she were a musical conductor, "It's *Fattoush*."

"What's Fattoush?" Jacqueline asked.

"It's a salad," I rolled my eyes, "Signe is just excited to

learn a new word." This happened when I asked if Signe was in the mood for salad today. When she asked me what kind, I responded with Fattoush, which is just a common salad found in Syrian cuisine.

"This was one of the best salads I have ever had in my life," Signe ignored my comment as she turned to give me her back, facing Jacqueline more directly, "Large chunky tomato, green onion, fried eggplant—which isn't gross like you'd think it'd be."

"I don't think eggplant is gross," Jacqueline's lips twitched in amusement.

"With crunchy little bread noodles—" Signe continued.

"—You mean deep-fried pita," I interjected.

"—And the *dressing*," Signe sighed dramatically before taking her pinched fingers to her lips and kissing them repeatedly to emphasize her love for it.

I was immediately jealous of her fingertips.

"So, in conclusion," Mary interjected from across the table, "It's a salad."

"But made with the love of Mama Ansara," Jamie added with a small smile as she took a bite of her muffin.

"That's right," Signe nodded as she stood to rinse out her bowl, "My compliments to the chef."

"Actually," I scratched the back of my neck, wondering if I should reveal this truth or not, "I made this one."

"You did?" Signe's mouth opened a little bit, like what I said surprised her. I immediately panicked that she was onto me.

I nodded, trying my best to look casual about it, "Yeah, I needed to use the produce before it went bad." She didn't need to know that I wanted something lighter for lunch today and went to the store last night specifically to throw this salad together for the two of us.

"Ah," Signe nodded before continuing over to the sink, "Makes sense. Glad I could help." Was that disappointment I heard in her voice? I immediately started spiraling. Was I *too* casual just now?

Signe sat back down in her seat before giving me a sly look and turning towards Jacqueline, "So, Jacqueline, I walked by your office this morning and saw you in the zone."

Jacqueline scrunched her eyebrows at Signe, taking a moment to chew and swallow her bite of teriyaki chicken before responding, "What do you mean?"

"You were focusing on something at your computer," Signe leaned back in her chair, crossing her arms over her chest, and not breaking eye contact, "With your earbuds in as you bobbed your head to the music you listened to."

Jacqueline's brow loosened as she nodded, "Yeah, I was finding the answer that Alice had about benefits and such."

Alice was the newest software engineer, something Mary was very excited about because moments earlier, she had been complaining about how there wasn't enough "fallopian energy" in the engineer's side of the building.

"What music were you listening to?" Signe asked; something about the question feeling a little sneakier than it needed to be.

"I can't remember," Jacqueline lifted a shoulder, and it was probably the only time I had seen the woman casually lift her shoulder.

"What do you normally like to listen to?" Signe pressed.

Jacqueline's body tensed, before she met Signe's eyes, "I don't know, a little bit of everything I guess."

"Speaking of music, want to hear my latest Taylor Swift theory?" Jamie spoke up, giving Jacqueline a friendly smile as she waited for our answers.

Signe gave up her interrogation of Jacqueline's music preferences, settling in her seat and giving me a look as if we were both in on some sort of secret.

I just stared at her, hoping for some sort of explanation, before she smirked and turned away, focusing on the conversation happening around us. So, I looked back at my food, quietly listening to the women chatting around us. I noticed while sitting at the table, observing the women chatting, how Jacqueline seemed to relax a little bit more as time passed.

She wasn't nearly as talkative as Signe or Mary, but she still seemed less...stiff.

I felt my phone buzz in my pocket as the conversation ensued. Pulling my phone out of my pocket, I saw that my family text thread was going off as my mother tried to plan dinner with my sisters and Ben.

As well as the separate sibling chat that I had with Raina and Salma.

Raina: Any updates on Red?

I smirked before thumbing back my response.

Me: No. Go away.

Raina: But I want to know if anything is happening, because she's still posting about the book. Did she tell you about it at all?

I furrowed my brows.

Me: No, not yet.

I felt my heart skip a beat in my chest at the question, remembering all of the times in the last few weeks that Signe had laughed and gently tapped my arm with the back of her hand. A few days ago, I said something to her laced with heavy sarcasm, and I'm upset that I couldn't quite remember what it was that I said because it made her bend over laughing as she grabbed my forearm to brace herself.

I was too distracted beaming from the grip she had on my arm to remember what made her laugh so beautifully.

"Is our conversation boring you?" I heard Signe ask from my side. I quickly checked the time and closed out of the text thread, shifting in my seat so I could slide the phone into my jeans pocket.

"No," I replied with raised brows, "I would much rather discuss Taylor Swift theories than get ready for my next meeting."

"I could write down the notes from this important discussion for you to review after your meeting," Signe winked at me, and I couldn't stop the jump in my pulse from the sight even if I wanted to.

I nudged her arm with my elbow, a move I hadn't done a ton in the last few weeks but was thrilled to find an excuse for whenever an opportunity arose, "I expect a full debrief on why Mary thinks every song in her newest album is about that one guy from that one band in an hour."

Signe gave me a thumbs up along with her bright smile,

making Mary and Jacqueline chuckle at our plan. Jamie's eyes bounced between us, a small grin on her lips.

"Enjoy your boring meeting," Signe wiggled her fingers at me as I stood up from the break room table, turning back to the discussion with the other women.

I met Jacqueline's eye behind Signe's back, a look on her face that I couldn't decipher, and decided that I didn't want to. The last thing I needed was for the head of HR to sniff out my inappropriate crush on our office manager. Jacqueline was loosening up the longer she worked at Sun Steer, but I didn't want to make her suspicious since I had already directly asked her about the ethics of workplace relationships.

I nodded politely in farewell at her, and excused myself, shoving my hands in the pockets of my jeans and wondering how much longer I could keep my attraction toward Signe a secret.

Chapter Fifteen

ZAID

EVEN THOUGH I assured my sisters that I knew how to woo a woman, the reality was, I had no idea what I was doing most of the time I interacted with her. My only hope in flirting with Signe in a way she appreciated, was by researching what women like Signe liked online.

I would rather shave my entire body with a dull razor than admit to my sisters that I probably could use some advice, and I didn't want to encourage them to take a page from our mother's book and insert themselves into mine and Signe's hypothetical relationship.

Salma already did enough with the whole babysitting fiasco.

So here I was, sitting in my bed, scrolling on my phone on my anonymous account that was filled with romance novels, women reviewing romance novels, and Signe Lange.

That being said, the confidence that people had on the internet would always astound me.

I wasn't referring to Signe, because her internet confidence was something enthralling. It drew the viewer in, not just because of her beauty, but also because of the way she delivered her content to viewers. Her personality showed through, even though most people made their presence on the internet something fake, like a persona. Not Signe, she was herself no matter if she was at work or online.

No, the people that shouldn't be as confident on the internet were usually men.

Specifically, men who felt the need to put down others.

There was a trending video, and I had seen a couple of people stitch already with their own sassy rebuttals. It showed a man walking through what looked like a construction site, and he claimed that when he brought dates over, he made them walk through a narrow passageway to ensure that they passed some sort of physical test. It illustrated that he wouldn't tolerate a woman too big to fit through the tight space.

"I make all the girls that I bring home walk through this," he started the video, "Because if they can't walk through this—" and then the video would cut off with someone else calling him a misogynistic prick. Because he was.

What caught me by surprise, however, was Signe's response to this video.

As soon as his clip ended, her flawless face filled the screen.

"Yeah, so," Signe cleared her throat while she nodded along as if agreeing with the man, "I make all the guys that I bring home play Xbox just to make sure that they can do this," She then lifted an Xbox controller and flicked her thumb against the joystick in a very sexual manner, "Because if he can't do this—" and then her video cut off.

And I threw my head back against my headboard to cackle.

Jesus, this woman was amazing.

I was still chuckling to myself and getting ready to call it a night before my phone buzzed with an email notification, and I adjusted my glasses to read it.

Brandon was cc'd on the email from a potential client in Tennessee, so I wasn't too surprised to see a text from him before I could check my schedule for the next few weeks.

> Brandon: Let's use this opportunity to update the photos on the website.

I frowned before responding.

> Me: If the photographer is willing to go to Tennessee, that's fine.

I hated getting my picture taken. I was uncomfortable in front of the camera, and no matter how hard I tried to smile, it always came off more like a grimace. Something about posing with a smile felt impossible.

> Brandon: Damn. I just called, and their voicemail said they were on vacation for the next month.

I smiled at that, good for the photographer. Sun Steer usually called the same person, since they knew our brand and vision and we had built a comfortable relationship with them.

> Brandon: Isn't Signe good with a camera?

I felt my heart stutter in my chest.

Signe had taken a couple of pictures at company parties and events in the past. She would just take her phone out and start snapping pictures of decorations and buffets and employees laughing and send them over to our marketing department for them to use.

They haven't used all of the images she's sent over, but they have used quite a bit for the company's social media account.

> Me: If the camera is attached to a phone, I believe so.

Based on what I saw on her social media account, she had a very good eye for aesthetically pleasing shots. How that would translate to the Tennessee landscape and tractors, I wasn't sure.

> Brandon: She can tag along since she'll book the flights and hotel anyway.

I didn't realize Nikhil was expected to go too, so I sent him a message to see.

While I waited for his response, I laid my head against my headboard and tried to calm myself, instead of getting too nervous about the idea of flying in a plane for four hours with Signe. Even with a third wheel there, what would we talk about? Would flying freak her out? Would she take her shoes and socks off as soon as she sat down? Would she clutch her seat as soon as there was a hint of turbulence, like me?

Perhaps I was overthinking the whole thing.

I didn't know why I was so worried about disappointing Signe on this trip. She wasn't the type of person to write off someone for being nervous about sitting strapped in a chair at fifty-thousand feet.

A new message came in.

Nikhil and Signe were included in the thread.

Brandon said that they both would be joining us in

Tennessee, instead of asking. The email left a bad taste in my mouth. Brandon wasn't always this bossy. I remember when we used to goof off back in college, but ever since this company started to take off, he suddenly became all business.

I wouldn't even go as far as to call us friends at this point. Colleagues made more sense.

The way he demanded that all three of us drop everything to meet with this potential client implied as much.

Nikhil: Unfortunately, I have that week off.
Mary has volunteered to go instead.

I smiled; glad Nikhil didn't fawn over Brandon's demands while also allowing Mary to step into her promotion a little bit more. If I remember correctly, Jacqueline should be emailing her the official offer letter this week as well. We were hiring more engineers, and an entire additional team needed a manager. Mary was perfect for the role. Nikhil's time off had already been scheduled weeks ago.

Brandon: That will work.

No form of thanks, no acknowledgment of how this changes everybody's schedules. Nothing. He just expected it to happen because he said so. Sure, he was the CEO of Sun Steer. But he wasn't a god. His employees were still people that deserved to be conversed with properly, instead of people waiting for him to snap his fingers and say jump.

That was the problem with a hierarchy like upper management. It was too easy to forget about all the worker bees that made every success of this company possible.

I didn't want to end up like Brandon.

I wanted to be part of all the work, not sitting alone in an office with everyone fawning over my next set of demands.

Though, to be fair, Signe never fawned. She treated everyone with kindness and respect. Minus that one time that I saw her flip off Brandon underneath her desk, though that was deserved. He's changed a lot since college.

All business.

Cutthroat.

Bonding and establishing rapport with employees is not something he bothered himself with.

I opened a separate thread and sent a direct message to Brandon.

> Me: We need to talk about alternatives for CTO soon.

It took less than a minute for his response to come in.

> Brandon: You're right, I'm getting ready to announce some changes in upper management, let's talk after Tennessee.

Relief relaxed my shoulders, a light starting to shine at the end of this long tunnel.

I scrolled on my phone some more, even though I hated how much more time I was spending on social media in general, I wasn't upset at all the information I was getting about Signe. How I was able to see the side of her that she kept hidden at work.

I wanted to know all sides of Signe, it seemed.

The thing about following Signe's socials as closely as I did in order to learn her likes and dislikes, though, was how it affected my algorithm.

I discovered this not two videos after Signe's, when a

blonde middle-aged woman with a septum piercing, whom I had never seen on social media before came on the screen and started the video with, "Are you fingering your wife or girlfriend?"

I raised my eyebrows at that intro, thinking to myself, *What ever happened to, hello? How are you?*

The woman continued as if that wasn't an insane thing to start with, "If you're not, you should be. If you are, you're probably doing it wrong."

Well, damn.

"Don't worry, there's hope. In this video I'm going to be discussing all the tips and tricks needed, and why. Your clit-owning partner will thank me." I paused the video, checking the time and seeing that it was late and that I should probably go to sleep.

But also...

"First..." the woman's voice rang after I hit play and continued for the sake of education. This seemed like a much better source than anything Pornhub might have to offer on the subject, and the no-nonsense way the woman delivered the information about the female orgasm made me realize I had a lot more to learn about it.

Was I being too hopeful about the opportunity to practice this new educational material with a certain redhead? Perhaps. Even though, if everything went to plan, I wouldn't have the chance to show off my, well, *skills* for a long time. Until after Signe finalized her book deal and quit. After I asked her out, and after I managed to "woo" her enough for her to confidently delete her dating apps.

Go big or go home, I guess.

An hour and a half had passed when I finally halted my research, after deciding to follow that blonde woman's account specifically because she made lots of videos on the proper way to please a woman. I felt much more educated on the subject of giving women orgasms, so I finally closed my eyes and went to bed.

My dreams about Signe weren't exactly tame that night.

I was scolding myself the next morning when my alarm went off and I realized that I needed to take care of some things in the shower if I was going to be able to handle being in the workplace with Signe again.

But I needed to be professional.

I was management, and it was inappropriate for me to be sporting an erection simply from learning how to take care of a woman properly with hopes that one day, in the far future, Signe would want to be that woman.

———

SIGNE

"I watched the show you recommended last night," I informed Mary as she settled into the back seat of Zaid's EV, "It was quite the titillating experience." I turned in the passenger seat to wiggle my eyebrows suggestively. Mary's eyebrows came down flat.

"Not a good enough reason to use the word 'titillating'," she shook her head once, already pulling her phone out of her pocket and settling into the backseat, still grumpy that I beat her to the passenger seat by calling "dibs."

The sound of another woman huffing in amusement made us all look to the other end of the parking lot where Jaqueline was walking towards us, a hand over her mouth for a moment before she removed it and revealed her professional but friendly smile, "Ladies, are you busy?"

Zaid was still on the phone, speaking low and resting his

hips against the hood of this fancy electric car. Mine and Mary's windows were rolled down, so we leaned closer to them to chat with Jacqueline.

"I just wanted to make sure the two of you feel safe with the travel plans," She gave me a pointed look, "And that the hotel accommodations are something you're comfortable with."

Mary and I exchanged a curious look before I nodded encouragingly at the head of human resources, "We feel safe, and I booked the hotel rooms myself. So it isn't a situation I'm worried about."

What was she implying, exactly?

Out of all the men in the company, Zaid was probably the one I had absolutely no reservations about traveling with at all. Nikhil an immediate second. If anything, knowing what I have written about the CTO, *he* was probably the one who should be checking in with Jacqueline like this. But Zaid didn't know what I had written about him, so here we were.

"Alright," Jacqueline nodded, thrumming her fingers on the car door, "If either of you need anything, please don't hesitate to reach out to me." She gave us a warm smile before stepping back from the car and wiggling her fingers goodbye. She then nodded her head at Zaid, who was still on the phone but nodded back at her and left.

"...Do you ever get the impression that Jacqueline has some trauma?" Mary asked.

"What do you mean?" I watched her walk back into the building, probably to interview more software engineers since hiring was chaos lately. I had helped her with a lot of onboarding paperwork in the last week.

"She's always very protective of the female-identifying

employees," I heard Mary shift in her seat behind me, "More so than I am used to from an HR rep."

I sat with Mary's thoughts for a moment.

She had a point.

"Didn't Jacqueline start just a few months before I did?" I asked as soon as the driver's side door opened and Zaid took his seat at the wheel.

"She started about six months before you," Zaid replied, inserting himself into the conversation, "Right after we got our Series A funding."

"Ah, that's right," Mary chimed in from the back seat.

"What's Series A funding?" I had heard this mentioned at the office a few times before, but I didn't understand all the terminology and details. All I knew was that Sun Steer was a "rapidly growing tech startup" and that seemed like enough information for me to do my job.

"It's just fancy terminology for the first round of funding from investors," Zaid explained, resting one hand on the wheel. I held my breath as he flipped the car into reverse, anticipating the classic "let me rest my hand behind your seat so I can look over my shoulder as I pull out of the parking spot" move, but that didn't happen.

Because we were in his fancy space car, which had several cameras to help him back out seamlessly without having to turn in his seat.

My chest deflated at the realization.

Because I was just embarrassing at this point.

"So, wait," I blinked as we turned onto Irvine Boulevard, heading towards the I-5 freeway, "Did Sun Steer not have an HR department before you had investors?"

Zaid and Mary both chuckled before responding, "No."

"Is that legal?" I pressed, "Can companies just...not have a human resources department?"

"That's not how startups work, Signe," Mary leaned forward when we finally started heading north on the freeway, the car's cameras making it easier for Zaid to merge into traffic, "When I first started a couple of years ago, there were probably only about twenty employees at Sun Steer."

"Whoa," I widened my eyes, "That's so small."

"When I first started," Zaid spoke with a small smirk on his lips, glancing in his rearview mirror before merging lanes again, "It was just me and two other guys."

"Okay," Mary scoffed, "That's not special. That's what happens when you start a company in your dorm room."

"Wait," I held my hand up, as if I was going to stop them both from moving forward even though we were all trapped in the car together, "You *started* Sun Steer?"

"Well," Zaid lifted a shoulder, his dark eyes flicking over to me behind his glasses before turning back to the road, "Brandon, me, and a guy named Rodney."

"Whoa," I sighed, "You're an OG employee."

"I'm employee number three, actually," He kept one of his large hands on the steering wheel before reaching into his jeans pocket and pulling out his company ID badge, showing me the "003" numbers at the bottom of it.

"Damn," I reached forward and grabbed the badge from his hands, "Nice picture."

You could immediately tell that he wasn't excited about having his picture taken. His smile was barely there, mouth closed, his head tipped back just enough to expose his solid neck and clavicle. It was genuinely a flattering picture of him, even if he didn't look happy about it. He didn't acknowledge the compliment at all.

"So," I handed it back to Zaid, and when his fingers brushed against mine since he was keeping his eyes on the road, I tried not to internally squeal from simple, accidental contact, "Jacqueline is a fairly new addition to the company. Like me."

"Yes," Zaid nodded.

"So, you've always been CTO?" I added after a second of silence. There was no way in hell I was sitting in this car with the two of them without chatting. I couldn't handle it.

"No, that is also a newer development," Zaid's brows scrunched a little, "I was in a position like Nikhil's until recently."

"Really?"

"Really."

"But we all know how much you love your position now," Mary added. You could hear the smile on her face laced with heavy sarcasm.

"I'm over it," Zaid didn't even bother playing along, "I'm ready for a change, that's for sure."

"I'd love to have you as my manager." Mary sighed, "I love having Nikhil as a manager, too. Alice has been nice so far, but I don't get to work with her much because she's on another team." I glanced over my shoulder to see Mary man-spreading in the back seat, her arms crossed over her chest as she stared out the window, "If you do step down as CTO, who would they hire to replace you? Nikhil?"

Zaid sighed, "If they wanted to hire from within, sure. Though Nikhil has made it clear that he doesn't envy my position in any way. Do you want it?" Zaid lifted his gaze to look at Mary in the backseat before she started gagging.

"Pass," She waved her hand, "Just give me my next promotion and give me raises from there. CTO sounds awful."

"Why?" I was full of questions today, "Doesn't CTO make bank?"

Zaid gave me a surprised look before settling more

comfortably in the driver's seat, "The pay is a big perk, but it's really a position that is nothing but meetings and meetings and more meetings that can just be emails."

"Oh," for some reason, I pictured CTO being more... involved. But a job that's basically just meeting with people all day every day does sound draining. Unfulfilling, even, "That's why you want to step down? Why did you even take the position in the first place?"

"Yes," Zaid nodded, before he squinted and tapped on the large iPad-looking screen on his car. A moment later, the storage compartment in front of me popped open, "We wanted Sun Steer to look organized. Like we had more money than we did so other people would want to invest. Having managerial positions like CTO filled, helped establish that image. I accepted the position under the condition that it would be temporary until someone better suited came along. Could you grab my sunglasses out of the case and hand them to me?"

"Sure," I reached forward to grab the glasses case and handed him the sunglasses, putting his regular glasses safely in the case instead and pushing the door closed, "Freaking space car."

"What was that?" Zaid asked.

"So do you think the next CTO would be someone from outside Sun Steer?" I focused back on the subject.

"Most likely," Zaid confirmed.

"Maybe I should tell Leo to apply again," Mary shifted in her seat to lean forward again, making me turn to look at her, "Since you losers considered him over-qualified for the role he applied for last time."

"That's because he was, from what Nikhil told me," Zaid's brow furrowed again in thought, "Now that you mention it...your cousin isn't a bad person to consider as my replacement..."

I widened my eyebrows, "Oh god, yes, please hire Mary's hot cousin."

Zaid's lips flattened a little as he turned to give me a heated look with a lifted eyebrow, "Mary's hot cousin?"

I lifted a shoulder, trying not to be too aroused by the sight of Zaid in sunglasses, driving, "He's very pretty to look at. I wouldn't mind filing reports for him, if you know what I mean." I wiggled my eyebrows suggestively, making Zaid shake his head at me.

"Maybe we should hire someone else then," Zaid's lips twitched like he was enjoying teasing me about this.

"Signe," Mary's hand smacked my arm, "Keep it in your pants. I'm trying to get my cousin a job here."

"Sorry, sorry," I held my palms up defensively, "I won't say anything else about—what the hell are you doing?"

Zaid had just flicked the handle that shifts gears on his car again, and after a low beep from the car in response, he took both of his hands off of the steering wheel to reach into his glove compartment and pull out a bag of peanuts. In the middle of the freeway.

He lifted an eyebrow at me when I immediately grabbed either side of my seat and held on for dear life as Zaid seemingly forgot he was driving.

"I put it on autopilot," Zaid chuckled a little at my nervous reaction as he tapped his index finger on the wheel before using both of his hands again to dig into his bag of peanuts, casually tossing a few in his mouth.

"Cool. Cool, cool, cool," I felt my hands clench in response as cars zoomed past us on our left, and we zoomed past cars on our right. I glanced down at Zaid's feet and noticed that neither of them were on the pedals.

"Signe, calm down," Mary squeezed my shoulder, weirdly, not helping me calm down.

"I'm still aware of the road, Signe," Zaid's voice was low and calm, but I could see his jaw twitch like he was enjoying seeing me like this, "I have to grip the steering wheel every couple of minutes to reassure the car that I am paying attention."

"But..." I slowly tried to pry my hands off of my seat, and settled for one hand releasing its grip instead, "the car is still doing this by itself?"

"Yes," Zaid nodded, "If it makes you feel better, the auto-pilot technology is fascinating, because—"

"I believe you!" I blurted before holding my breath as our vehicle turned on the blinker all on its own and proceeded to change lanes on the freeway to pass a car going five under the speed limit.

"Do you want me to turn it off?" Zaid asked. He reached out a hand for me before stopping halfway over the console. He quickly put the bag of peanuts down and flipped the car out of autopilot, putting both of his hands back on the wheel.

"Signe, the technology is mostly safe, and as he said, he's still paying attention to the road."

"Sorry!" I slammed my hands over my face, feeling more embarrassed that I freaked out so easily over the thought of something like an autopilot, "It's just my first time in a space car. I wasn't prepared for the hands-free experience." I mumbled behind my palms.

Zaid just released a low laugh at my words.

"If it makes you uncomfortable, I won't use autopilot."

I parted my fingers to look at him in the driver's seat, one of his arms resting against the car door while the other gripped the steering wheel confidently, his eyes on the road behind his dark sunglasses.

He looked like a movie star.

"Just give me a minute," I inhaled through my nose, "We can try autopilot again. I just wasn't prepared before."

"We don't have to—"

"I trust you." I interrupted him, "It's my first time in a robotic space car—"

"It's just a car—" Mary added before I ignored her.

"And I want to experience it, now that I know what to expect." I inhaled through my nose before calmly folding my hands in my lap, and sitting straight in my seat, "Give me a minute, and we can try again."

"No rush," Zaid responded as he turned to give me a reassuring smile, "I can wait."

I glanced over at him, feeling something in his words that I couldn't quite identify. He quickly faced the road again, though. Nothing but casual confidence in his posture as he drove us out of Orange County towards LAX.

Perhaps it was the romance author in me that wanted to add more weight to his words.

Maybe it was because I was harboring a very inappropriate crush on him.

Possibly even the idea that he might be feeling this tension between us, too.

Whatever it was, I forced myself not to focus too much on it as Mary asked Zaid a question about programming that I tried to keep up with but immediately became lost as the conversation continued. The rest of the drive went smoothly, and when we eventually arrived at LAX, all we focused on was getting through TSA and getting to the gate where Brandon was waiting for us, having already driven to the airport himself instead of carpooling with the rest of us.

"WHAT DO YOU WANT?" I asked Zaid as we stood in line for dinner. We had about forty-five minutes before our flight boarded, and we all agreed that we were hungry. Brandon was busy thumbing away on his phone and basically ignoring us, and Mary was FaceTiming Jamie.

When Zaid and I asked them what they wanted, we all looked over at the pizza place just a couple of gates down. It had a long line, but it looked the most delicious. So here we were.

"I like a plain cheese," Zaid replied. We stood next to each other in line, but the queue for it wasn't designed for people to comfortably stand side by side. I was a step ahead of Zaid, but I turned my body so we could still converse while we waited. It looked like we would be here a while.

"Isn't your dad a literal chef?" I asked, stepping forward once when the line moved. Zaid followed me, his arms folded across his chest and standing tall. When I slouched, and he stood straight like that, he felt significantly taller than me. Even though normally I barely had to look up at him to meet his eye. He was only three inches or so taller, so while he was a big guy, I never exactly felt small in comparison. But watching him stand with his feet shoulder-width apart, in the middle of the queue, ignoring the line of people desperate to get one more step closer, I felt small.

I couldn't remember the last time all five feet and eleven inches of me felt small.

"Yes?" Zaid asked, raising a dark brow at me and shoving his glasses farther up his nose. God, I loved those glasses on him.

"So shouldn't you like fancier pizza or something?" I countered, trying not to stare at his exposed clavicle under his plain t-shirt for too long. His muscles popped on his arms when he folded them like this, and I was a simple woman.

"I don't understand your logic," Zaid's lips twitched with amusement while his gaze studied the menu above the crowd of people, "Because my dad is a chef, I'm not allowed to like cheese?"

"No," I shook my head, "It's just weird that you don't like other things with it. Like anchovies or spinach or whatever fancy people put on pizza."

"Pizza isn't a fancy person dish," Zaid shook his head and stepped forward, crowding my space for half a second before I realized I needed to step forward too, "It's made with whatever your heart desires before getting tossed in the oven."

"And your heart desires cheese?" I pressed.

Zaid lifted a shoulder, "Among other things."

I raised my eyebrows, "Like?"

He lowered his gaze from the menu for a moment, his dark eyes locking with mine directly and making my breath catch in my throat. I felt my skin heat under his stare, and while his expression didn't inherently look sexual, my body reacted as if he had just told me to get on my knees.

Zaid held my gaze for one, two, maybe three moments, before shaking his head once and murmuring, "Wouldn't you like to know?"

I grinned, "I see how it is."

And then Zaid smiled while biting his bottom lip with his teeth, and I thought my pants were going to burst into flames from the image.

This was getting dangerous.

By the way his eyes drifted over to me while he gnawed on that plump lip, how his hooded gaze dropped the slightest degree towards where my mouth was, I was moments away from convincing myself that he was just as into this as I was. That he was right there with me, experiencing this chemistry between us.

How he and I would be so, so good together.

"The line moved," someone said behind Zaid, shattering the heated moment I could have sworn we were both experiencing just then.

My heart was still racing, and I used the excuse of being surrounded by dozens of people also desperate enough to wait in this line for pizza to fan myself with the collar of my t-shirt. I turned to study the menu, deciding that saying something would be the best way to move on from whatever that was a few seconds ago.

"...I'm getting a cheese slice, I think," I finally added.

I heard Zaid chuckle next to me before he replied, "Sounds like a plan."

Chapter Sixteen

SIGNE

We flew in late that night since Tennessee was three hours ahead of us. All of us immediately checked into our hotel rooms before the next morning, when we officially visited the manufacturer for Boson Tractors, a company that competed with well-known brands like John Deer.

Their manufacturer was located in the small town of Newport, Tennessee. The population was barely seven thousand people.

Why I was tagging along again was beyond me, but I did my due diligence and snapped photos of the property and all the pretty tractors as Brandon instructed.

As the four of us toured the large warehouse of Boson Tractors, and I actively tried to ignore how freaking humid it was, I realized how good at his job Brandon was.

He was a schmoozer, which was wild to see.

He easily built a rapport with the representative from Boson, shaking hands and throwing cheap dad jokes to crack a smile.

Even Zaid smirked a little at the performance Brandon

was putting on, as the two men discussed what a possible collaboration with a company of this size could look like.

It was clear that Zaid was much more comfortable with a behind-the-scenes situation. Brandon took charge for most of the conversation, whereas Mary and Zaid were clearly only present to answer questions that Brandon might not have been able to on the spot.

Sure, Zaid was professional and seemed succinct when the Boson representative had a question about the specific technology Sun Steer built, but he was clearly here under duress like I was.

Mary also seemed to be struggling with the humidity, some stray strands of her dark hair that came out of her ponytail stuck to her neck. We smiled at each other in comradery a number of times throughout the hours-long meeting that actually ended up taking two whole days.

I got my ten thousand steps in each day, that was for sure.

All while taking notes of the meetings, even though my notes only really made sense to me at the moment. I would have to spend the rest of the evening in the hotel room rewriting the notes so that when I forwarded the run-down to the others, they would be able to make sense of it.

Typing notes on my phone, while keeping up with two businessmen who didn't bother to notice that Mary's shorter legs were probably sore or that I loathed cardio and was sweating through my blouse, was more difficult than I thought.

If it wasn't for Zaid checking over his shoulder, letting Brandon and the Boson rep walk ahead of him before asking loud enough for everyone to hear if Mary and I, "needed a minute," we would have been left in the dust multiple times.

The rep from Boson was just as excited to show off their new machines and models as Brandon was excited to tell them all the ways Sun Steer's technology could help take their business to the next level.

Cool, good for them.

At the end of the second day, after standing in the shower for about an hour to hopefully wash the humidity off of me, I collapsed onto my back on my hotel bed and appreciated not standing on my feet.

And then my phone buzzed, making me curse as I patted my hand aimlessly on the comforter in search of it.

If it was from Brandon, I was pretty sure I was going to type a very inappropriate and rude message back to him.

But it wasn't Brandon, it was Zaid.

I felt my smile tug at my cheeks as if it were a reflex to do so now.

Zaid: Have you eaten?

Me: I'm too exhausted to eat.

I set my phone on my stomach, refusing to get up off of the bed in search of food. I just wanted to sleep for a week straight, maybe find a tub to soak my feet in. Unfortunately, the small town of Newport didn't have the fanciest hotels with tubs. The hotel were staying at was pretty basic.

I felt my phone buzz again.

Zaid: What room are you in?

I raised my eyebrows, checking the time on my phone to see that it was 9:03 pm.

I texted him my room number and nothing else, wondering what he would possibly say in response.

I waited and waited.

At some point, I was pretty sure I dozed off, because I was startled by a knock on my hotel room door, and I felt cold drool on the side of my mouth that I quickly tried to wipe away.

According to my phone, it was now 9:37 pm.

I stood, wincing at my poor achy feet as I padded over to answer the door, embracing the fact that I was wearing a comfy light grey shirt with the words "Hello darkness my old friend, I stood up too fast again" in black lettering, and black bike shorts.

After opening the door, I had to struggle to keep my jaw from falling in shock at the sight of Zaid in grey sweatpants, a white t-shirt that hid nothing about his physique, holding a takeout bag of food that immediately made my mouth water.

He smelled like he also recently showered, his cologne mixing with the scent of barbeque making my head spin.

"I brought nourishment," Zaid held the bag up with a playful grin on his face, his dark eyes shining behind his glasses.

I almost broke down in tears, not realizing just how hungry I was after two days of chasing Brandon around a massive warehouse for the sake of my job.

"You're my hero," I sighed as I opened the door wider, allowing him to come in.

Zaid smirked as he crossed the threshold, setting the food down on the entertainment center because there wasn't a kitchen table to eat at. Just two wooden chairs that he grabbed with each hand and moved to the front of the entertainment center, creating a makeshift eating area for the two of us before he started pulling boxes of food out of the takeout bag.

I just stood there, watching him make himself at home in my hotel room.

God, what I would *give* to be a victim of the only-one-bed trope right now.

No, Signe, I scolded myself, *we're behaving. We're professional and I don't want to see anyone from management naked.*

"Signe?" Zaid asked, making me snap out of my fantasies and take a seat in one of the chairs.

"What's on the menu?" I asked, playing it cool after he caught me staring at him. Probably with a very horny gaze.

"Um," Zaid got back to assembling the paper plates, which must have come with the takeout and plastic cutlery, "I just got brisket, mashed potatoes, coleslaw, and these buttery garlic rolls this place was known for."

"Sold," I snagged a roll out of his hand before he could put it on one of the plates, taking a large bite and feeling my eyeballs roll into the back of my head at the taste of buttery, garlicky carbs.

"It's good?" Zaid asked with a huff of laughter at my reaction.

"So damn good," I took the plate he handed me with everything else, not wasting time.

We didn't talk much as we both ate, which would normally embarrass me, but I realized I felt comfortable sitting in silence with him while we ate our meals. We could exchange small pleasantries here and there, more along the lines of "this is delicious" and "I've never had brisket this good" and "what is in this barbeque sauce?"

Only about twenty minutes later, after my stomach felt like it was going to burst because I ate so quickly, did I take a moment to appreciate how intimate this moment was between us.

Sure, we had been alone together before. In his office, at his sister's house in her living room, but never in a hotel room.

Not with a king-sized bed mere feet away from us, as if it was a bright red sign reminding me what consenting adults liked to do when a king-sized bed was present. Days after the heated looks we exchanged with each other at LAX. Minutes after he bought me food.

"So," I cleared my throat as I set my plate in the takeout bag that was now serving as a trash bag, "Do you think the meetings with Boson went well?"

"I hope so," Zaid sighed, taking the last few bites of potatoes before also discarding his paper plate, "Otherwise, sweating to death in that warehouse was all for nothing."

"Oh my god," I leaned forward in my seat, "Why the hell did we conduct business like that? Why couldn't we all sit in a boring conference room like normal people?"

Zaid chuckled at my reaction, shrugging his shoulders in commiseration as he searched for the moist wipes the restaurant must have thrown in. There were four little packets of moist wipes, and he grabbed them before also snatching up the complimentary breath mints the restaurant threw in to offer to me. I took one of each and watched intently as he popped the other breath mint into his mouth.

Watching his mouth work as he crunched the breath mint between his teeth, the muscles in his jaw and throat working as he chewed through the breath mint in seconds, made me want to moan.

There was something seriously wrong with me.

"According to Boson, they like a more 'personal approach'," Zaid lifted his fingers into air quotes in between wiping his hands clean of the greasiest yet most delicious barbeque I had ever eaten, "And Brandon really wants this deal to go through, so we were at their mercy."

"I would have said no," I shook my head, "It was torture. I should sue."

"Don't let Jacqueline hear you joke like that." Zaid grinned, wiping his mouth, and ensuring his beard was clean before leaning back in his chair and resting one of his ankles over his knee, "Damn, it was exhausting though."

"I'm just a girl," I whined, "I'm not meant for so much walking."

"Next time we'll bring a little red wagon to drag you around in. I'm sure Zeki wouldn't mind if you borrowed his," Zaid winked, and the action made my heart skip a beat. Perhaps it was also due to the grey sweatpants he was wearing, but I had a feeling I would react viscerally any time Zaid Ansara winked at me.

"You say that like you're joking," I raised my eyebrows at him, standing to grab the trash bag of takeout and tossing it in the small trash bin near the front door, "But don't set my expectations so high like that."

"I wouldn't dream of it," Zaid replied, making no move to stand up from his chair and leave now that dinner was over.

I grinned and sat back down in mine, actively pretending like there wasn't a big ol' comfy bed that could hold two of us as we let the food that we just devoured settle in our stomachs.

"What are your thoughts on Tennessee so far?" I asked him.

"It's hot, and wet." Zaid shook his head, "I'm a spoiled California man through and through."

I laughed, tucking my legs underneath me in my chair to

get more comfortable, "I'm glad I'm not the only one. I'm happy living in Orange County for the rest of my life."

"Me too," Zaid stretched his arms behind himself, resting both hands behind his neck as he kept that one foot crossed over his knee, looking as if we had shared a dinner in our lounge clothes dozens of times. As if this was normal for us to do in my hotel room, and not the very first time that it happened.

I wondered if this was his way of trying to act casual about being in my hotel room right now. If he was letting his body language display how *not* worried he was being near this bed. How he had no worries about jumping on me.

Wish I could say the same.

"I do want to travel some more, though," Zaid thoughtfully added as he glanced around the hotel room, "Lately I've wanted to visit Iceland."

I tilted my head at him, "What's in Iceland?"

He grinned, "Really cool renewable energy technology," he lifted a shoulder, "Plus spas and volcanos and cool views. I don't know, it just always interested me."

I hummed my agreement, "That does sound like a cool place to visit, as long as southern California is my home to come back to."

"Yeah," Zaid smiled, creating a wrinkle in the corners of his eyes behind his glasses, "Agreed."

It was too easy to picture going on a vacation like that with him.

Both of us bundled up in layers as we hiked through Iceland or soaking in the hot spas I'd heard about. Or visiting some renewable energy plant that would fill him with way more excitement than I'd ever understand, but watching his face light up from the experience would be worth it.

How I wanted that to be my reality so badly.

Ask me, I begged him in my mind, *ask me to run away to Iceland with you.*

I felt my heart jump at the realization of how wrong that thought was.

We were coworkers, friends.

Zaid and I weren't lovers.

As far as I knew, he didn't view me with romantic interest in the slightest. He was just such a nice, down-to-earth guy. He was a man that women could feel safe around.

And then there was me, someone he might not feel safe lounging next to in that chair, if he knew what I was doing. How often I objectified him.

I thought I was going to be sick.

I stood up from my chair suddenly, the urge to run away and escape making my muscles tense.

"Signe?" Zaid asked, standing up from his chair and trying to meet my eyes, "Are you alright?"

I huffed a laugh of disbelief, rubbing my palms on my cheeks as I stepped away and paced around the room a little bit.

I wanted him.

I wanted Zaid *so* badly.

It was too easy to fantasize about what it would be like to have him, even though he wouldn't want me at all if he knew what I did.

This was so inappropriate.

I have to tell him.

"Signe?"

"I'm—I'm okay." I waved my hand in the direction I left him, still walking back and forth, shaking my hands out as if I could wiggle the anxiety out of my body.

God, what was I even doing?

I have to tell him.

"Signe, Signe stop," Zaid stepped forward and grabbed both of my forearms with his large warm hands, crouching just enough to force me to meet his eyes, "What is going on? Are you alright? Can I help?"

His thumbs started mindlessly tracing circles on my skin where he held me, and I felt myself shiver at the contact.

I tried to pull away, shaking my head once as I tried to avoid his eyes, but he didn't let me go. He wouldn't let me escape.

"I'm just freaking out a little bit," I admitted, looking everywhere but him. I had to tell him. I couldn't look at him and tell him at the same time.

"What is it? Are you having a panic attack?" His eyes scanned the entirety of my body, because my feet were shifting as if desperate to run away.

"No," I thought about it some more, "Well, maybe. I don't know." I caught a whiff of his scent, and I wanted to lean into his body. I wanted to run my mouth over his neck, his shoulders, his jaw. I wanted to feel his beard under my lips, find the soft pillows of his own.

"How can I—"

"I need—I need to tell you—oh god," I was pretty sure I was wheezing, it seemed very difficult to breathe.

"What?" His dark brows furrowed with a shake of his head, "Breathe, just breathe. You're safe."

"I—I need to—" I was watching his mouth as he frowned, my body screaming at me to *kiss him, tell him, kiss him.*

"I'm here. How can I help?" Zaid looked so genuinely concerned for me, my heart melted. I glanced down at his hold on my arms, how he tugged me a little closer to his body when he saw where my eyes landed.

I looked back up into the dark depths of his eyes and realized how quickly my control was leaving with every moment that passed.

His body was so close to mine, his spicy cologne once again invading my senses and scrambling my brain. It was difficult to think rationally.

"Signe?" Zaid asked, stepping closer into my space, and placing a gentle hand on my forehead as if to check my temperature.

I want to climb you like a tree, I almost blurted out. But I gently grabbed his hand and moved it off my forehead before I pasted on a hopefully believable casual smile and replied, "I'm fine. I'm just..." *I'm just what? Procrastinating on telling him about the book? Picturing him naked? Wondering what it would be like to earn the affection of a good man like him?*

Zaid's dark eyes glanced down between us, and it took me a moment to understand what he was looking at. It wasn't until I felt his rough fingers lace through mine that I realized I never let go of his hand. I had simply removed it from my forehead and held my grip.

The feel of his fingers intertwining with mine made my heart skip a beat, and I inhaled a deep breath that, frankly, felt more like a gasp. My blood was rushing in my veins, and I found myself blinking more often as I struggled to understand what was happening. How Zaid stepped a little closer into my space as our hands held each other, his eyes lifting to meet mine.

"You're just...?" Zaid asked, his voice lowering. It was so intimate, and the tone he used immediately reflected just how alone we both were. How we were in this hotel room, away from the office. It was deceptive. It didn't feel like I was with Zaid Ansara, Chief Technology Officer. It felt like I was just with Zaid. This wonderful, kind-hearted man I had been insanely attracted to since day one. The man who loved his nephew more than anyone else. The man who opened up to me more and more every day, and dammit if my heart didn't pitter-patter at the hopeful thought that he was just as worked up as I was.

"I'm sorry," I whispered, sounding much more panicked than I intended to. Probably due to the inability for me to regulate my breathing.

His hand tightened its grip on mine as he replied, "For what?" his brows drew together, his dark eyes desperately trying to meet mine through the frame of those glasses that were driving me crazy, "I'm here. You don't need to talk—in fact, don't talk—"

"I didn't mean to..." I shook my head once as I stepped closer to him, our chests almost touching as I reached up to place a hand on the side of his glasses, pausing as I finally met his eyes and hoping he understood.

He seemed so confused and anxious, before taking his free hand that wasn't gripping mine, and slowly removing his glasses himself. My other hand landed on his shoulder, and my fingertips gently pressed into the glorious muscle underneath his cotton shirt.

"Signe?" Zaid asked, his dark eyes widening a fraction. It was his body language that did it for me. How after he gently set his glasses on the entertainment center to the side of us, his gaze dropped to my mouth. How his eyes dipped slightly, growing hooded as I quickly wet my lips. How his hand still held mine tight, as if not wanting me to let go. How when my hand on his shoulder gently dragged a path up to the side of his neck, he seemed to lean towards me even more.

He was with me.

Zaid was right here with me.

"I—I—" I tilted my face back just enough for him to tilt towards mine.

"Tu'burni," Zaid mumbled as his chest expanded just enough to brush against mine. I didn't have time to ask him what the hell that meant because suddenly he met my lips with his own and nothing else mattered.

Chapter Seventeen

SIGNE

I TOOK everything I could get. Within a second, I had both of my hands gripping either side of Zaid's strong neck, sliding themselves higher to tangle my fingers in his thick hair. Our bodies were flush together, and the feel of his large warm hands on my waist made me sigh in relief as we continued to brush our lips against one another again and again.

It was immediately apparent that this was a man who had done a lot of kissing, and after taking a few seconds to get a feel for each other's lips, I decided to be greedy by nipping at his bottom one and brushing my tongue against it.

Zaid groaned before he gave me what I was asking for. His hot mouth was over mine, our tongues sliding against each other in slow, painfully sensual passes that made my stomach warm and tighten in anticipation all at the same time.

He separated our mouths just long enough for me to inhale a deep lungful of air. I was getting dizzy, which could have been from the experience of making out with Zaid after months of imagining it, or because he was so talented at making out that I genuinely forgot to breathe. Either way, I wasn't upset about it.

I felt his hands grip my hips before he quickly turned the two of us and took a couple of steps needed to make it over to the hotel bed. The backs of my legs hit the foot of the mattress, and when I reached up to wrap my arms around his shoulders, Zaid's hands barely skimmed over my backside to grip the backs of my thighs.

With one swift movement, I was suddenly on my back on the comforter.

This man had just tossed me down on the bed like I was nothing, and the heat in my belly burned hotter from acknowledging that.

My hands were already reaching out for him again when Zaid lowered his large body over mine, our mouths meeting in the hungriest, most desperate kisses I had ever experienced.

"Ya amar," Zaid murmured against my mouth, his tongue stealing any chance for me to reply. "Ya alby."

"What?" I finally managed to breathe out in between our lips. I didn't care, because the reality was that he could be giving me the most unhinged insults in Arabic, and I would still be wet from the sound of his voice against my mouth alone.

Zaid ignored me, which was fine because his arms were supporting his weight so he didn't crush me, while still managing to roam one hand up and down my sides. Every time he got closer and closer to my ass, I found myself thrusting my hips up against him like the horny woman I was.

Eventually, his hand finally, finally made its way to grip my backside, and the moan I made as I locked my arms around his neck and shoulders was nothing but encouragement.

"Goddamn," Zaid groaned as his lips left mine, brushing themselves across my jaw and near my earlobe, "I *knew* you'd feel so good."

"Oh god," I exhaled as I tilted my head back, giving him all the access he needed to explore my skin with his mouth, "I love finally knowing that you also thought about this."

Zaid shifted, rolling our bodies so that we lay on our sides facing each other. One arm of his was cradling my head, his fingers in my hair and angling my face so that he could nip and kiss and taste as much of my neck and shoulder as he wanted. His other hand kept exploring my ass and hip and thigh, and when I ground my pelvis against his I gasped when I felt the hardness in his sweatpants.

Those fucking sweatpants and their thin material were going to be the death of me.

I immediately dropped my arms, one of them supporting my weight underneath me while the other wrapped itself around his waist and felt all the ridges and planes of his back. As soon as my hand started to lower more, towards the waistband of his sweatpants, his hips thrust against mine in a way that made me moan desperately.

"Of course," Zaid spoke against my neck, remembering the conversation even though I had forgotten about it, "I'm always thinking about this, Signe."

Oh god, the way he murmured my name against my skin.

I was a goner.

I threw my leg over both of his, allowing his hard length to rest against where I wanted him. One thrust against him like this and we were both moaning from the friction.

"Yes, yes," I panted against his mouth, pulling myself up

so that I could push him onto his back and straddle his hips. His eyes were half open, beautifully glazed, and when I rolled myself over his erection again, I was rewarded with the sight of Zaid's teeth sinking into his bottom lip. His hands gripped my hips so tightly that I was positive my skin might be a little bruised afterward.

"You're so fucking hot, Signe," Zaid moaned as I rolled my hips again, leaning down and pressing kisses along his neck and bearded jawline, "Goddamn."

"Oh please," I grinned against his short beard before I continued to speak against his skin, "As if you're not one of the most attractive men I have ever met." I captured his lips with mine again, my hands running over the planes of his chest and arms with greed as I angled my hips just right against him.

There was a very good chance that I would come from this alone.

"...I can't...think of a clever response to that..." Zaid admitted before his tongue desperately traced the inside of my mouth, "You're too distracting." His hips were bucking underneath mine in time with the roll of my hips, and when I slid my hands underneath his shirt I melted into the touch. The feel of his hot skin, the planes of his abs and chest, the light dusting of hair across his pecs. It was too much. This man was unraveling me.

"Just to be clear, it's not just your body, though," I admitted in a whisper near his ear, nipping at his earlobe with my teeth and tugging the slightest bit, "I'm turned on by everything about you." I was drunk on power, loving how Zaid was breathing and how his hands couldn't find a place to hold still on my body. As if he was desperate to map me out, to feel everything I had to offer him. I eventually grabbed one of his wrists and guided his hand underneath my shirt, slowly dragging it up my side until I pulled his palm forward to wrap itself over the underside of my breast, his rough fingers tracing the edge of the bra cup.

As soon as his thumb found the stiff peak through the material, I admitted defeat. I was someone I didn't recognize, using my hands to brace myself on his shoulders as I rubbed against his shaft in quick, determined strokes. His thumb encouraged me as his other hand wrapped itself around my hip to hold me against him. As if he was encouraging my movements on him.

We were both still fully, completely clothed.

I eventually sagged against his chest, my hands bracing themselves on his waist as I continued to roll my hips against him. I thought I caught myself sucking on his neck as I did, but I couldn't quite tell. I was lost, desperate to reach the crest that was so close.

"Are you going to come for me, Signe?" Zaid murmured in my ear. His hand left my hip and tangled itself in my hair on the back of my head, holding me against his shoulder as his other hand kept up its ministrations under my shirt, even with it crushed between our chests.

"Yeah?" I was mostly confused by my actions. I couldn't believe I was already so close, the edge barreling towards me at a rate I hadn't experienced with a partner in quite a while.

Zaid groaned, barely flexing his own hips in time with mine, "Use me."

His demanding tone caught me off guard in the best way, but the problem was I was not in the best physical shape like he was. After whatever amount of time I spent on top of him, supporting my own weight and dry humping like teenagers, I felt my muscles start to ache and my orgasm slowly, slowly start to slip away.

Zaid noticed the shift immediately, along with the

desperate little whimper I made when I realized that I wasn't going to cross that line.

"Fuck, fuck," I was desperately trying to gain the friction again, but the muscles in my legs were starting to shake on either side of his hips.

Zaid grumbled something incoherent, and the next thing I knew, he flipped us again, so my back landed on the mattress. I barely had time to think before he yanked my shirt up, pulled the cup of my bra down, and lowered his head.

"Oh!" I gasped, my hips searching for his while my hands knotted themselves in his hair.

"That's it," Zaid spoke around the tip of my breast, his tongue gently teasing as his hand ran down the front of my bike shorts, "Just relax and let me help."

I could not have possibly gotten any wetter.

"Please," I whimpered like I wasn't a grown woman capable of bringing myself to orgasm, "Yes, I need—" my words were cut off when his hand made its way into my bike shorts, into my panties, and brushed a finger against my core.

"Fuck, Signe," Zaid groaned, shifting his focus over to my other breast and tasting me there too, "Say my name when you come."

He traced my opening for just a moment, wetting his finger, before dragging it up and tracing small, tight circles against my clit.

"Yes," I panted, feeling the muscles in my core starting to tighten after every circle his finger made.

"Say it," Zaid demanded, his tongue starting to flick my nipple in time with his finger.

Heat rushed through my core, snapping a string that was tightening inside and releasing fiery pleasure behind my eyes, before I miraculously managed to breathe out, "God, Zaid."

"Good, just like that," Zaid kept his finger steady, never once changing the pressure or pace as my orgasm rolled through me, a second overwhelming wave coating my body at his praise. I felt my grip on his hair tighten as I moaned through the orgasm, stars spinning in the peripherals of my vision because he just wasn't letting up on me.

"Okay," I gasped, using my grip on his hair to get him to let up on my breasts, "I can't—no more." I was barely able to get the words out, and when Zaid lifted his head to gaze at me, air escaped my lungs again at the sight of him. His flushed face, his mussed-up hair, and the lazy grin he gave me before leaning forward and kissing my lips again.

He was like the human embodiment of my personalized aphrodisiac. I had just orgasmed harder than I had in a long while, and yet I still found myself tucking my fingers into the waistband of his sweatpants, searching.

Zaid groaned on top of me before shifting his weight and wrapping his hand around mine to remove it from his waistband. Then I found my hand pinned to the mattress on the side of my head.

"Sorry," I mumbled against his deep kisses, "Do you want—"

"I'm okay," Zaid mumbled, his tongue dragging against mine, "I'm okay."

"I want to," I turned my head just enough to speak, but he didn't stop kissing me. He brushed his lips against my cheek, my jaw, my ear, "I want to make you feel good."

"I know," I could feel his lips curl into a smile against the shell of my ear, and I shivered from the contact, "I'd like to have something to look forward to."

I sighed as his lips started to drag themselves back towards mine, and I allowed one more, deep, drugging kiss from him before I voiced the worry that was tingling in the back of my mind, "This wasn't a one-time thing?" Why did I sound so insecure? If it was a one-time thing, I would respect Zaid's decision, put on my big girl pants, and deal with it.

But I didn't want it to be a one-time thing.

I had just barely gotten a taste of what our chemistry was like, and I was nowhere close to finished with him.

"No," Zaid sounded a little dangerous as he replied, his grip on my hand tightening as he nipped at my bottom lip just like I had done to him earlier, "I don't do casual hook-ups, Signe." He released his hold on my hand to cup my cheek, his thumb brushing against my jawbone as he leaned back to meet my gaze, "This means something to me, I hope it does for you, too."

I felt myself bite my lip under his intense gaze. The fluttering that was taking place in both my heart and my stomach at his words was nauseating in the best way. Zaid had just given me a toe-curling orgasm, and now he was telling me that he didn't do casual. As someone who had only done casual the last few years, I couldn't deny the giddiness that unfolded in me at the mere thought of someone being interested in me beyond sex.

"I think this might mean something to me, too," I whispered, taking in his masculine features in the lamplight of the hotel room, "But...are we allowed?" Maybe it was because I had just experienced a mind-blowing orgasm, but my anxiety and breathing were much more regulated now than it was before Zaid and I kissed.

"Allowed?" Zaid asked, pressing his lips against my cheek once more before pulling back again. It was as if he couldn't help it. Like he had to keep kissing me. Once that dam between us broke, there was no going back.

"Like…because of work?" I pressed my lips together nervously. He was my superior, which usually came with a ton of complications. However, I wasn't concerned with Zaid's position at the company. If everything went well, I wouldn't be working there too much longer anyway.

Oh frick…

What the fuck is wrong with you, Signe? Do you think he'd be interested in this if he knew all the filthy things you've written about Zayne?

I was quite literally just about to tell him about my book, but now I knew what his lips tasted like. What his hands felt like, and how loving his touch was. But…he and I were just starting something. Something that I hadn't ever let myself daydream too much about, because the disappointment of not having this with him was too much to bear.

It was still new. Minutes old.

As wonderful as this was, it was still too soon to know if this could turn into a serious, long-term relationship. Even if Zaid "doesn't do casual". Plus, there is still the possibility that now, if he found out about the book, he wouldn't be interested in this between us anymore.

And if anyone else at work found out what I wrote about him, especially if he was turned off and not interested in me anymore, it's not unrealistic to expect me to lose my job over it. Following that logic, while still being wrapped up in Zaid, I figured it would be better to wait until Michelle has sent the manuscript through the first round of submissions to publishers in a few weeks. Depending on how that is looking, I could start looking for other part-time work and quit Sun Steer whether I was still involved with Zaid or not.

If all of that lined up, and Zaid and I were getting

serious, I was convinced that *that* would be a better time to tell him about the book.

"It's not against the rules for us to explore this, no," Zaid shook his head once, his hand on my jaw dragging down towards my neck so that his thumb could brush against my collarbone, "I also don't consider it anyone's business but ours."

I felt my smile become wobbly, knowing I was still recovering from the high of Zaid's magical lips and fingers.

"That being said," Zaid's eyes were focused on his finger's path as he spoke, "If you want to disclose this to Jacqueline, I wouldn't be against it. For your safety, I mean."

"What about *your* safety?" I asked, my head spinning with the horror of having to sit down in Jacqueline's office and let her know that the CTO and I were hooking up.

No, not hooking up.

Exploring this.

"I'm not worried about my safety in the slightest," Zaid sighed, reaching over me to grab my phone that was left on the bed, and checking the time, "I should get back to my room though. Our flight is early."

Okay, so at least that answered the question of if he was staying the night with me or not.

"I guess," I shrugged.

Zaid tossed my phone back down and gave me one last kiss, this one calmer and lingering, not indicating at all that he still had a very noticeable erection in his sweatpants.

"I like you, Signe," Zaid said as he brushed his thumb against my cheek after pulling away, "I know this was unexpected," he stared into my eyes for a moment, before nodding his head once and saying, "I'm okay letting you take the reins here, to decide what makes you most comfortable."

I just stared at him, my heart still racing for so many different reasons, "Okay."

"I'll see you in the morning?" Zaid asked, the tiniest hint of nerves sounding in his low voice.

I whispered, "Yes." Before leaning up and kissing him back, something he met with enthusiasm before forcing himself to pull away.

"Sleep well," Zaid whispered as he stood from the bed, adjusting the rod in his sweats attempting to conceal it, before giving me one last lingering look and letting himself out.

I just lay there, my head spinning.

In summation, I had just been happily and successfully finger-banged by the Chief Technology Officer of Sun Steer Technologies. I had just enthusiastically sucked face with the man who was the picture-perfect inspiration for the male lead in my romance novel.

And I wanted to do it all again.

Chapter Eighteen

ZAID

I DIDN'T PLAN to barge into Brandon's office today, but after sitting at my desk and seeing the email he sent out to the entire company, I decided I needed to. I was fueled with irritation as I reread the email a few times, taking a moment to breathe through my nose before I decided to confront my old friend in person.

Brandon had hired a Chief Financial Officer. Something he figured we needed with how rapidly our company was growing every day. While I agreed that having a person in a position like that was probably a good move to make at this point, because we were in the process of receiving another round of funding for our tech, and dotting the Is and crossing the Ts with Boson Motors, I was annoyed that I was somehow *still* the CTO.

Brandon knew my position was supposed to be temporary.

If he was in the mindset to hire a CFO, which must have been the big announcement he mentioned during our texts before the Tennessee trip, he could probably be persuaded to take my request for a replacement more seriously.

I rapped my knuckles on his door before walking in.

He sat at his desk; his dark blonde brows furrowed as he thumbed away on his phone with both of his elbows resting on his desk. His office space screamed CEO of an up-and-coming tech company, with fancy plants, abstract paintings, and a hammock in the corner. While I wasn't comfortable being in a managerial position this high up in the company, it was obvious that Brandon was living for it.

His blue eyes flicked up to me as I entered before he gave me a friendly grin and continued to look at his phone, "What's up, Zaid?"

I cleared my throat, wondering how to toe the line of college friend vs. professional colleague during this conversation.

"I saw the email you sent this morning," I decided to start with that, taking a seat on his leather couch and sitting back, trying to look relaxed, "You think she's a good fit?"

"Oh yeah," Brandon nodded his head before frowning once more at his phone and finally setting it down, giving me his attention, "She actually used to work at the same company that Jacqueline came from." I raised my eyebrows at that. That was now two employees we had hired from Blix, a massive social media company that competed with others like Facebook or Instagram. They had millions of users worldwide, and younger generations were much bigger fans of Blix. I was positive they were going to change the entire social media game.

"Wow," I replied, "What made her want to come here? We couldn't possibly pay her as well as Blix could."

"No," Brandon lifted a shoulder, "But she isn't exactly hurting financially either. I guess she had been with Blix since the start and got a pretty good stock investment. I think she's cashed out and is interested in working at a smaller company now."

"Huh, what was her name again?"

"Nicole Young," Brandon replied, "She's starting in the next few days, I believe." He sat back in his chair and crossed his arms with a friendly expression on his features, "She'll take the office next to mine that is currently being used for storage."

"Alright," I rubbed my hands on my thighs as I sat forward, trying to force the confidence in me to say the next thing, "So, have you considered it might be time for me to step down?"

Brandon's eyes widened a little at me before he leaned forward to rest his elbows on his desk again, "You really don't want to be CTO?"

I shook my head, "I don't think I'm the best fit for the position." Why he was sounding so surprised made something bitter rise in my chest. I had made my feelings very clear, why he was acting obtuse about it was beyond me.

Brandon was already shaking his head by the end of my sentence, "You're great. The board and the investors love you. You explain the tech so well, and it's helpful that the man who built it can be the one selling it."

I frowned a little, "I can see the benefit, but this isn't a position I'm interested in keeping. I'd rather be a step or two down, reporting to the CTO or managing a smaller team of my own. Getting my hands dirty with the code that's being developed, brainstorming new features that clients want. That sort of thing."

Brandon looked genuinely confused at my words, which made irritation simmer inside of me because this wasn't the first time we had had this type of conversation.

"I hadn't been thinking about it," Brandon admitted,

"But I will now that I know you're unhappy making more money."

I wanted to roll my eyes at his passive-aggressive comment. It was all about money to him. Forget what the job description entailed; it came down to the dollars in his account. Not that Brandon was unethical for being so focused on money, because it wasn't like he made an excessive amount as CEO. In fact, Brandon took a pay cut compared to other tech companies our size, because he didn't want the lowest-level employee at Sun Steer to need to get a second job to make ends meet.

However, he clearly still struggled with wrapping his head around me also wanting to take a pay cut in the form of stepping down from a position he personally loved.

"I'd love to help with the process too, I understand that we can't just hire anyone to replace me. I'd love for Nikhil to want the role, but he's made it very clear that he is happy with where he is...There was a man we interviewed for a different position a while back, who was overqualified. He might be a good alternative to consider, too."

Brandon's expression was almost comical, filled with evident confusion while still trying to be polite about other people's wants, "Yeah, I'll talk to Jacqueline and see what kind of candidates would be interested in taking over your position."

"That would be appreciated," I nodded as I stood from his desk, "I'll let you get back to your day."

"Thanks," Brandon smiled as he adjusted his desk chair to face his computer, grabbing the mouse and bringing the screen to life.

I had just stepped out of his office and started walking towards mine when I heard Signe's familiar two-knock rap on my door. I lifted my head to see her frozen mid-stride as she was passing my office on the way to Jacqueline's, a company iPad in her other arm.

"Oh," Signe grinned, but her cheeks slowly became stained pink, "Hi."

"Hi," I grinned, glancing around and seeing only a few engineers down the way chatting. We weren't alone, but we were far enough from other employees to probably not be heard. I double-checked Jacqueline's office to see that her door was shut.

"I thought you were in your office," Signe explained, jutting her thumb behind her to my closed door. Through the glass next to my door, you could see how the sun shining through the office window lit up the room.

"Ah," I nodded, stopping a pace or two away from her. Her cheeks were still pink, and I realized that this was the first time we had seen or spoken to each other at work since Tennessee. We had sat in separate seats on the plane ride home the following morning, and Signe took the rest of the workday off because she didn't think it was worth it to go back into the office for two more hours of the workday. Plus, jet lag.

I had gone back and worked with Brandon and Jacqueline on the deal we had agreed on with Boson Tractors.

That brought us to today, a Friday.

Looking at Signe, wearing a dark green sweatshirt with light wash jeans that hugged her thick thighs and impeccable ass, while falling loose around her knees and calves, made me realize how difficult it would be to see her in the office without thinking of our kiss in her hotel room.

There was writing on Signe's sweatshirt again, and I made a point of reading the text.

"Are you really staring at my boobs right now?" I heard Signe whisper in surprise, a smile in her voice.

I smirked, pushing my glasses up my nose a bit as I read out loud, "I closed my book to be here."

Signe's lips parted as she glanced down at her sweatshirt, pulling it away from her body to confirm the text I had just read, "Oh, duh," she palmed her forehead, her cheeks turning an even darker shade of pink, "Of course you were just reading my shirt."

"But if I was?" I asked, stepping forward again to get closer to her but far enough away that others wouldn't be suspicious, "Just staring?"

Signe grinned while pressing her lips together, her hazel eyes glancing around the office space we were in before looking back up to me, "It wouldn't exactly be professional." She replied with a whisper.

"This is true," I leaned against the wall, crossing one of my ankles over the other, loving how her light eyes tracked the movement and how she seemed to shift closer to me in response, "Though, neither is what you begged me to do to you in Tennessee."

Her eyes widened as she swiveled her head around, double-checking that nobody was around and listening to our hushed conversation. I tucked my bottom lip in between my teeth, delighted that she was blushing as much as she was. Did our time in her hotel room also replay in her mind every spare moment? Did she also get off to the memory of what we did as soon as she was in her own bed?

"You're...bolder about this than I expected you to be," Signe replied, hugging her iPad close to her chest as she also leaned against the wall I was on, looking at me with mischief in her eyes, "I enjoy this side of you."

Thank fucking god.

"Have you thought any more about that night?" I asked, trying to swallow around the dry gravel that masked my voice every time I got close to this exquisite woman.

Signe's eyes met mine for a moment before they dropped to my lips as she parted her own, "All the time."

"All the time," I agreed with her.

We stood there, the murmurs of distant voices of other Sun Steer employees echoing around us as we took the other in. I wondered how I could go about my day without wanting to touch her. To feel her skin under my hands. To pull those desperate sounds from her lips that haunted me in the best possible way.

"Come to dinner with me," I tried not to visibly wince at my choice of words, making my request sound like a demand. I wanted it to be Signe's choice, not like I was pressuring her to do so.

Signe grinned, gnawing on her plump bottom lip I could still remember the taste of as she eyed me up and down, "I'm free tomorrow night?" was her reply.

I smiled in relief; glad she wasn't thrown by my over-eager wording.

"I can pick you up at seven?" I questioned, my eyes flicking up to some sales reps behind her that were making their way toward the managerial office wing.

"That sounds nice," Signe smiled at me, before pulling the iPad away from her chest and glancing down at it, "I should get this over to Jacqueline before I forget."

I nodded, shoving my hands in the pockets of my slacks because it took every muscle in my body not to grab her by the shoulders, shove her against the wall I was leaning on, and taste her lips again.

"Have a good day, Ms. Lange," I stood straight as she started to walk away. She glanced over her shoulder, her eyes taking their fill as they dragged up and down my body, before grinning to herself and facing forward. Turning her back to me, she knocked on Jacqueline's office door.

I was wrecked for this woman.

No matter what happened in my workday, if I stepped down as CTO tomorrow or a month from now, I only had one objective in my mind.

Figuring out how to get my lips on Signe's again as fast as humanly possible.

SIGNE

The amount of effort it took for me to smile normally at the camera was embarrassing.

I sat in my little studio apartment, on a video call with my agent and editor, getting ready to tell them why I called this random meeting.

"So," I gulped, before wincing the slightest bit and deciding to rip the band-aid off, "I think we should change some things about Zayne and his character." I nodded once, and flipped through my notebook as if this was a super serious decision I had planned. And not a decision I made because I crossed an ethical boundary by writing fanfic of a very real person, but I also made out with him.

And was currently "exploring things" with him.

Changes had to be made.

"What kinds of things?" Michelle asked.

"Um," *everything*? "His name, for starters." It was a change I should have made a long time ago. Except I sucked at naming characters in my books. Names were the bane of my existence. I usually just googled a long list of

names and slapped one on that didn't remind me of anyone
I hated.

Except for Zayne.

Because it sounded like Zaid.

I was such a loser.

"This again? To what?"

"Um...well..." I inhaled through my nose, "I am
wondering if we should change Zayne's background a bit,
too."

Michelle and Layla stared at me in silence for a moment
before Layla chimed in, "Like, his trauma?"

"No, like," I shrugged my shoulders, "I'm thinking I want
to write a male lead with a different ethnic background.
Maybe someone Eastern European—oh, south Asian would
be good, too."

They both just stared at me.

"But why?" Michelle started clicking on her computer,
her eyes shifting to stare at whatever she pulled up on her
screen, "Do you not feel like you're doing a good job writing
a Middle Eastern lead? Because we have sensitivity and
authenticity readers who say otherwise so far."

I inhaled a nervous breath through my nose, "No, no," I
shook my head once, "I'm just wondering if Zayne even fits
in this story. I'm wondering if I should save his character for
another story, is all." I lied. I had no intention of using
Zayne at all in any future writing if I could get away with it.

My editor winced a little bit at my words, "I disagree,
and frankly, it's a bit late to be making such drastic changes
in the story. I'm in the middle of my last round of
proofreading the manuscript."

"Agreed," Michelle nodded, "As I've mentioned before,
the hype from this story is specifically because of Zayne.
How you wrote him, how readers felt about him, and how

artists felt the need to illustrate him and bring him to life. You became popular because you're an excellent writer, Signe, don't get me wrong," I felt my stomach churn at her words, "But we can't pretend that the love readers have for Zayne's character wasn't also a huge draw to your book."

I nodded; I wasn't threatened by her assessment. It was true. Readers fell in love with Zayne. Artists fell in love with Zayne. Hell, I was dangerously headed in that direction with Zayne's inspiration if I was being honest with myself.

"I see," I nodded, "I get what you're saying. I was just wondering if I should save Zayne for another book. Maybe write a different love interest for this one."

"Is there a reason we shouldn't be using Zayne's character that we're not aware of?" Layla asked, almost mindlessly. She was also scrolling on her iPad, a small smile on her face as she read whatever she was looking at.

I felt my throat tighten with nerves.

Michelle and Layla never once asked me about the Zaid/Zayne livestream fiasco all those months ago, and I have to assume that's because they never saw anything. They were busy and trusted me to run my social media how I saw fit. I doubt they actually scrolled through my page often.

My social media had been completely Zaid-free the last couple of months though, except for the one rogue account that will DM me asking if I wrote Zayne based on anyone else.

I just left that reader on read.

Could I just tell my agent and editor that Zayne resembles my coworker too much and it feels icky to proceed with the story as is? At this point, I felt like I had no other choice. But I didn't need to give them all the nitty gritty details. Instead, I could give them as much of the truth as I felt comfortable with.

"The thing is," I sighed, feeling the heat pool under my cheeks and neck, "Zayne is inspired by a real person. Someone I know." I felt my shoulders scrunching in on myself, and I tried to straighten in my seat and look less anxious than I felt, "I just don't want to create any complications for you both, knowing the inspiration behind the character."

"Oh, thank god," Layla grinned and slumped back in her seat, "So we don't need to make any big edits after all."

I wanted to throw up, "We—we don't?"

"No," Layla shook her head once and pulled a hair tie off of her wrist, sitting forward and pulling her hair back, "Correct me if I'm wrong Michelle, but if the similarities between Zayne and whoever you based him off of are really that blatant, I think all we'd need is some form of written consent from him that we can continue with the story as is."

I held my breath, not relieved in the slightest to hear that solution from her.

"That's right," Michelle nodded, "Authors write characters based on real people they know all the time, but if you're really this worried about it, securing his written consent will help ease that anxiety you're clearly feeling right now. The anxiety that looks like it's giving you some cold feet before we move forward."

I tilted my head side to side, "I guess that's a good way to describe it." I would have gone with crippling panic, but tomato-tomahto.

"Something else to keep in mind," Layla added, "Is that you're not in a position that normal trad authors are in. People are already familiar with a big portion of the story. Like Michelle said, they already love the characters.

Changing things like Zayne's ethnicity could be very problematic and put a bad taste in reader's mouths—even if you gave him an alternative minority background."

"Oh," I felt my shoulders slump, "I didn't consider that aspect of making those changes..." In other words, I was in deep shit and needed to see it through.

"But we don't need to change anything," Michelle chimed in, "Because all we need is that form of written consent from Zayne's inspiration because if submissions are successful, publishers would want that confirmation anyway. That way the publisher can avoid any potential lawsuits."

"That makes sense," I nodded, feeling completely steamrolled but not having any idea how to avoid this.

"Is there anything else you wanted to talk about while we are all here, Signe?" Michelle asked, clicking away at something on her computer.

I sat for a moment, wondering if I should put my foot down, but feeling a large lump form in my throat instead, so I just shook my head and eventually, we all said our goodbyes before ending the call.

Fuck.

How did I get out of this?

Was there a way for me to start any type of relationship with Zaid without him knowing about this? According to these women, no, no there wasn't.

The man didn't even know I was a writer, let alone that I wrote a character that closely resembled him.

I was nothing but a meat suit of anxiety at this point.

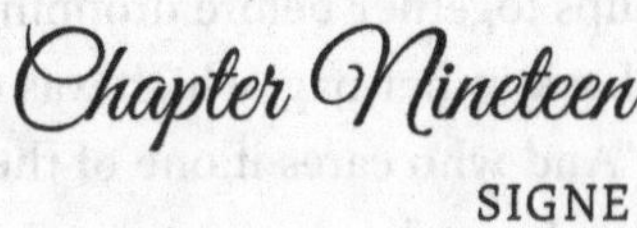

"So, how's your book going?" Mary randomly asked me one morning. It had been a little over a week since my dinner date with Zaid, and we had gotten together after work twice since. Once to walk the bluffs of Laguna Beach to watch the sunset and another time to try a new ice cream joint that had just opened up a few blocks away from the office in Irvine.

I held my finger up to my lips immediately after Mary's question, panicking as I checked the surroundings to make sure nobody else was nearby.

"Cool it," I hissed, "You and Jamie are the only ones here that know about it."

Mary rolled her dark eyes before setting her bag on my desk and rummaging around in it. She pulled out a red lip stain and a compact mirror, applying the makeup with an effortless swipe before saying, "So, are you no longer writing the book?"

I grimaced, pulling the crew neck of my sweatshirt up over my face in embarrassment, "No, we're getting ready to send out the first round of submissions to publishers to see if anyone is interested in the rights to it."

Mary snickered, "Nice. I respect this decision."

I pulled my sweatshirt down just enough for my eyes to reveal themselves, "Why is that?"

"Because writing a book is kickass," Mary smacked her lips together before dropping her stain and compact mirror back in her bag, which was covered in buttons and stickers, "And who cares if one of the characters looks like someone we know."

I bit my lip and dropped my hold on my sweatshirt, drumming my fingers on my desk.

Mary stared pointedly at my fingers before narrowing her dark eyes at me, "Spill."

"I don't wanna." I whined.

"Do it." Mary leaned forward on my desk, "Or I'll tell Jacqueline about the book."

I glared at her, "You wouldn't dare."

"Try me," Mary glared back at me.

I held my breath, kind of hoping that I would just pass out to avoid telling Mary anything but knowing that wouldn't actually fix any of my problems.

Who knew, perhaps Mary would have some advice for me?

"I...think I'm dating Zaid," I whispered as quietly as I could.

Mary's jaw dropped, "What? Since when?"

I closed my eyes and whispered again, "Since we made out and he finger banged me in Tennessee."

Mary released the girliest gasp I had ever heard from her, before she ran around my desk and sat on the lower ledge, leaning in, and wiggling her eyebrows at me, "Was it amazing?"

Perhaps Mary wouldn't have advice for me.

"Of course it was amazing," I hissed, "It's all I have been able to think about. That, and the fact that he and I are going out to dinner tonight."

"Oh my god," Mary's eyes widened, "It's not just sex?"

"No," I shook my head, my hands tugging on the back of my neck in the stress, "It's *feelings*. We haven't even had penetrative sex yet. He keeps being all sweet and respectful, and it's ruining my life."

"Wow," Mary deadpanned, "What an asshole."

"I'm serious," I was sweating under my sweatshirt, "What do I do? I can't keep dating him and publish a book about him without him knowing!"

"Well," Mary lifted a shoulder, "Maybe it's time for you to just tell him."

"But what if he hates me?"

"Then that's his loss," Mary crossed her arms, "He's allowed to be upset about you writing a book about him without his knowledge, if that's how he chooses to react. But you can't have it all, Signe. You can continue to date him or keep the book a secret from him. You can't do both. That's just weird."

I groaned before leaning back in my chair and swiveling back and forth.

Mary studied her chipped black nail polish while I let her words settle around me.

The elevator doors dinged, and the man himself waltzed through.

Zaid had his phone to his ear, but that didn't stop him from smiling at me and nodding his head at Mary as he passed my desk on the way to his office.

Once Zaid finally turned the corner out of sight, Mary leveled me with a look, "You need to tell him at some point.

Unless you plan on ending this relationship with him and ghosting him, of course."

I frowned at her words, my mind spiraling around her words before I breathed out, "I want him."

Mary shrugged, standing from her seat on my desk and rubbing my shoulder as she passed by me, "Then grow a pair of ovaries, own up to your choices."

She was right, of course.

I needed to come clean to Zaid about my current career goals. Hopefully, secure that written consent from him so Michelle could give it to anyone who bites.

I was just hoping to have a little more time with him before I needed to face the consequences of my actions.

For now, I wanted to focus on other things.

Like the fact that tonight I was going out with Zaid again.

He had texted me to ask if the restaurant he had in mind was a good option for me or not. I agreed because Indian food was always a fun choice. Learning what amount of spice the two of us could tolerate, and also loading up on naan, sounded like a fun time with a man like Zaid Ansara.

I was at my desk, gently trailing my fingers along the thick leaves of the snake plant he gave me, when the doors to the elevator dinged and two women approached.

One was around my height, an older woman with olive-toned skin and dark hair and eyes. A beauty mark on the side of her lip. She had a very lean form and wore pressed slacks and a silk blouse with bracelets on her wrists. A colorful (and probably expensive) necklace completed her outfit. She had her arm looped through another woman closer to my age with the prettiest caramel colored hair I had ever seen. It reminded me of Jacqueline's, though it was clear that where Jacqueline had natural caramel highlights from the sun, this woman had colored her hair for the same effect.

She also had dark eyes with long thick eyelashes, and her lip color was a fun light shade of pink. She also wore slacks and a blouse, as if the two women came from the same place.

"Good morning," I glanced at the clock on my computer to ensure that it was, still in fact, morning, "How can I help you?" I smiled at the two women who approached my desk. The older woman rested her free hand on the ledge of my desk.

"Is Mr. Ansara busy?" she asked with a polite smile of her own.

I turned towards my computer, opening his schedule, "It looks like he is in a lot of meetings all afternoon, but there is a thirty-minute window before lunch," I checked the time again to confirm that that free window was in the next few minutes, "I can call him and see if he's available—"

"Could you let him know his mother is here?" She interrupted me, patting her hand on the arm of the woman she escorted through the elevators, "I have someone I want him to meet."

I hesitated, just for a moment, as I realized a couple of things seemingly all at once.

I was speaking to Mama Ansara, the woman who cooked my lunches for the past few weeks and raised the man I was going out with later tonight.

The second thing I noticed was that the woman Mama Ansara had her arm looped through looked very nervous and almost uncomfortable. The younger woman gave me a small smile as I took her in, brushing some of her shiny hair behind her ear as a blush stained her cheeks.

"Oh, um, yes," I nodded as I grabbed my desk phone and

dialed the extension to Zaid's office. Part of me hoped he wouldn't answer, because even though I had very little evidence to support my claim, I was instantly feeling very territorial of the CTO.

Nikhils words from a while back started ringing in my head, *she is desperate for him to find a woman to bring home.*

And even though this woman looked visibly uncomfortable, as if Mama Ansara had dragged her here under duress, I couldn't help but notice how entirely different she and I were. She was shorter than me, had a petite frame, and dark hair that probably required a hair care routine I could only dream of affording. Her olive-toned skin was flawless, and her makeup looked like it was applied by professionals. Even her professional attire was flattering, and I couldn't help but glance down at my sweatshirt and jeans combo which ended up being the equivalent of my work uniform most days.

This was the kind of woman Mama Ansara picked out for her son.

It was unsettling to note.

"Signe," Zaid's voice sounded through the phone, and I jumped a little in my seat because I hadn't expected him to be on speaker. I removed the phone from my ear and gently set it down on my desk as I replied.

"If you're not too busy," I tried my best to sound casual, but probably didn't, "You have a visitor in the front here to see you." I winked at the two women. Mrs. Ansara smiled at me in appreciation, whereas the younger woman looked almost defeated behind her thin smile.

"...Who?" Zaid asked, his deep voice making my heart rate spike. Hearing his voice while being in the presence of his mother did odd things to my nervous system.

"Bisbous," Mrs. Ansara leaned over the ledge a little so

she could speak into the phone, "Come say hello to your mother. There is someone I'd like you to meet."

The line was silent for a moment before the telltale sound of the phone being hung up rang through, and the line was dead.

I set the phone back on the receiver as I turned back to the women, "Can I get either of you anything? Water? Coffee?"

"We're fine, thank you," Mrs. Ansara nodded as she tucked the woman's arm tighter against her body as if securing her to this spot.

I nodded, and we sat there in what I felt most as uncomfortable silence while we waited for Zaid to join us.

"I like your shirt," the younger woman finally spoke, gesturing to my shirt of the day. I glanced down to remember what I wore; it was just a picture of an open book with flowers and birds and greenery flying out of the pages. Thank god, because I wasn't sure if Mrs. Ansara would have appreciated my, "anti-social book club" t-shirt I almost wore instead.

"Thank you, do you read?" I asked, leaning my elbows on my lower desk ledge and looking up at the women.

"I do," she smiled, an accent similar to Nikhil's coating her words, "Mostly fiction, though."

Mama Ansara's eyes were going back and forth between the two of us, curiosity on her features.

"I prefer romance myself," I lifted a shoulder.

"Oh, I *love* reading romance," for the first time since she entered the building, the woman looked a little more relaxed. A little more open, "Have you read anything good recently?"

"Oh yeah," I nodded my head enthusiastically, "Most recently I read—"

"What are you doing here?" Zaid's voice made me lean back in my chair as if I had gotten caught shooting the shit with someone when on a deadline. I wasn't, but Zaid's tone wasn't exactly friendly.

I threw a quick glance at the younger woman, who had immediately tensed up again as Mrs. Ansara pulled her forward, facing the CTO who finally approached my desk.

"Zaid," his mother gestured towards the younger woman, who looked like she wanted to crawl into a hole, "This is Aarna Pandya, she works with me at the hospital, and—"

"It's very nice to meet you, Aarna," Zaid interrupted his mother, an action that made her snap her mouth shut with a firm press of her lips. Zaid held his hand out, only waiting a second for Aarna to offer her hand to him in a shake.

As soon as he gave the woman a polite smile, he pulled his hand away and turned towards his mother, "May I have a word?"

His mother adjusted her grip on Aarna's arm before saying, "We didn't want to take up too much time, I just wanted to introduce—"

"If you wouldn't mind," Zaid interrupted his mother twice, making visible irritation tense her facial features as she nodded and patted Aarna's arm once, before following her son down the hall and just around the corner.

Aarna and I both turned to look at each other with wide eyes before I couldn't help it and a small giggle escaped me.

Thankfully Aarna's lips pulled into a grin in response to my inability to hold it in, and she covered her face with her hands, "This is humiliating."

"I'm so sorry," I whispered back to her, "Do you need to make an escape? I can cover for you." Even though the offer was entirely based on my own personal interests and only marginally based on the discomfort Aarna was experiencing.

"I think I'll be okay," she turned to face my desk, leaning her elbows on the top ledge, "I was ambushed. She asked me to lunch and announced that she was going to make a quick stop on the way back to the hospital. I had no idea she was playing matchmaker today."

"I could tell," I grinned, "I feel for you."

"Thank you," she sighed, "I guess now might be a good time to let Mrs. Ansara know that I am already happily in a relationship."

"No way," I widened my eyes, "You must have *really* been ambushed."

"Yes," Aarna huffed a laugh as she palmed her forehead, "She means well. I don't want her to feel too bad. She's clearly a mama who wants her son to be happy." Then the sound of footsteps was approaching, and the two of us turned to see Mrs. Ansara walking towards us without Zaid, who must have gone back to his office.

"I apologize," Mrs. Ansara spoke to the two of us, "Thank you for letting me take this detour."

"Of course," Aarna stood taller, looking up at Mrs. Ansara as she met us both at my desk.

"Thank you for letting us interrupt my son's workday." Mrs. Ansara spoke to me with a kind smile attached, her eyes lingering on me in my seat for a moment longer than she had before.

I gave her a bright smile in return, the anxiety in my body leaving me in waves as I settled in the knowledge of what a flop this whole situation was. How I was still the one going out to dinner with Zaid after work. How Aarna wasn't even remotely interested in, who I considered, the sweetest man in Orange County.

"Any time," I desperately wanted her approval, which seemed silly considering she had no idea who I was, but I couldn't stop myself from adding, "Also, Zaid has been sharing your leftovers with me. I know we just met, but I wanted to let you know that I think you are a *phenomenal* cook. The days you send him home with too much food to eat on his own are my favorite ones."

Mrs. Ansara hesitated her departure at my words, her body only partially turned to face me as she studied me with her dark eyes that matched her son's in color.

"Oh," Mrs. Ansara looked like she had to gather herself, which made me feel a little self-conscious for the unsolicited compliment I attempted to throw her way, "Yes. I'm glad that he's not letting the leftovers that I give him go to waste."

Something about the way she emphasized certain words in that sentence threw me off, but she smiled and waved as she and Aarna finally stepped back on the elevators and left the building.

As the doors closed behind them, I released a very heavy exhale of relief, right when my cell buzzed with the arrival of a text.

I glanced down and grinned.

Zaid: Sorry about that. My mother won't be bringing random women to the office again.

Me: It's alright, I'm not worried about it. That must have been jarring for you to deal with in the middle of your workday though.

Zaid: A little.

> Zaid: But there's only a few hours left before we clock out and I can have you all to myself.

I felt my heart take off in my chest, fanning my collar away from my neck as I asked myself, *is it hot in here?*

> Me: Looking forward to it.

ZAID

"Can we talk about the weird thing that happened today, or do you want to keep ignoring it?" Signe asked right after the waiter set our dishes in front of us.

"Um," I cleared my throat, wondering what exactly her thoughts were on my mother obviously trying to set me up on a date, "Sure." I reached for my glass of water, an attempt to hydrate my throat so I didn't panic throughout the entirety of this conversation.

"You can unclench your butthole," Signe replied, making me choke on my drink for the second time in her presence, "I know that you were super uncomfortable with your mother showing up."

I patted my chest to help me inhale a breath of air before giving her a smile, "I was. Very much so."

Signe nodded, casually stirring her curry with her spoon, "I was, too. I didn't picture meeting your mother like that."

I paused my own movements to give her a look, "You've pictured meeting my mother?"

"Well, yeah," she took a quick bite of her curry before

swallowing and grinning at me, "Obviously I want to meet the woman who has been feeding me the past few weeks." I grinned at her, "I told her I loved her cooking."

That made my heart jump in my chest, "What did you say, exactly?"

Signe ripped a piece of naan and dipped it into her curry as she replied, "Just that I loved her cooking, and how I appreciated her giving you more leftovers than you can eat yourself."

Shit.

It was a small detail, perhaps a detail that could go past my mother.

Hell, who was I kidding? My mother was a very intelligent and observant woman. She would remember that *I* had been the one specifically asking for extra leftovers the last few weeks and that she hadn't forced the extra food on me at all.

To hear Signe claim that *she* was the one giving me extra leftovers, she would start to put some things together before I was ready for her to.

"And what did she say in response?" I asked, wondering if my mother had blown my cover.

Signe furrowed her brows a bit, before chewing her bite and saying, "She just said you're welcome."

I relaxed my shoulders, knowing my mother was probably going to be a little snoopier for the time being, but it was worth it. Hopefully, if things went according to plan, she would be seeing a lot more of Signe anyway.

Though, I wanted to see more of Signe first.

I wanted her to get to know me, to trust me. Which, now that I thought about it...

"I asked my mother for the leftovers," I rushed the words out, unable to take them back as Signe froze with a piece of naan hovering above her mouth, "She didn't push them on me."

Signe blinked a bit, before lowering her bread and asking, "You did?"

I nodded, in for a penny, in for a pound, "It was an immature act of jealousy, on my part."

Signe's eyebrows rose at my words before she shook her head once and asked, "What do you mean by that?"

"Hearing you talk about your lunch date," I found myself tightening my hold on my water glass before loosening my grip, "It made me jealous. I didn't want you going on another one. I figured if I could take up your time during lunch, you wouldn't feel the need to. That, I don't know, we could have our own lunch dates."

Signe was silent, her wide hazel eyes staring at me. I squirmed in my seat under her stare and added, "I'm sorry. I shouldn't have overstepped like that."

Slowly, Signe shook her head just once at me.

"I'm not sorry," Signe's voice was lower, a grin tugging at the corners of her tempting lips, "I'm flattered, mostly. I'm not against what you did." She released a small, breathy giggle before taking a sip of her own water.

I returned her smile, "That's a relief to hear." I felt the muscles in my shoulders loosen at the admission, glad I could be honest with her.

I knew what she was about to tell me in Tennessee, but I tried to stop her from blurting out anything about her book. It was clear she was in distress at the time, and for some reason, I realized I didn't want her to tell me like that. I didn't want her to tell me about the book out of fear, but instead out of trust. Excitement for it, even.

Hopefully, me admitting this small piece of our history to her will help her lean in that direction more.

The dark green dress she was wearing made it very difficult to remind myself that I wanted to wait before sleeping with Signe. Something I momentarily lost control of in Tennessee, because I was seconds away from ripping all her clothes off and taking her right then and there.

The deep V-neck plunge of her dress made my mouth water when I picked her up at her apartment tonight, a small studio space. I could see all the furniture she owned when she opened her front door, including her bed. Which, because I was obsessed, made me visualize how she'd look in that bed if she let me touch her in the way that I dreamed about.

How it would look if I was the type of man who planned to take her back to her apartment after this dinner and slowly peel her dress off of her body.

I was desperate to see her curves, especially now that I knew how soft she was under my hands. I was entranced.

"Zaid?" Signe's voice interrupted my thoughts.

"Hmm?" I asked, quickly taking another bite of food to hopefully distract myself.

"You're staring at my cleavage."

I felt heat, that didn't come from my meal, stain my neck and ears, "I apologize."

"You don't have to," Signe smiled, "I wore this specifically for you, so, it makes sense for you to look."

I gave her a heated look, which made her eyes widen as she slurped another bite of her curry, her breathing hitching when my eyes locked on hers.

"Did you, now?" I asked, pushing my glasses farther up my nose.

"Is...is that all right?" It was one of the most self-conscious tones I had ever heard Signe use. I didn't expect it. Signe had always given off an air of confidence I had desperately tried to match. I studied her as she avoided my gaze, a small but nervous smile on her lips as she studied the way her spoon dragged across her curry.

"Signe," I leaned forward, my elbows resting on the edge of the table to provide a little more intimacy in this restaurant, "I have struggled to keep my eyes off you for a long time now." At that, her gaze snapped up to meet mine, her lips parting a small fraction, "The thought of you choosing that dress," I lifted my chin towards her, "with the motive of gaining my attention, makes me want to throw cash down on the table, drag you out of this restaurant, and lock us in the back seat of my car."

Her breathing had picked up in speed, making her breasts heave behind the satin fabric of her dress, "Oh... what would we do there?"

I lifted an eyebrow, making her raise both of hers in challenge as she took a sip of her water.

"In this fantasy," I glanced down and gathered another bite of food on my fork, "You'd be on my lap, both of your legs around my waist." She glanced around, similarly to how she did yesterday in the office. I took a bite of food as if this was a very normal, appropriate conversation for a public space, and swallowed before continuing, "No one would see inside because of my tinted windows," I let my fork drag across my food as if I was preparing another bite, "But I'd see you. I'd see everything you're hiding underneath that mouthwatering dress," I grabbed my glass again and took a sip, meeting her eyes that were looking more hooded as she watched my throat work around my drink, "I'd feel everything. Hear everything. Every little sound you made back in that hotel room, and more."

Her breathing caught before she reached for her own glass of water again and took a drink.

"But we're not going to do that," I shook my head, my lips tipping up in a smile as I saw her shoulders slump and her eyes widen in disbelief.

"We-we're not?" she asked.

I shook my head before leaning back in my chair and taking another drink of water, setting the glass down on the table, "No, we're not."

She sat there, nodding her head once as a small pinch in her brow formed, her hands falling into her lap, "Can I ask why?"

I grinned, "I don't like to rush things."

She nodded again, taking another sip of water, and fanning her neck afterward, a self-deprecating smile tugging on those pink lips I desperately wanted to taste again.

"You didn't consider what we did at the hotel rushing things?"

"I actually do," I forked another bite, before locking eyes with her, "I was a man unprepared for your attention. But this is our first date, Signe. I want to savor it."

Her expression softened a little at that, and as she watched me take another bite of food and chew it behind my closed lips, her shoulders relaxed a little bit before she nodded for the third time.

"I think I like the sound of that," she grabbed her spoon and scooped another bite of curry before adding, "Though, you need to cool it. Otherwise, I'm going to soak through my dress here soon."

I didn't choke on my food this time; I just gave her a hungry look that I'm sure conveyed how desperate I was for her.

"So," I cleared my throat, the straining in my pants desperate for me to change the subject, "What else is there to know about Signe Lange?" I took another bite and stared at her. I noted the look of nerves that flickered across her features, and how she adjusted in her seat as if she was momentarily uncomfortable. Because she didn't know that I was already fully aware of how she was in the process of writing a book with me in it.

How I wasn't supposed to know it even though that knowledge of mine is what led us to this dinner tonight.

Signe recovered after squirming in her seat for a moment, grinning at me and straightening her back with confidence as she pointed to the plate of naan, "Signe is a huge fan of carbs."

I smiled and nodded, "I'll make note of that."

"...And I guess free food in general."

I hummed noncommittally.

"...And you."

I felt something warm bloom in my chest at her words, wondering how much longer I could keep up this charade of mine. Part of me was curious how long we would see each other before she felt the need to bring up her book. I remembered my sister's warning from a while ago, about how it would be important for me to inform Signe that I was fully aware of her book, to avoid any conflict the longer our future relationship lasts.

But a part of me also struggled with the thought of why Signe was still keeping it a secret from me, I didn't want to push her to share with me before she was ready. Surely, if this relationship we were exploring together were to become more serious, she'd have to share it with me at some point. Then I could let her know that I loved the idea of her pursuing her dream, even if I unintentionally helped inspire her to do it.

Maybe she wouldn't be upset with me for keeping her secret just like she was?

But I didn't let those thoughts spiral out of this moment I was having.

After months of pining, and longing for her, I was here. Having dinner with Signe.

I didn't want to ruin this experience by focusing on both of our deceptions.

...I just wanted to focus on Signe.

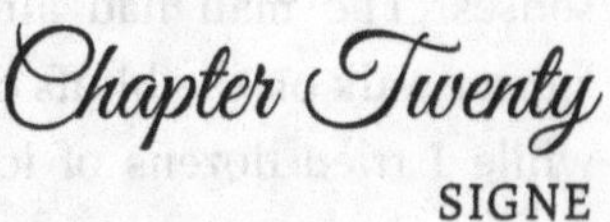

"OH MY GOD," I felt my eyes widen in alarm.

Actually, I think the proper term for my eyes was, "bulging out of their sockets."

"I can't believe you just did that," Zaid caught up to me, breathing heavily at my back as I stood there, frozen on the threshold of his bedroom door.

When I arrived at his apartment with takeout, he suggested I get comfortable on the couch while he went to his room to look through his selection of Blu-rays. He asked what I was in the mood to watch, and like a normal person, I asked what he had. It was insane to me that the man still had Blu-rays and DVDs instead of just any streaming service.

I wasn't sure I even had something to play a CD or DVD with in my entire apartment. My laptop didn't even have a CD drive.

Anyways, Zaid had given a very vague answer of "lots of options," which made me stand up from the couch to just follow him down the hallway to his bedroom where the movies supposedly were.

He immediately got nervous, his hands up defensively as he insisted that I sit on the couch while he grabbed some options.

My spidey senses started tingling.

By spidey senses, I meant my "what the hell could he possibly be hiding in his room that he didn't want me to see" senses. The man had already invited me on a romantic sunset walk on the bluffs of Laguna Beach, patiently waited while I tried dozens of ice cream flavors before choosing one, and even went out of his way to ensure I still had delicious leftovers to eat for lunch.

But now he was hiding something, and as much as I didn't want to shatter the illusion that he was perfect, I couldn't let this go.

I had no idea what to expect when I bolted underneath his large arms and sprinted down the short hallway, determined to see what he was so nervous about. Was his room unusually messy? Did he have plush animals on his bed? Unfolded laundry? Skin suits? I needed to know. There was no chance that I was going to sit on his couch all evening and not wonder what warranted such a nervous reaction from him.

I couldn't have guessed this even if given the chance.

What I walked in on was so out of left field, that I had to blink several times to make sure that I was seeing things correctly.

"Um..." I took a few steps into his room, my gaze bouncing all over the place because it was impossible to land on one thing. Every time my eye landed on a new area, details stuck out to me.

The dark red accent wall that his bed sat against.

The giant Captain America symbol on his comforter.

The movie posters—sorry—the *signed* movie posters. Avengers, Iron Man, Captain America, and even the Hulk.

The framed dolls.

The framed playing cards.

I walked over to a large floor-to-ceiling bookshelf that had some books, but mostly DVDs. A glance let me know that they were all organized by release day. The man had every single DVD in the Marvel universe, as well as some mint edition comic books that were also framed or kept in some sort of glass housing.

"So..." I heard Zaid speak behind me, making me turn around to see him leaning in the doorway with his arms crossed over his chest defensively, "...This is my bedroom."

I stared at him, trying to wrap my head around this additional information I had on him.

"This is your room," I repeated, trying to maintain eye contact with him but also getting distracted by additional Marvel Universe merch on the wall near his door, the side of the room I didn't immediately see upon entering.

"I'm sweating over here, Signe," Zaid said, genuine concern on his expression as he watched me look around.

"I just..." I shook my head a little bit as I took a few steps toward him, getting distracted by an out-of-the-box action figure sitting on a shelf near the doorframe he leaned against, "Didn't expect—"

"For me to be a geek?" Zaid interrupted with a nervous smile.

"For you to be a *huge* geek," I corrected, pointing to the new shelf of merch beside him, "Did you leave any toys for the other kids in the store?" I was giggling by the end of my sentence, my smile taking over my features as my shock evaporated into complete, utter adoration for this side of him.

Zaid rolled his eyes at my snarky remark, "These are adult toys."

"Tell me more," I widened my eyes in exaggerated interest as I gently snagged one off of the shelf, careful with my hold in case it was valuable and fragile, and started to inspect it, "Where's the button? How many vibration settings does it have?"

Zaid choked as he snatched his action figure out of my hand. He couldn't hold back his laughter, even though he tried. He righted the toy back on the shelf before mumbling to me, "You're a menace."

"You have the biggest boner for the Marvel Universe that I have ever seen."

"All I heard," Zaid gave me a sly look as he reached forward to grab my forearms and tug me towards the door, "Was that I have the biggest boner."

I snickered as I ripped my arms from his grip and stepped backward towards the bed, wiggling my eyebrows at him, "You need to walk me through this."

"Do I?" He asked, giving a nervous glance at his surroundings as if he hoped he could conceal any aspect of this room.

There was no hope. I had seen it all. I wasn't ever letting this go.

"So, you're at a bar, you see a woman you want to get naked with," he slid his dark eyes over to me, a look of exhaustion with his grin, "She, obviously, wants to get naked with you too—"

"I'm going to stop you right there," Zaid lifted a hand as he marched towards me, and I skirted his reach again by side stepping quickly to the other side of his bed, creating distance between us. Zaid's eyes narrowed a little bit as he followed my retreat, trapping me in the corner, near his end table, "Women don't come home with me."

"Because they see your room?" I asked, gesturing dramatically to the Captain America shield comforter.

"No," Zaid came to stand in front of me, something flashing in his eyes before he halted and stood a foot away, "Because I don't bring women back to my room."

"Ever?" I asked.

He lifted a shoulder, "I don't do casual hookups, Signe."

I stared at him for a moment, a question that was none of my business at the tip of my tongue. I slammed my lips shut as I thought better of it.

"What are you thinking, ya amari?" Zaid asked, his voice lower. Intimate.

"What does that mean?" I whispered. He had dropped a few terms of endearment in Arabic now, and I had been too nervous to ask. This seemed like a good alternative to asking whether or not he was a virgin before we got together.

Zaid gave me a longing look for a moment before he released a heavy sigh, "The moon."

I tilted my head, "You called me the moon?"

He smiled before taking a seat on the edge of his bed, stretching his long arms behind himself, "It's an affectionate name."

"That's nice...Mars."

Zaid rolled his eyes.

"Specifically, I called you *my* moon," Zaid leveled me with his gaze, his voice softening, "My most beautiful."

I stood there, frozen.

I was all too aware of the blood pumping in my veins from my rapidly racing heart. I stood in Zaid Ansara's bedroom, with his nightstand with an Iron Man lamp just inches behind me, while he called me his most beautiful.

Something inside of me both melted and cracked at his words, and I was hopelessly muted as I processed. How this lovable man I had originally written off for being too shy had quite possibly the geekiest bedroom a thirty-four-year-old man ever had.

"So..." I stopped because even though I was a writer when the sun went down, words could still escape me in very real moments like this, "You don't bring women back to your room," I couldn't focus too much on Zaid casually throwing out *ya amari* without getting emotional, so going back to the original topic was the best I could do, "Because you don't do casual hookups."

Zaid shook his head, his arms still supporting his weight on the bed behind him, "No."

"What if I told you," I swallowed around the painful lump in my throat, nerves building inside of me, "That I have only done casual hookups for the last...little bit."

Zaid lifted a shoulder.

That was it.

"Nothing?" I pressed, casually leaning against the wall near his window, and turning my body so that I could trace my finger down the shade of his bedside lamp to avoid looking at him.

"What do you want me to say?" Zaid asked.

"What you're thinking."

It was silent again, so I folded my arms and lifted my eyes to stare at him. He was studying me, his dark eyes wide and hiding nothing. And yet, even though he wasn't trying to hide any emotion, my nerves still kept me from reading him accurately.

"I think that it doesn't matter to me what your sexual history is," Zaid lifted his shoulder again, and I wanted to smack it down.

"At all?" I asked, "Even though you don't..." I waved a hand vaguely in the air.

"I don't what?"

"Fuck around?" I blurted out, feeling the heat stain my cheeks as I slammed my mouth closed.

Something flickered behind Zaid's gaze, and as I watched him stand from his bed to step into my space, lifting his hands to uncross my arms, I thought my heart was going to jump out of my throat.

"I don't fuck around, no," Zaid murmured, keeping hold of my wrists as he brushed his thumbs gently against my pulse. The touch sent a shiver down my spine, "I used to, but not anymore."

Well, that answered my ridiculous question about his virginity.

I didn't even believe in the social construct of virginity, so why I wanted to know how experienced Zaid was made me hate myself a little bit.

"Are you waiting to settle down?" I asked, staring at the collar of his shirt, the slutty little wide-neck t-shirt he wore that showed off his clavicle.

"Yes," Zaid nodded once, making something flip in my stomach at his words. I immediately remembered our conversation on his sister's couch all that time ago. Watching that children's show with the Australian dog family I had watched more episodes of on my own.

"So, like," I rolled my eyes as a small smile twitched on my lips, "When you invited me over to your apartment to watch a movie...?"

Zaid's lips twitched a little bit in return, "I invited you to *just* watch a movie. No other expectations."

"Even though I'd be a very willing participant?" I whispered. I knew it was wrong to entertain sleeping with him right now, considering the big fat secret I was keeping from him. But I was only human.

I must have been very inside my own head, because suddenly I felt Zaid's warm fingers skim over my jaw so he could cup my face in his palm, tilting my head to look up at him. I thought he was going to say something, the way his lips parted, and his eyes darted between both of mine. But then he shook his head once before lowering his lips to mine.

The kiss was gentle and sweet.

Heartwarming.

And all the other words I could also use to describe Zaid.

He brushed his warm, soft lips over mine once more before pulling away, just enough for him to rest his forehead against mine, "I'd like to wait, Signe."

I felt my breath release from my lungs, a myriad of emotions coursing through my body. The first emotion, though I tried to dismiss it as quickly as it came, was rejection. How Zaid wasn't trying to seduce me tonight and would reject me if I tried to seduce him instead. The other emotions were fairer to him, I thought. Admiration for Zaid not jumping into bed as soon as a woman expressed interest in him. For upholding his own boundaries. To not feel pressured to jump into this goofy-ass Captain America-themed bedding and go to pound town.

"Until you're married?" I ended up asking for clarification, my voice barely audible because it took so much effort to calm my voice into something he wouldn't feel offended by.

In response to my question, Zaid chuckled, and I felt that deep sound of his all the way to the tips of my toes.

"No," Zaid whispered back, matching my low voice,

almost like he was giving our talk reverence, "Just until things aren't casual."

I lifted my head up to look at him better, forcing Zaid to lift his forehead off of mine, "When do you decide things aren't casual?"

Zaid pressed his lips together, the only sign of nerves I could see on him, "When you and I chat and decide that not only are we exclusive, but we're also endgame."

"You did not just make an Avenger's reference right now," I giggled my question at him, making his lips pull into a grin.

"I didn't mean to, I promise," He pressed his lips against my forehead, his mouth lingering for a moment before looking down at me, "I'm not waiting for marriage, I'm waiting for someone who wants to be just as committed to me as I want to be committed to them. I can casually date you without sleeping with you."

I stared up at him, a pang of hurt stabbing my chest, "So..." I ended up closing my mouth and looking down at the ground. I let my wrists fall out of his hand, having momentarily forgotten he was holding me like that.

"Signe," Zaid's voice fell over my shoulder, both of his hands cupping my face now to get me to focus back on him, "What did I say?" His eyes looked so concerned, having immediately picked up on the shift in me.

"I'm just being ridiculous," I mumbled, trying to look away even though his grip on my face tightened to keep me from doing so. He wouldn't let me escape, determined to hold my gaze before he tried a new tactic.

Zaid's lips brushed against my ear, slowly dragging down my neck in a way that made goosebumps erupt across my skin. My heart was racing from both fear and arousal.

"Why do you think you're ridiculous?" Zaid asked,

kissing the pulse point between my neck and shoulder in a way that drove me insane.

"I-I just—" when I first met Zaid all that time ago, I never would have guessed that the man would eventually be using his kisses to get me to spill my guts to him, "I'm a little embarrassed at how easy it is for you to not have sex with me. H-how I'm not exactly someone you see yourself s-settling with yet."

Zaid stiffened, his lips ghosting over my skin near my collarbone. My head was lifted and bent back to make room for him to explore me, but as he froze, and I held my breath as I waited for him to respond.

"I thought I made it clear how *difficult* it is for me to not sleep with you right now," Zaid spoke against my skin, making me exhale my breath on another shiver, "Signe, I—" his hands came back up, and gripped either side of my waist, and I had to give up all pretense that I could regulate my breathing "Goddamn, I want you *so* badly."

I felt myself huff a disbelieving laugh, "You do?"

"Do you not remember our first kiss?" Zaid asked, his kissing losing its sweetness and being taken over by something else. Something hungry, "How you straddled me? How I touched you?"

You mean the kiss that ended with me coming in my pants? Yup, I sure do.

I was meeting his kisses eagerly, my hands sliding up his chest and tangling in the roots of his hair behind his neck. I remembered our first kiss. I couldn't think of a time recently when I wasn't thinking about our first kiss.

"Yeah," I managed to respond once he pushed me farther against the wall, his lips ravaging my neck, "I remember."

"I couldn't resist you then," Zaid grumbled, pulling away

and tugging me with him as he twisted our bodies to sit me down on his bed, "I'm barely resisting you now. Do you know why I'm resisting, Signe?"

I wheezed my response, "Because you're waiting."

"Because I'm waiting for *you*," He corrected, sliding his hands up my arms and gently pushing my shoulders so I fell back on his bed. Zaid bent over me, one knee bracing himself on the edge of the bed as he pressed his lips against mine again. Once. Twice. "You, and only you, Signe." Every time he said my name like that my heart swelled, "As soon as you kissed me in your hotel room, I was a goner."

I sighed as his lips trailed against my jaw, my cheeks, my temple.

I melted underneath him.

He said he was a goner, but I was the one who was completely hopeless for him.

"I don't want to make you wait too long," I whispered, surprised at myself for getting so emotional during this conversation.

"That's okay," Zaid lifted a hand to brush some of my hair away from my face and neck, "I can wait. You're worth it."

"Are you sure?" I asked, "Because I am scared easily, too." I giggled awkwardly, trying to brighten some lighthearted humor into a very serious conversation.

"That's why we aren't disclosing our relationship to Jacqueline quite yet," Zaid replied into my neck, making me addicted to the feeling of his lips on my skin, "Not until you tell me you're ready."

I gently gripped his wide shoulders, pushing him back so I could look him in the eye, "You really see me as the last person you'd ever date?"

"Habibti," when I raised my eyebrows at his newest term

of endearment, he shook his head once, unwilling to translate for me, "I've seen you for a long time. I want you to *confirm* that you're the last person I'll ever date—but unfortunately—" he leaned down to plant a firm, drugging kiss against my lips again, "We need to get to the actual date part first."

With that, Zaid pushed himself off me, not bothering to conceal the erection in his pants as he grabbed my hands and pulled me back up too.

I was dizzy from a whirlwind of a conversation, and from suddenly being tugged into a standing position from a prone one. Zaid wrapped me in his arms against his chest for a moment, letting me get my bearings after stumbling into him, before finally loosening his grip and nodding towards the bookshelf, "You still need to pick a movie."

"You don't want to cuddle up under the Captain America bedding and read comic books together instead?"

Zaid nudged me towards the bookshelf, a low chuckle in his chest as he kept his hands on my hips, brushing his lips against my ear while I faced the shelf of DVDs, "That's the hottest thing a woman has ever said to me."

"Maybe we can go online and see if anyone is selling first editions of your favorite comics?" I continued, using my finger to skim the names on the spines of the DVDs. Behind me, with his hands still gripping my hips, Zaid let out a very low and very sexual moan.

I whirled on him, every inch of my skin blushing from the utterly erotic sound he just made, only to see him grinning at me.

"Is this something you're always going to tease me for, Signe?" Zaid asked, reaching behind me, and tugging a movie off the shelf.

It was a comedy, one of those mindless ones where the

plot was thin, and the actors probably relied on improv for all of the dialogue.

Perfect.

"Just for the first little while, but if I'm being honest," I tugged the DVD out of his hands and strutted for his bedroom door, throwing over my shoulder at him, "I loved learning this little secret of yours."

Zaid hummed behind me, "Now I just need to learn some of yours to even the scales."

He meant it playfully, probably not realizing that I currently did have a very big, very problematic secret of my own. A secret that involved him, much more than it should.

But I was a selfish, conflict-avoidant woman.

So, when Zaid quickly ushered us out of the room and asked me what kind of seasoning salt I preferred on my popcorn, I let the moment pass.

Even though I could have sat on his couch the rest of the night, spiraling about how he and I were doomed before we even had a chance to start, I refused to. Instead, I let my delusions take hold that evening. I watched the silly comedy, laughing with him, cuddling under the throw blanket, and actively pretending that my underwear wasn't damp from our previous make-out in his bedroom. I sat with the knowledge that I would love nothing more than to try out committed monogamy with Zaid Ansara. How I wanted to earn this man's love because there was no chance in hell that he didn't love with his entire being.

I sat there on his couch, nurturing a small piece of myself that desperately, longingly, wanted this all to work out.

Chapter Twenty-One

SIGNE

TODAY MICHELLE HAD a handful of meetings with potential publishers.

Submissions had officially started, and I was going to be glued to my phone.

The first text I received from her said that the first publisher decided to pass on my story. I wasn't too worked up about it, it would have been insane if the first publisher Michelle spoke to made an offer.

Perhaps it was the text from Zaid asking about our date tonight that made it easier for me to brush off the first rejection.

Later, Michelle texted me again that she still hadn't had anyone bite on the story, and I felt a little discouraged.

However, I needed to accept one major fact.

Submissions had officially started on the story, and whether or not publishers were showing interest in it yet, I needed to tell Zaid. It was time to come clean.

I was determined to tell him on our date tonight, when it was just us and we weren't in the office. So, when I reread his text and typed out a reply to confirm, I hesitated and ended up deleting the message, instead choosing to walk over to his office.

Seeing Zaid throughout the day always lifted my spirits and would help with the emotional rollercoaster that was submissions.

I forced a skip in my step, which is why the moment I halted to a stop felt a little cartoonish. Almost comedic. However, the moment that made me come to a stop was far from humorous. Perhaps I would be able to look back on it and find a little humor in dealing with the consequences of my actions. In the moment, though, all I could focus on was the nausea pooling in my stomach. The rock forming in the base of my throat made me wonder if I would stop breathing. If I would die from humiliation right then and there, feet outside of Zaid's office, hiding to the side to shield my presence while still being able to observe my self-destruction taking place inside.

"...a romance novel," Jacqueline said. The words made an icy panic shoot down my spine. My body froze and instinctively backed away a step or two before either of them could see me waiting outside of his office. Before I heard her say anything else, I knew what they were talking about. Deep down, my soul knew that my time had come.

I could see Zaid with his elbows on his desk, his fingertips rubbing at his temples as he exhaled a tired sigh. Jacqueline sat pencil straight in the chair on the other side of his desk, her back to me, with her iPad displaying a very familiar social media account.

My social media account.

While Zaid processed what she had just told him, she was swiping through screenshots of that account. Screenshots showing character art, my face, and the historical moment of Zaid walking through my live feed so long ago.

Dread consumed me. Anxiety and embarrassment heated my cheeks at the same time the lump in my throat grew.

"Did you tell Signe yet?" Zaid asked, his head still down while he pinched the bridge of his nose. I could see the anxiety rolling off of him in waves. Why was I so hurt by that? Why was I surprised to see him react in such a way to my secret?

"No, I came to you as soon as I saw her account," Jacqueline had swiped again to what looked like a document, "I wanted to let you know what we can do so that you feel safe in the workplace—"

"Ya ilahi," Zaid groaned, sitting up in his chair and scraping one of his hands down his face.

I quickly stepped behind the tall potted plant near his office, my breath barely escaping me. I felt like I was suffocating. My heart was racing in my chest. Ice was coating my veins, and my muscles all felt stiff. My stomach was tightening in knots which made me wonder if I was going to throw up.

I need to get out of here.

I stiffly forced my legs to take me back to my desk, replaying the scene I had just witnessed, over and over again. Zaid hunched over his desk, distress coating his body language. Jacqueline swiped through all the evidence proving that I used Zaid's appearance, both inappropriately and without his consent. The light seemed too bright at my desk, and I kept either closing my eyes or squinting them against my computer screen.

I'm having a panic attack.

Zaid probably is too.

Oh god.

Zaid didn't ask for this. He didn't ask for any of this. Jacqueline was probably walking him through the procedure as I spiraled. He probably had no intention of speaking to me ever again, and I couldn't find a part of myself that blamed him one bit.

I had crossed the line.

Hell, I had *sprinted* across the line.

I had even come back over, just to dance across the line multiple times in the last few months. I could have pulled the project as soon as I realized how messed up it was. I could have demanded to my agent and editor that I change the appearance of Zayne's character. I didn't. I actively chose to stick with the original inspiration, because I cared more about my selfish desires. I cared more about finally landing my dream job than I did about Zaid's privacy. His peace of mind. The peace of mind that comes from working with employees who *don't* write smutty fanfic about you.

It was my own fault.

I had no one to blame but myself.

Surely, I would be fired. I was replaceable. My job was fairly entry-level, and even though I was sure that there would be growing pains between firing me and hiring someone else and training them to do everything I did, it would be worth it to the company. Firing the lower-level employee who, for all intents and purposes, sexually harassed the CTO would make more sense than fighting to keep me on.

Zaid was valuable to the company.

I wasn't.

So, what did I do now? Did I just...wait to be fired?

A new wave of embarrassment and dread filled my chest, and when I glanced at the time and saw that I only had about an hour left of my workday, I decided that sticking around was a bad call.

I stood from my desk, not remembering sitting down at it, and started shoving everything in my bag. Charger, earbuds, gum, ibuprofen, and Midol that I kept in the drawer.

"Signe," Jacqueline's voice made me jump and snap my head up towards where she stood over me, her iPad that had my sins clutched in her arm against her chest, "Do you have a moment?"

"I—I," I closed my eyes, feeling my chin wobble and desperately trying to control my chaotic emotions, "I don't know."

Jacqueline's dark eyebrows rose a hint, "Are you busy?" Her eyes glanced at my computer screen, "I'm sure whatever it is can wait."

"Actually," I felt my heart racing in my chest, my fight or flight instincts at war with one another as I shook my head and shouldered my bag, grabbing the desk plant that Zaid had given me.

I felt my eyes sting with tears when I remembered how I got this cute little plant.

Part of me wondered if I should throw it in the garbage instead.

A bigger part of me hated the thought of that.

"Actually," I swallowed around the lump in my throat, attempting to speak again, "I think it's best if I just go."

Jacqueline's brows came down this time, "Are you feeling alright?"

"No," I shook my head, a smile tugging my lips as my bottom lip trembled, "I'm not. But that's okay. I'm okay. You don't have to worry about me."

"Worry about you?"

"I heard you, just now," I jerked my head in the direction of Zaid's office, making Jacqueline's eyes widen as she straightened her posture.

"Did you?" She seemed a little nervous, and part of me truly felt bad for putting her in this position. I had just started to crack that armor of hers. We had just started becoming friends. And yet, she had to do her job.

I couldn't blame her for that either.

"I did," I nodded, stepping around my desk and inching my way toward the doors, "I can write out a formal resignation letter if you'd like."

Jacqueline stared at me; her open mouth snapping closed as she stiffened at my words.

"I'm so sorry," I felt a small tear trail down my cheek, something Jacqueline glanced down at as she followed me to the elevators. It wouldn't be until the doors shut behind us and I punched the button for the first floor that I realized it was part of her job to walk me out. It was probably part of the plan of reassurance to protect Zaid, so he could confidently know I wouldn't be coming back to his office again.

"Signe," Jacqueline sighed and pinched the bridge of her nose, like how I saw Zaid last.

Oh god, don't think about the last time you saw him.

I sniffed, aggressively wiping another stray tear.

"Look," Jacqueline had created a long pause after saying my name, so I took the opportunity to interject, "I know I fucked up, alright? I know I shouldn't have, well, you know," I nodded towards the iPad she was still clutching in her hands, "I didn't mean to be this unethical about it. I never expected to become friends with him. I never expected to —" I stopped myself because telling HR that I had developed very real feelings for the man that I indirectly harassed probably wasn't a smart move, "But, that doesn't excuse my actions."

Jacqueline just stared ahead at the elevator reflection, letting us sit in silence until the car stopped and the doors opened. She waited for me to step out first before following after me. It wasn't until we had made it to the parking lot that I spoke up again.

"I do wish," I swallowed around the lump in my throat once more, adjusting the strap of my bag before I turned to face Jacqueline directly, "I wish that you had come to me first."

Jacqueline tilted her head to the side, "Why is that?"

I shrugged, keeping my eyes on the cute little plant in my hands, "I thought we were becoming friends."

Jacqueline stiffened again, making me lift my gaze to meet hers.

She looked a little wounded. Not so wounded that my words made her have more empathy for me than she should have, but wounded enough to where I could see her struggling a little more to keep her professional mask in place.

"Signe," Jacqueline sighed, "I was just doing my job."

"I know," I nodded, "I understand. It's selfish of me but, maybe if you approached me first...I could have just left, and I wouldn't have had to see Zaid like that."

A touch of softness creased the corners of Jacqueline's eyes at my words before she quirked her lips to the side and nodded at me once, "I can see that you aren't feeling well," her eyes trailing up and down my almost trembling form confirmed her statement, "I hope you feel better soon. You will be hearing from us shortly."

I nodded, "I'll send my resignation by tonight or tomorrow."

Jacqueline hesitated, her mouth opening before she closed it and relaxed her shoulders. She nodded at me once more, before she turned and marched back towards the building.

I was such a fuckup.

Desperate for a distraction, when I felt my phone buzz in my pocket again, I immediately pulled the phone out and opened the latest update from Michelle.

Michelle: Still no takers, but this is to be expected. Stork Press didn't think the story had anything special that hadn't already been written in the genre. Unfortunately, we are going to have to comb through several publishers, and it might take a few rounds of submissions before anyone bites. Don't let this discourage you.

When I got in my car, I practically threw my phone in the passenger seat in frustration. Fully discouraged. Heartbroken. Emotionally unwell.

It wouldn't be until later, when I walked through the door to my tiny studio apartment, that I realized what else I had to do.

Because if I continued with this story, if everything continued as it was, I would be at serious risk of getting into more trouble. Zaid, and Sun Steer, had the funds to come after me.

I had to tell my agent what was going on.

Neither Michelle nor Layla were keeping track of my social media.

Would this end with my book being scrapped? Would potential publishers even want to continue working with me after I openly admitted to basing my love interest on a very real person like I have?

I wasn't sure, but I couldn't find the will to sit down at my laptop and start drafting emails to figure it all out.

Instead, I laid down on the couch. Kicking my shoes off, pulling a throw blanket off of the back, and mourning the one thing that I was truly upset about.

Beyond losing my job at Sun Steer.

Beyond potentially losing my book deal.

No, what was upsetting me the most out of all of this, was losing Zaid.

Chapter Twenty-Two

ZAID

I PACED my office back and forth, blatantly ignoring the person on the other end of the call monologuing into my earbud. I couldn't focus anymore today. I checked my watch and saw that it was six-thirty.

This was ridiculous.

I tapped my phone and saw that Signe hadn't ever responded to the message I texted her this morning, asking if we were still on for continuing our Marvel marathon tomorrow. Her idea, not mine.

Nothing.

Sure, she probably had work to do. I didn't expect her to

319

respond right away, but she hadn't taken *this* long to respond before. Not since our relationship went from friends to more. Not since she's seen my bedroom.

Not since I learned what her lips tasted like.

I finally heard words that sounded like the end of the discussion, and I forced myself to tune back into my call to make sure that it would end soon. As soon as we all agreed everyone was on the same page, I ripped my earpiece out and shoved my phone into my pocket.

I grabbed my coat off of the back of my chair, shoved my laptop in my bag, and stepped around my desk to leave right when there was a knock on my office door.

Jacqueline let herself in, her hand still on the handle, "Do you have time to talk now?"

"What?" I asked, glancing at the time on my phone again.

Fuck, why hadn't Signe responded?

"About Signe," Jacqueline asked, stepping in and leaving the door open a few inches, "Everyone else has gone home, but I stayed because you said we needed to talk about this later. When you were done with your meetings," she stared pointedly at my bag and coat, "It looks like you're done now."

"Damnit," I squeezed my eyes shut and demanded the headache I felt starting to pulse behind my eyes to hold off, "Can't we talk about this another time?"

"I guess," Jacqueline shrugged, "Though I'm going to be busy trying to find someone to replace her."

I froze, shooting Jacqueline a look that made her eyes widen a little in shock and stop whatever tapping she was doing on her iPad, "Whose replacement?"

"...Signe's," Jacqueline was nervous at first, but I saw her straighten her spine as she confirmed my fear, "I need to fill her position."

"Jacqueline," my voice did not sound kind, but I only felt a little bad about it when Jacqueline winced at the tone, "Did you fire Signe? After I specifically told you not to mention any of this to her?"

"No," Jacqueline glared at me, "Signe quit, told me herself that she'd send me her resignation letter later," I felt my heart sink at the words, "Because she heard me talking to you about what she did."

No.

She did?

I didn't see her; I didn't see anyone outside of my office when Jacqueline ambushed me earlier. I had just finished a call with Nikhil when Jacqueline asked if I had a moment. I nodded and invited her in, only then to be informed that Jacqueline had found Signe's social media accounts. Her accounts that talk about her book, her book about me. Jacqueline showed me several screenshots showing just how sexualized my character was and asked if I was aware that Signe was using my appearance in such a way.

I was terrified, frozen.

Jacqueline took my silence as if I wasn't aware.

Then she tried to tell me everything she was planning to do. Everything from relieving Signe from her position to filing paperwork disclosing the harassment Signe had caused.

My ears had started ringing from stress before I snapped at Jacqueline to stop. She seemed surprised but agreed. I told her that we would need to discuss this all later, but that she was *not* to approach Signe about this yet. That I wanted to talk to her first.

Clearly, that all went to shit.

"Fuck," I scraped my hand down my face, my palms getting a little clammy.

"We're at work," Jacqueline scolded. I rolled my eyes at her, a movement that she was visibly surprised to see me do since I usually was more collected in the office.

"We need to fix this," I was rubbing both hands on the sides of my neck, pacing back and forth in the small space of my office. Jacqueline stayed put, near the cracked office door as her eyes watched my movements skeptically.

"What do you mean? It looks like the problem solved itself. She quit. We don't need to worry about severance or—"

"If she quits, she can't finish the book!" I snapped, deflating a little when Jacqueline jumped and showed a little fear on her face from my outburst, "I'm sorry. I'm sorry. This isn't your fault. I'm just trying to figure this out."

Jacqueline studied me, always with a calm and professional face.

"You...want Signe to finish the book?" Her voice was coated with disbelief. I gave her a desperate look before I decided that I should take a seat in one of my office chairs. Making myself smaller relaxed Jacqueline a bit more, instead of her staying glued to the wall as she watched my larger self, pacing and stressing.

"I've known about the book for months, Jacqueline," I sighed, dropping my head in my hands. My glasses got in the way, so I pulled them off and tossed them on the seat next to me before digging the heels of my palms into my eyes, "I've always known."

Jacqueline was silent for a few moments.

I took the time to inhale a few deep breaths and relax myself.

Signe knows that I know.

She quit.
She hasn't responded to my texts.
Signe quit.

"You've...known..." Jacqueline's voice reminded me that she was still here.

"...Why did she quit?" I asked myself, ignoring the head of HR watching me panic about what my next steps should be.

"...Why *wouldn't* she quit?" Jacqueline countered. When I snapped my head up to look at her, her face softened a little bit as she took a tentative step towards me in my seat, "She heard me talking to you. She saw how you reacted...I assumed the same as she did."

"What did you assume?" I asked, desperate for details.

"That you were upset," Jacqueline frowned, "Upset that she crossed a line and that you wanted the situation dealt with. When I sought her out after meeting with you, she was already packing up her desk."

I glared at Jacqueline, who immediately held my glare with one of her own, "I told you not to talk to her about this."

"You don't have the authority to demand that of me," Jacqueline squared her shoulders, "I know how to do my job, even if it makes employees uncomfortable. It's my job to ensure that the company practices safe and ethical procedures. So, when you told me to drop it, I ignored you and went to approach Signe about her behavior directly."

"Jacqueline," I leaned back in my seat, glaring at the ceiling, "She can't quit."

"She actually can," Jacqueline lifted her shoulder, "I'm not going to stop her. She crossed a professional line, even if you knew what she was doing and seemed to be okay with it."

"If she quits," I gritted through clenched teeth, "She can't finish her book. She'll need to find a new job, which will take time away from publishing the novel, which delays accomplishing her goal of writing full time."

The head of Human Resource's face shifted to surprise, before relaxing into a studious expression. I swear for the first time since I've known her, I saw Jacqueline's eyes soften the tiniest bit at my words.

"I didn't say anything," I continued, "because if Signe finished the book, solidifying her book deal, she could quit her job here. Then, I would no longer be her superior."

Jacqueline blinked at me, and I held her gaze. I chewed on the inside of my cheek before I decided to come out with it, "I'm in love with her, Jacqueline."

Her eyes widened, her mouth parting in bewilderment before she cleared her throat and tried to compose herself, "You're...involved with Signe?"

"Yes," I admitted, rubbing my jaw with my hand, "That, however, is a very new development."

Jacqueline's eyes narrowed at me the slightest bit, "So, when you approached me about romantic relationships in the workplace—"

"I was not involved with her then," I cut her off, "I wasn't planning on ever being involved with her while she was still an employee. I understand the ethics of the situation."

"And yet..."

"And yet..." I sighed, my shoulders slumping, heaviness pulling on my body as I struggled to explain things to HR while also stressing about the fact that *Signe still hadn't texted me back*, "I found out that my feelings weren't so one-sided."

The sound of Jacqueline's shoes against the carpeted floor made me lift my head to watch her move my glasses to the side table and take the other chair in front of my desk, "Signe loves you, too?"

"Well," I felt myself blushing, an insane reaction given the situation, "I have no idea if she feels that strongly for me. I was originally waiting for her to quit just to formally ask her to dinner. I wasn't planning on kissing her at a hotel," Jacqueline's eyebrows rose, "I wasn't intending to start anything while we were both still employed. But we did start something. And I'm scared as hell about what she wants to do."

"Well," Jacqueline said, "If she quits, you two can date."

"This isn't how I wanted that to happen," I groaned, resting my forehead in my hands, "I wanted her to quit because she was following her dreams. Not because it's unethical for her and me to be romantically involved, or because she felt like she had no other choice."

We sat in silence for a few moments in my office.

The sound of my heartbeat and breathing was the only thing echoing off of the walls, and it took a while for me to finally lift my head from my hands and face the head of HR.

"Look," Jacqueline spoke up first, cutting me off before I could get a word out, "This is a messy situation." I nodded, "So I advise that you and Signe talk—outside of this office."

I blinked at her, before nodding again, "All right."

"Once you and Signe reach an understanding," Jacqueline inhaled a deep breath, before closing her eyes and exhaling it through her nose, "If Signe is interested, her job is still available to her. I haven't processed any of the paperwork for her resignation yet—but you two *have* to come in and disclose your relationship to me."

I stared at Jacqueline, my lips twitching a little bit at her words, "You're not going to lecture us about the dos and don'ts of workplace relationships?"

Jacqueline rolled her eyes before standing and heading for my office door, "It's useless. There's a reason it's a word of caution and not a hard rule. I can't control two consenting adults." Jacqueline paused at the doorway, one of her hands resting on the doorframe as she turned to look at me, "And Signe...she's a good person. You both are...you deserve the best."

With that, Jacqueline left, making a smile start to tug on my lips as I realized how much of a *relief* it was to have HR's blessing going forward.

I pulled my phone out of my pocket once more to check the time. It was just after seven o'clock, and Signe still hadn't responded to my text from this morning.

Which simply wouldn't do.

Chapter Twenty-Three

SIGNE

THAT NIGHT there was a knock on my door, and I barely had the energy to move my eyeballs in that direction.

I ignored the knock.

I hadn't ordered anything, my mother was out of state at some artist's retreat, and I was ignoring the incoming messages and notifications on my phone for the time being.

Wallowing alone in self-pity was needed at the moment.

The knock sounded again, followed by a familiar voice I hadn't heard in a long time, "Signe, I'm going to pee on your doorstep if you don't answer!"

I immediately jumped off the couch and ran, throwing open the front door to see Eloise St. James standing there in all her pregnant glory.

"Hi—"

"I'm going to pee my pants," Eloise interrupted my greeting by quickly elbowing me out of her way and making a beeline toward my bathroom.

I laughed, after righting myself. Eloise was a smaller woman than me, in every way, and yet she almost knocked me on the ground to get to the bathroom in time.

After slamming the bathroom door closed, there was a sigh of relief that echoed in the bathroom as she relieved herself, making me laugh out loud again as I walked back to the couch.

A minute or so later, Eloise emerged from the bathroom, giving a grateful smile as she wandered over to me. A significant bump was already pushing against her shirt, and I clapped my hands excitedly as she noticed where my gaze landed and posed side to side for me to admire her pregnant belly.

"You're so cute!" I squealed, "You make pregnancy look adorable."

"That's nice," Eloise smiled as she finally settled herself on the couch next to me, throwing her feet up on my coffee table just like I was sitting, "But I'm always one sneeze away from either peeing or shitting my pants."

I snorted and took a moment to laugh some more, "Is that why you decided to stop by without notice?"

Eloise shrugged her shoulders, "I knew I wouldn't make it home from shopping with my mom in Newport, and when I realized how close your apartment was and how long it's been since we've hung out, I decided to insert myself into your Friday night."

I gave her what tried to become a grateful smile before my lip wobbled and I felt the threat of tears start to sting my eyes.

Eloise's clear blue eyes widened at me in response, and she quickly tucked her light blonde hair behind her ears before throwing herself at me in a hug. I didn't start sobbing or anything, because I was determined not to wallow too much about facing the consequences of my own actions, but I did hug her back while some traitorous tears escaped.

"Is everything okay?" Eloise asked against my hair. She smelled so good, like roses or something.

"No," I sniffled, pulling back from her hug, and wiping my eyes with my sweatshirt sleeve, "I quit my job today."

Eloise raised her eyebrows for a moment, nodded once, and waited for me to elaborate. When I didn't, she asked, "... The job you've wanted to quit since starting?"

I smiled and huffed a laugh because she wasn't wrong. I probably was giving off a lot of mixed signals.

"It's more complicated than that."

Eloise waited, so I released a heavy breath and made myself fill her in on everything regarding Zaid.

Everything including the live stream, the desk plant in apology to women everywhere, and the homemade lunches, until this afternoon. When Jacqueline discovered my deep dark secret, told Zaid about it, making me panic and quit so that I wouldn't have to face his disgust with me.

"So, you haven't spoken to him since you overheard Jacqueline telling him?" Eloise asked, "Has he reached out?"

I shrugged, "My phone is silenced in my bedside drawer." I nodded my head in the direction of my bed against the other wall.

"...But what if he's not upset about it, though," Eloise pressed.

"Call me crazy," I gave her a deadpan look, "But the look on his face really made me doubt that the man who wanted to wait to lay his pipe inside of me until we were serious was happy to hear that I had been writing a romance about him. A romance that includes some not safe for work, explicit content."

Eloise was already giggling before I finished my sentences.

I smiled at her, waiting for her to catch her breath. Her

face turned bright red with her laughter, a sign of the high blood pressure she had been struggling with since becoming pregnant a second time. "Hold on," Eloise breathed through her giggles, trying to regulate, "Laying pipe. Good god."

"Would you prefer dipping his wick? Entering my castle? Filling me out like an application? Putting his wand in my chamber of secrets? Shooting his meat rocket into my—" I was stopped by Eloise's hand slapping itself over my mouth as she cackled.

"I'm going to pee again, you need to stop," Eloise giggled some more. I listened to her warning because even though my couch wasn't the nicest one around, I still didn't want to clean her pee out of it.

After giving Eloise a few moments to catch her breath, I shifted and rested my fist on my cheek, my elbow on the back of the couch, "How are you doing with this pregnancy? You already have a little one this time. Do any of you need anything?"

Eloise rested her head on the back of the couch, her hand resting over her heart as she grinned at my question, "I don't think so. Logan being retired is probably the best thing that happened for us." I grinned, jealous that someone in their early forties could retire and be financially secure for the remainder of their lives. Perks of playing in the NHL, I guess, "Plus my parents are super helpful with Iris, thank god. She's the most energetic four-year-old I've ever met."

I believed her. Eloise used to work at a facility that provided therapies for babies and toddlers before teaching an exercise class at the gym where I met her. I went to it for a one-week duration, before never going back again. Because I hated sweating.

We became friends almost immediately though.

"Logan is excited to have a boy, too," Eloise rubbed her bump thoughtfully.

"Was he nervous about having Iris?" I didn't remember him having a nervous attitude at all during Eloise's first pregnancy. I just remembered the gigantic man fawning over his pregnant wife the entire time, making my heart explode from the cuteness. Big men being doting husbands and loving dads always did things to me.

Zaid would probably be just like Logan, should he ever have kids like he wants.

"Not at all," Eloise shook her head once, "He was thrilled at the news of having a girl. I think he would have been more nervous having a boy as our first. His dad is...well, who knows where he is. But he wasn't a great father figure, to put it bluntly. So, he was worried he wouldn't know how to be a good boy dad himself. Going to personal therapy again, and having Iris first, I think, gave him the parenting confidence he needed to be the kind of boy dad he knows he wants to be. Plus, one of our close friends is a good example of being a supportive father figure with their little girl and soon-to-be boy."

"Oh, so your kids have built-in friends to play with too," I clasped my fingers together, thrilled to watch Eloise live her best suburban life. Watching what it was like to be a parent, and to have a support system nearby.

"Yeah, my friend Courtney is currently pregnant with their first son, too. We're due around the same time," Eloise shook her head once, "But you're distracting me by asking a lot of questions about my life. So let's fix that." Eloise gave me a look that she probably gave her daughter when she was acting up, "I think you should check your phone and see if Hot Marvel Nerd reached out to you at all."

I snorted, "His name is Zaid."

"Zaid, of course," Eloise grinned, "What if he texted you saying he's totally happy with you writing erotic fanfiction about him?"

I tried to smile, but it was wobbly again. The anxiety I had been desperately trying to shove down into nothing for months was catching up to me. I could feel it in every muscle in my body. It was exhausting just sitting here trying to wrap my head around the entire situation. The anxiety I felt about it all made me freeze, which is probably why I decided to just hide my phone for the time being. My life was already a disaster, how terrible could holding off on responding to messages be?

"...Maybe I'll check my phone tomorrow," I shrugged noncommittally, "But for now, I'd love to watch a movie with you."

Eloise gave me a small smile as she reached behind us and grabbed my throw blanket, covering both of our legs in it as she snuggled closer to me, "As long as it isn't anything sexy, I'm down."

I gave her a look, "So like, nothing with sex scenes?"

"Or sexual tension," she lifted a hand and started listing off requirements on her fingers, "Or longing looks, or hand flexes, or wet clothing, or hot people, or—"

"Eloise, that's every movie ever."

"Well," she shrugged, "I'm reaching the crazy horny stage of the second trimester," she gave me a wide-eyed look, "I can't keep jumping Logan every day."

I cackled, "I think he's fine with it."

"Well of course he's fine with it," she lifted a hand and gestured vaguely down her body, "I'm a hot piece of ass carrying his gigantic baby. However, I also have things to do. Places and people to see. I can't spend all day in bed with him. Someone needs to feed Iris."

My shoulders were shaking with laughter, before I offered, "If you're comfortable with it, I'd love to spend some time with Iris. Maybe she and I can spend the day together and have a sleepover while you and Logan get a hotel room for a night."

Eloise stared at me in silence for a moment, making me wonder if my offer was out of line in some way, before she eventually said, "I'm trying to convince myself to turn this down since my parents literally just had a sleepover with her at their house, but I don't think I'm going to. I'm taking this opportunity. I'll talk to Logan and let you know what dates work best for us."

I patted her thigh over the throw blanket, "Perfect."

After going through my favorite streaming services, Eloise vetoing every suggestion I had because it was all just too sexy, we decided to land on a nature documentary about dolphins and whales.

It was nice, sitting on my couch with my friend, having some sort of company after the shittiest day ever. Throughout the documentary, in between Eloise trying to mimic the whale and dolphin's noises to the best of her ability, I kept staring over at my nightstand where my phone lay.

Perhaps Eloise was right, and Zaid would be the kind of guy who didn't mind what I did. Or at the very least, would be willing to let me apologize for crossing a boundary? But I just kept picturing the visible anger on his face when Jacqueline showed him all the damning evidence, and I squashed that hope.

So, I decided to embrace my need to freeze things for the time being. I focused my energy on my friend living her best life, sitting on my couch, taking a ton of pee breaks, and giggling with me at our ridiculousness.

Tomorrow was a new day, and even though I had no real plans on how to address anything, I knew I couldn't do any of it without a full night's sleep. Eloise eventually left at the end of the documentary, hugging me tightly in her arms again. Once I closed the door behind her, I popped a gummy to ensure that I didn't toss and turn all night from stress.

Chapter Twenty-Four

SIGNE

I FINALLY FELT ready to come out of my cave of self-pity. Twenty-four hours seemed like a reasonable amount of time to wallow and grieve and mourn. To process whatever complex feelings I had that were no one's fault but my own.

I had just brewed a cup of coffee and sat down at my laptop, ready to type out my resignation letter and email Michelle and Layla gently explaining what a fucking creep I am, and to ask if there was still time to completely alter my main male character's appearance.

Instead, when I finally retrieved my phone from its place charging in my nightstand drawer, I noticed that it was flooded with social media notifications. As well as several missed calls and messages from Michelle. Probably to inform me of more rejections, which I just wasn't in the headspace to read at the moment.

I took the opportunity given to me to delay confessing my sins to Michelle and Layla, and instead skimmed all the likes and comments I had gotten on my social media account in the past day or so.

What I was surprised to find all the likes and comments linking to, however, was a video that showed Zaid's face.

I double-checked the account that the video was posted on, and I was immediately confused when I realized it was *my* account that had his face. His face, sitting in his nerdy-ass Marvel-themed bedroom.

I felt my stomach drop, wondering if I had been hacked by a fan who had stolen footage of Zaid. *Great*, I thought to myself, *yet another reminder that my actions have consequences.*

I tapped on the video because I hated myself.

Zaid cleared his throat, propping the phone up on his desk. He leaned back, his dark eyes darting between the image of himself and the camera at the top of his phone before he pulled his glasses off and rubbed the inside corners of his eyes with his fingers.

"For the love of god," Zaid spoke behind his hand that lingered on the bridge of his nose, "Signe. Change your fucking password."

I felt my heart stop as I tapped the screen to pause it, my coffee that I was sipping went down the wrong pipe and I choked for a couple of seconds before I set the mug down and restarted the video.

Holy shit.

Zaid was talking to me?

On my *account?*

I hesitated for another moment before tapping the screen again, resuming the video.

"Or, better yet," Zaid shrugged, a smirk tugging at his lips as the man struggled with looking at the screen versus the camera, "Answer your phone so I don't need to get your attention like this." He eventually settled his gaze on the camera, and it felt like he was staring directly into my soul. Those dark, beautiful eyes that I thought I wouldn't have the privilege of admiring again, made my heart skip a beat through the phone screen.

"Signe," he shook his head once, tsking his tongue, "I know you're upset. I know you're probably a little embarrassed," he sighed as he settled more comfortably in his seat, resting his forearms on the desk in front of him, "But I need you to talk to me. And this is me desperately coming up with a last resort."

I was holding my breath, and it wasn't until I started to feel a little dizzy that I forced myself to inhale and exhale like a normal person.

"I know you told Jacqueline you quit," Zaid shook his head once, "I know you probably think I have no interest in you after learning about your book." He let that sentence hang there a second, gnawing on his lip once as he looked contemplative about what he wanted to say next, before soldiering on, "But I am. I am still in this, Signe. I'm all in." He chuckled at himself, looking a little sheepish as he smirked at the camera, "And I've known about your book for a while."

I felt my heart drop.

He *what*?

"I knew the day that I intentionally walked through your live stream—" *intentionally*? "—and I've been very aware of your publishing journey since then. I stayed updated on your posts. I deep-dived everything that you wrote publicly about this story, about the characters. About me...because I love you."

I squeaked and threw my phone to the opposite end of the couch.

My blood was rushing in my ears, and butterflies erupted in my chest and stomach.

He *what*?

I crawled like a crazed woman across the couch to retrieve my phone and continue watching, "You weren't the only one keeping secrets, Signe." Zaid glanced to the side for a moment, before focusing back on the camera, "I knew I was good at hiding my attraction to you. I bent over backward to avoid looking at you for too long," I felt a flattered blush stain my cheeks, all those instances where he broke eye contact first playing in my mind, "Because I was your superior, and that would be wrong. So, I avoided you. Like I knew I should...but then you wrote a book about me —well—about a man that looks an *awful* lot like me." He smiled as he pulled up his iPad to show the infamous character art of himself, zooming in on the veins the artist illustrated, making me want to crawl into a hole to escape the cringe of it all, "And as I sat there, listening to my sisters who have been followers of yours for a while now, filling me in on the fact that their brother was the inspiration behind a very popular story rising in online romance communities, I realized...I don't know, I thought maybe I had a chance. That maybe my attraction wasn't so one-sided after all." He shrugged casually as he set the iPad down and returned his gaze to the camera, making my breath catch in my throat.

"I tried to take a page from Zayne's, or I guess your, book," his expression turned a little self-deprecating, "I tried to put myself out there with you a little more. Baby steps. I wasn't trying to change who I was just to get your attention," he huffed a laugh, "I just tried to show little pieces of myself to you here and there, wondering if you'd like what you saw. Because the reality was, Signe, that even though I had been avoiding interacting with you in the workplace due to my inappropriate crush, I couldn't stop myself from constantly seeking you out."

I squeaked again, noticing that at some point my hand

had come up to cover my mouth in shock at what I was watching.

"Any time you entered a room, any time you laughed, any time you made someone else in the office laugh, I noticed you. I noticed *everything* about you. How could I not? I had no choice in the matter. Falling for you, even when I tried so desperately to fall for you *correctly*, had always been out of my control. I had given up on trying to contain my feelings a while ago. I think," he made a comical expression as he rubbed his bearded chin thoughtfully and stared off to the side, "I had completely relinquished control of my heart the moment you grabbed my face and kissed me as if your life depended on it."

I huffed a laugh to myself, both humiliated and enthralled at what I was watching.

"I'm going to assume that no man would stand a chance against that," Zaid chuckled again, embarrassment coating his features before he gathered himself, "Look...I know we probably shouldn't be together." I felt my heart sink at his words, "I know that it will always be frowned upon for someone in my position to be with someone in yours." I frowned, hating that he was right, "I have thought a lot about this the last day or so, in between desperately begging for you to *answer your phone*."

He held my stare through the camera, and I removed my hand from my mouth in surprise, "Jacqueline said that your job is still yours if you want it. That if you wanted to come back to work, you could. You could still have a steady paycheck and finish your book—keeping the male lead *exactly* as he looks in that beautiful head of yours—and quit later on when you settle into this career."

I was smiling, warmth filling my chest.

"And I will quit now, instead."

Wait, what?

"Because I am privileged to be in a position like mine at the age that I am. I can find work anywhere. My skillset gives me job security no matter where I go."

What? Zaid, no.

"I will admit," Zaid held a finger up as he chuckled to himself in his nerdy bedroom, "Part of me is willing to quit just so Jacqueline's eye doesn't twitch the entire time we are both working together... However," Zaid cleared his throat, "You know I'm not happy in a managerial position like this. Hell, everyone we work with knows. So, if quitting my job makes me get out of my own rut and pursue something that brings me more fulfillment, *and* I get to be with you on top of that? Well, that's a no-brainer." Zaid shrugged, smiling at the camera.

I was so in love with Zaid it wasn't even funny.

I was sitting up on my couch now, my phone with his video posted to my account still playing while I glanced around my apartment, getting ready to go find him, "So, let me know if this sounds good to you, or if I just publicly humiliated myself on the internet in front of your entire fanbase for no reason. No pressure either way." His smirk made me pause my frantic pacing around my apartment in search of clean socks to smile back.

"I'll be waiting to hear from you. But, Signe, in case it wasn't clear," Zaid leaned forward as if he was about to tell a secret, "I love you."

"I love you, too," I found myself whispering back. Zaid hesitated for a moment before shaking his head to himself once and reaching forward to end the video. The fact that he had hacked into my account to do so was of no concern to me while I closed out of the app and quickly found his contact to dial.

I meant to FaceTime him, but a traditional phone call was what came up. I ran with it.

"Signe?" Zaid's voice sounding over the speaker of my phone sent butterflies through my veins.

"Where are you?" I finally shoved my feet into sneakers, with only one sock on one foot, before grabbing my hoodie and reaching for the door.

Zaid inhaled a breath, "Where are you?"

"My apartment, but I'm coming to you—"

"Let me come to you." Zaid cut me off, and I froze, halfway out the door with my hand on the knob. My hoodie slung over my arm. I didn't even close the door behind me yet.

"But—I'm walking out of the door now."

"Well, I'm walking up your staircase now," Zaid countered. I heard the exterior building door shut below, and I gasped as I ran to the staircase to look down two floors. As soon as Zaid stepped into view, holding his phone to his ear as he smiled up at me, I squealed.

"Fine!" I grinned as he started ascending the stairs, the same moment I glanced down at myself and noticed that I was wearing the same sweatpants and t-shirt with holes in the armpit that I put on last night.

Frick.

I raced back to my apartment, stepping out of my sneakers, and skidding to a halt before I entered the bathroom to backtrack and prop the door open with one of my shoes so Zaid could come inside.

"Signe?" Zaid asked, reminding me that he was still on the call.

"Come in! I'm just changing. Or showering. Or something," I panicked. Glancing at myself in the bathroom mirror and cringing at the dark circles under my eyes and the unbrushed hair. The zit forming near my temple.

"Or something?" Zaid asked, his steps echoing through my open apartment door.

"I want to look cute!" I set the phone down and started yanking a hairbrush through my hair.

"Weren't you just leaving to come find me?"

"I didn't realize how...I looked," I widened my eyes at myself in the mirror. *Good job, Signe. Way to sell yourself to the equivalent of a sports-illustrated model.*

"Signe," Zaid's voice was low, not quite a warning, but teasing enough to let me know my time was running out, "I'm coming in."

"The shoe is propping the door open," I admitted, taking my bottle of mouthwash, and swishing it around for a couple of useless seconds before spitting in the sink.

The sound of my front door creaking open made my pulse spike, adrenaline and excitement and a whole other mess of giddiness making my hands shake as I struggled to apply deodorant as quickly as humanly possible.

"Signe?" Zaid's voice sounded in my living room, and I quickly tugged my shirt off to put a different, less-hole-y shirt on in its place. I was just grabbing a clean one when the bathroom door I had left cracked open, opened wider, revealing the man himself.

I was in my purple bra, a cream-colored shirt halfway up my arms before I lifted them to tug it over my head, my sweatpants hanging low on my hips, revealing the men's boxers I bought for myself to wear. Half of my hair was brushed, and I thought I felt a drop of mouthwash drying on the side of my mouth.

And yet, the way Zaid's eyes darkened as he stood in the bathroom doorway holding a pothos plant in one hand, his other gripping the doorknob after seeing me, made me feel like the most tempting thing alive.

"Hi," I squeaked.

"Hi," Zaid smiled, his eyes meeting mine after taking in, well, everything.

"I'm pulling myself together."

"Okay." He left the door open and leaned against the doorframe, his free hand going into the pocket of his slacks while he still held the little pothos plant in his other large palm.

"What's that?" I asked, nodding towards the plant.

"It's for you," he gestured towards me with the pothos, reaching forward and setting it down on the countertop next to the sink, "Are you stuck?"

"Huh?"

"Your shirt," He nodded towards my shirt around my arms, stepping closer.

"Oh," I glanced down at my arms, still halfway shoved through the arm holes of the shirt that I hadn't pulled over my head yet, "I—well—I was going to put it on."

"You were?" Zaid's low voice was teasing, making butterflies spread in my chest and throughout my body, his steps closing in on me in my tiny bathroom.

"Yup," I nodded, still not moving to finish dressing myself.

"And yet," Zaid stepped closer as he reached out with one hand to rest his index finger on the cream-colored shirt, gently tugging it off my arms, "You don't seem like you want to."

I swallowed around a dry but excited lump in my throat, "I'm distracted."

"By?" Zaid asked, successfully tugging my shirt off my arms and holding the garment up with his index finger.

"You are standing in my bathroom," I straightened a little bit and tried patting my hair down into place, "Bringing me plants, hacking into my social media—"

"I'd hardly call it hacking when you use the same password for everything," he raised his eyebrows at me, scorn coloring his expression for a moment, "Something you told me yourself."

"Yeah, well," I lifted a shoulder, reaching forward and tugging my shirt off of his finger to toss it to the side, "It's still taking advantage of my platform."

"It's almost as manipulative as writing a fictional character whose appearance looks an awful lot like someone you work with," Zaid met my eyes, a nervous smile tugging at the corner of his lips, "And trying to hide it from said someone."

"Did you really know the entire time?" I felt nerves skitter in my belly, insecurity creeping in. Perhaps that was partly due to still being topless in my bathroom with Zaid Ansara.

"Ever since my sisters cornered me the night of your livestream and told me all about it," Zaid smiled, stepping closer and taking my hand in his.

"And *they* knew the whole time?" I asked, my mind reeling, "When Salma came to your office? When I babysat—"

"The entire time," Zaid's gaze was bouncing between my eyes as he tugged my hand and guided us out of the bathroom, towards the couch, "They meddled a bit, trying to convince me that I needed help wooing you."

I stopped in my tracks right as Zaid took a seat, tugging on my hand to get me to join him, "Wooing me?"

"Wooing you, courting you, charming you," he tilted his head in mock contemplation, "Seducing you." He tugged on my hand once more, firmer, making me stumble onto his lap on the couch. Before I could adjust, he wrapped both of his arms around my waist and held me tight as I awkwardly lay bent over his lap. He lowered his head to brush his lips against my ear as he said, "I needed all the help I could get, Signe."

I felt shivers race down my spine as his breath fanned against the side of my neck. I squirmed, and he loosened his hold on me enough for me to turn around and seat myself properly on his lap, wrapping one of my arms around his shoulders.

"You aren't upset?" I asked, tracing my fingers across his hairline on the back of his head.

"No," he confirmed with a shake of his head, "I'm mostly annoyed that you ran away and ignored all my calls and texts."

"I ignored everyone," I ducked my gaze, staring at my hand that was tracing the shape of the tendons in his arm through his jacket sleeve, "I wasn't ready to face your rejection."

"I'm not rejecting you, Signe," Zaid sighed, shrugging out of his jacket, and revealing a simple t-shirt underneath, "I am doing whatever the opposite of rejection is." His large hands grabbed either side of my waist, his fingers splayed to hold as much of me as he could, "I'm claiming you."

"Claiming me?" I snickered as I adjusted my side saddle position to swing one of my legs over his lap, straddling him and wrapping my hands behind his neck, "That sounds a little overbearing."

"Declaring my intentions?" Zaid leaned forward, his gaze on my mouth, "I poured my heart out for you, Signe. And you have said very little in response to it." He halted, his dark eyes lifting to meet mine. A spark of insecurity lit in them, and I reached forward to press my lips to the side of his mouth while he held perfectly still. His hands didn't roam, they stayed put on my waist as I gently brushed my lips across his cheek, to the point of his jaw, up towards the shell of his ear.

"I love you," I whispered, making him suck in a sharp inhale, "I'm so sorry that I plagiarized your appearance, but I'm not sorry that doing so gave you the confidence to talk to me. To expose pieces of yourself to me. To be my friend at work. To share your mom's cooking with me. To share *yourself* with me...and to let me attack your handsome face that one night at the hotel."

I could feel Zaid smile as he ducked his head into my shoulder, and I continued to leave featherlight kisses down his neck, "I love you, Zaid. Geeky-ass, Marvel-themed bedroom, and all."

I squealed when his fingers on my waist immediately started tickling me, shifting so that he could let my back land on the couch cushions next to us.

"My decorating is still not nearly as embarrassing or cringeworthy as writing an entire romance novel about me," Zaid grumbled in my neck, his tongue tickling me as well.

"So, what you're saying is," I grabbed his head and pulled him away from my neck so I could look at him, "We're both equally embarrassing and there's no reason to hold what I did over my head?"

Zaid's eyes softened, his smile tugging his cheeks as he rested his forehead against mine, "I'm flattered, Signe," Zaid pressed a kiss to my nose, "I wish you could hear what was going through my head at the time, learning that the woman I had been longing for at work had written erotica inspired by me."

"It's not *erotica*," I leaned back into the cushions to meet his eye again, "It's just open-door, explicit romance with a man who looks a lot like you."

"Remember the Halloween party, when you handed me your phone with smut on it—"

"Oh my god!" Humiliation washed over me, having perspective on the situation now. It was already mortifying to have Zaid read a smutty scene I had written; it created an entirely new level of humiliation knowing that he *knew* it was about him. I covered my face with my hands in embarrassment, "I'm the worst."

"Stop it," Zaid grasped my hands and pinned them on either side of my head, his body resting entirely on mine. His hips settled in between my legs, "I loved it."

"Shut up," I giggled as I playfully glared at him.

"I'm surprised you didn't see the tent in my pants then, knowing that *you* wrote that. That you visualized *me* doing that."

I smiled up at Zaid, loving how we were having this conversation with me pinned underneath him. One of his feet rested on the floor while the other leg was resting on the couch. Both of my legs folded up on either side of his hips.

"Well..." I smiled up at him, "We don't have to just visualize it anymore."

His chest expanded over me as he breathed, his smile slipping just a hint as a predatory gaze coated his features, "I don't do casual, Signe."

"I know, Zaid," I bit my lip at him, loving the tension between us in this moment, "I'm very aware of what being with you like that means," I inhaled a shaky breath, "I have no interest in anything casual either...I love you."

A look of intense relief washed over his features as he

huffed a breath of air across my neck, his smile reaching his eyes as he leaned down and kissed me hard.

My lips parted for him, getting lost for a moment in the feel of his mouth against mine before he pulled away from me just enough to say, "I'm always going to fight to keep you, Signe."

"You don't have to fight," I rolled my eyes, "I'm with you of my own free will."

"If I mess this up," Zaid shook his head, "If I ever mess this up, promise me that you'll try to help me fix it." I could see his insecurity again, as he removed his grip on one of my hands to cup my face in his palm, "That even though it might be hard, or I might say the wrong thing, or do the wrong thing...that you'll still want to try to make it work. To make it right."

"Zaid," I turned my head to kiss his palm, my free hand coming up to grip the wrist, "I promise." I squeezed his wrist for good measure, "I promise I'll *want* to make it work. I haven't felt this way about a man in, well, ever. I've never wanted to commit to someone so fully." I smiled, "How can I make you understand? You're *it* for me. It's like you said, I'm all in."

"All in?" Zaid repeated, his thumb stroking my cheek as he locked eyes with me.

"All in," I smiled up at him, "Want me to prove it?" I reached up to peck him on the lips, "Want to run away to Vegas and elope?" He chuckled once before I gave him another quick kiss, "Want to have a traditional engagement and wedding instead?" I kissed him again, lingering only because he nipped my bottom lip back, "Want to knock me up?"

Zaid froze during our third kiss, making me stiffen in response.

Oh no, too far, Signe.

I collapsed back onto the couch cushions as Zaid's lips parted and his dark eyes drank me in, "I know you're joking," Zaid breathed, "But I don't think you understand how tempting it is to take you up on that offer."

I bit my lip.

Holy *shit.*

Zaid *did* have baby fever.

"I knew it," I whispered to him with a smirk, "You're *dying* to be a dad."

"I only want to be a dad if *you* want to be a mother," Zaid shook his head once, his hips grinding a little in between mine, "Otherwise, I'm happy to just practice making kids for the rest of our lives." He gave me a devilish smirk that made my heart skip a beat. When Zaid found his confidence and knew what he wanted, he was lethal. I was boneless against him. I melted, I swooned. I wanted nothing more than to be one of those heroines in historical romance novels who lay there and let themselves be ravished.

"Well..." I quirked my lips to the side as if I was considering something casually, "Why don't we use condoms for the first while? Just to practice, to make sure we *really* get it right. Then, after some time, we can consider the idea of creating life a little more seriously."

Zaid's lips crashed down on me, and I had a feeling that we suddenly had more important things to do than discuss plans and commitments. Instead, we needed to focus on us.

Chapter Twenty-Five

ZAID

"AS COMFORTABLE AS MY COUCH IS..." Signe mumbled against my mouth after I lost myself in the feel of her lips against mine.

I didn't bother responding. Instead, I pulled her up and practically dragged her to her bed. I pulled off my shirt in the process, and when I used my grip on her hand to plop her down on the mattress in front of me, I started undoing the button and zipper of my slacks.

"Oh my god," Signe's hazel eyes growing heavy-lidded as she took in my naked torso made me want to pose for her. Something that would probably just be cringey and ruin the moment for most women.

But Signe wasn't most women.

So I halted, pushing my pants down and settled my hands on my hips, giving her an unobstructed view of myself shirtless.

"Let me know when you're done," I spoke, my voice growing thick at the sight of Signe reaching her thumbs into her sweatpants and pulling them down. Her eyes never left my chest.

350

"Done with what?" Signe asked, breathless.

"Ogling me."

"Ridiculous," Signe shook her head, still not meeting my eyes, "I'm never going to be done ogling you. You should know this by now."

I couldn't stop the smile that came from hearing that before I stepped forward and tugged her sweatpants down the rest of the way. I kissed each ankle when I freed it from her pants, noticing that only one of her feet had a sock on it. I tugged that off too, before gently trailing my fingers across her skin to reach for the next layer I desperately wanted to remove.

Signe braced her weight on one hand, to lift herself enough to assist me while using her other hand to grip the back of my neck and pull my face toward hers.

Kissing Signe Lange would always scatter my thoughts.

Feeling her lips coax mine open, her tongue sliding into my mouth to dance with mine, had been euphoria every single time. I never grew too accustomed to kissing her. I decided that I would never grow tired of it, ever. I was convinced that kissing her would be a religious experience in and of itself.

But now, she was naked.

"Lay back," I whispered against her lips, nipping at her top one before I let her go. I stood to my full height while she grinned at me and scooched herself back to the center of her bed, stretching her legs out and crossing them at the ankles.

Nope.

I reached forward and wrapped both of my hands around her calves, kneeling on the bed and spreading her wide enough for me to fit in between them. Signe really needed to get used to me fitting between them.

Not wanting to push her legs too far apart, I slung each leg over each of my shoulders before skimming my hands down the outside of her thighs and settling in.

"Zaid!" Signe gasped as I wrapped my hands around the tops of her thighs. I had been so focused on what I intended to do that I had completely forgotten to communicate such. I glanced up at Signe, panicked that I may have assumed some things before I noticed the way she bit into her bottom lip, the flush coloring her cheeks and neck, and the heavy rise and fall of her chest.

That still had that purple bra on it for some reason.

"Is this okay?" I rasped, holding myself back as much as I could.

"You mean oral?" Signe replied, her voice a thick whisper as she struggled to play it cool, "I don't think I'll ever tell you no to that."

"Good," I lowered my head right when she reached her hand up and gripped the roots of my hair, halting my descent when I was centimeters from where I had been dying to be for months.

"Is this okay for you?" she asked me.

"What?" I asked, the fog of arousal making it difficult to keep up with the conversation at this point.

"You don't have to, you know," she waved vaguely towards where I was desperate to taste her, "If you don't want—" she gasped, cut off by my tongue swiping through her slowly, tasting everything.

"Unless the next words out of your mouth are—" I paused to lick her again because I was already addicted, "— my name, or 'oh god', or instructions for me, stop interrupting."

"Okay," Signe groaned when I pressed my lips against her.

At that point, I was willing to swear on all things holy, that I wanted to spend the rest of my days with my face in between Signe's legs.

My version of heaven was the taste of her on my tongue, the sounds of her whimpers when I licked her just right, echoing in my ears. The feel of her soft legs underneath my hands, positioning her perfectly for me to devour her.

The feel of her thighs clenching around me as she got closer and closer.

"Don't stop," Signe panted, "Please, please don't—"

As if stopping was a realistic option for me right now.

As if I would ever be willing to waste this experience with her.

I had been fantasizing about this exact moment with her for too long.

"I'm—"

"Say my name, Signe," I murmured against her center, continuing my ministrations as her breathing became rapid and her body became taut. I slowly dragged my fingers towards her opening as I focused my tongue on her clit, so fucking grateful for that one random woman's educational videos I stumbled upon weeks ago. Signe was responding exactly how she said women would, and when I slowly dipped my fingers inside of her, I was rewarded with wetness that definitely wasn't coming from my own mouth.

I gently, gently eased my fingers into her. Coating them in her wetness. Feeling her clench around me made me grind my own hips into her bed to keep myself contained. I was so hard I thought I was going to die, but if I died with the taste of her release on my tongue, it would be worth it.

Once she was used to my intrusion, I angled my fingers up and inside of her as I flicked my tongue against her clit in a rhythm that made her chant my name.

Fuck yes.

"Shit, shit, shit," Signe was groaning through clenched teeth as her thighs trapped me where I was, her grip on my hair just painful enough to keep my own release at bay, "Zaid, oh god."

Suddenly her entire body went stiff as her muscles contracted against my fingers and mouth, soaking my hand.

I made a groan of approval while I worked her over again and again, doing my best to drag every single minute of her orgasm out as long as she could handle it.

All too soon, Signe tugged on my hair and begged me to stop.

I lifted my head and took in the sight before me.

Her red hair disheveled in a halo around her head, her chest rising and falling in heavy dramatic breaths, the flush that coated her skin as she let her arms flop out on either side of her.

I stared at her purple bra as if it was a personal attack.

Without warning, I crawled up her body and slid the straps down her shoulders, making her giggle as I grunted my annoyance with getting the garment off.

"I can help—oh—okay," I had already slid my hands underneath her body to unclasp it before I finally removed the garment and tossed it elsewhere in the room.

I immediately palmed her breasts, fascinated by the freckles that dotted the tops of them. My thumbs brushed against the hardened tips, and she gasped before grabbing both of my wrists with her own hands.

SIGNE

"I'm still crazy sensitive," I wheezed. Zaid released a disgruntled groan as he made himself stop teasing my nipples. My already warm body was starting to heat again.

"Do you need water? A snack?" Zaid asked, his dark eyes so hooded I thought I might orgasm again just from the look of him. How many times did I fantasize about this part of him? How many late nights were spent with me imagining what he would be like in bed?

The answer, apparently, was perfect.

"Um, no?" I asked, curious about his line of questioning.

"You sure?" he asked as he stood up and finally, finally started pushing his pants down. Unfortunately, he left his boxers on, "Because it's going to be hard for me to stop from this point on, I think." His eyes only met mine briefly, before he scanned my body again. I couldn't remember when he took his glasses off, but something about him without the glasses, his hair mussed up from my grip on it moments ago, shirtless, really did things to me.

"Wait," I was finally able to breathe regularly as I lifted myself on my elbows, "How much longer are we going?"

"As long as you'll let me, Signe," His voice was rough with his reply, and I grinned wide as he reached his hands out and palmed my shoulders to get me to lay back again. As if he didn't want me running off too soon.

"If you're expecting me to be able to come again, I probably won't—oh my fucking god." Zaid had slid his boxers off, revealing everything. He quickly reached down to dig around in the pocket of his pants before pulling out a square foil. I couldn't see what kind it was, but I assumed he got it from a box with the label, "baseball bat" or "third leg."

I crossed my legs in response to finally seeing what exactly the man was packing.

"Don't hide from me," Zaid shook his head with that confident male smirk that made my insides melt. After he covered himself with the condom, he slowly knelt on the bed and started crawling over my body, "Please don't hide from me."

"I'm not hiding," I lied with a nervous breath of laughter, "But, you understand my hesitation, right?" Zaid chuckled as he started licking and kissing my shoulder, his hands grabbing firm handfuls of my hips as he settled his erection against me.

"I'm flattered," he murmured against my skin, "But you have nothing to worry about."

"Says the man," I rolled my eyes even though I was smiling, pausing to appreciate the attention he was giving the pulse point in between my neck and shoulder. I wrapped my arms around his shoulders and pressed my hips against him, surprised at how much heat was already pooling in my lower belly again.

"I don't want to hurt you, habibti," Zaid sucked my skin a little after that sentence, making me whine in appreciation, "That's why we're going to take our time. Get you used to me," he dragged his lips up my neck and across my jaw as one of his hands snuck underneath me to both squeeze my ass and grind himself against me, "Because if you feel as good as you taste, and I know you will, we're going to be stuck here all night."

I tightened my arms around his shoulders, closing my eyes at the euphoric feel of his hard body against my soft one. How his fingers splayed out to grab as much of my ass as possible, and how his other hand was supporting his weight on the mattress so he wouldn't crush me.

"You," I had to pause as he released my ass cheek to drag his hand forward, his large fingers tracing circles around my clit, "You think it'll be that good?"

"I fucking know it will be, Signe," He pushed himself back a little to get a better look at me, "No one can convince me that we weren't made for each other at this point."

I mean, the man had just eaten me out as if he was starved. Like I was his last meal, and he wanted to savor every bite. I wasn't worried that sleeping with him would be a bad experience at all.

"You're right," I whispered, my hands tracing up and down his arms and shoulders, before finally tangling themselves back in his thick silky hair, pulling him back towards me, "You're all mine."

He moaned, his hips jerking against mine, his erection rubbing against my clit in a way that sent sparks throughout my body. I angled my hips, guiding him where suddenly I desperately wanted him. Size be damned. I knew deep down that vaginas were magical things that adjusted to anything and everything, and I was ready, so ready, for this next step with him.

"Are you ready?" Zaid whispered, nudging my opening.

"Slowly," I breathed back. He listened, gently, gently allowing himself in. I definitely stretched, but watching Zaid adjust positions so that both of his forearms rested on either side of me, so that he wouldn't crush me in missionary, was insanely hot. Everything about him was attractive, but finally being able to see his body braced over mine, his brow furrowed with concentration as his dark eyes studied my face, made me adjust more quickly than expected.

I was already fluttering around him, something he responded to with a groan and his eyes squeezing shut.

"You were right," I breathed as he pushed himself in a

little deeper, "You're made for me." I playfully clenched around him again, making a rough gust of air escape his lungs as he pushed his hips some more.

"Fucking hell, Signe," he grumbled through a smirk, "You feel like home."

I felt my eyes start to water at his sentiment. In response, I lifted my hips a little more to help guide him in more on his next thrust.

After some more time, he bottomed out, and I was still fluttering around him.

"I'm going to go off like a rocket," I admitted. Zaid's eyes widened a little bit in surprise before a burst of laughter escaped his lips, his body shaking over mine and definitely not aiding my predicament.

"Can you take it?" Zaid asked, his brow scrunched as he squeezed his eyes closed in concentration.

"Absolutely," I nodded, lifting my legs to wrap themselves around his hips, "Give it to me." Before I even finished my sentence, Zaid had pulled almost completely out before slamming his hips against mine.

Penetrative sex had never been so amazing.

"Oh fuck," Zaid groaned as repeated the thrust, "Damn, Signe."

I couldn't respond, my brain could only process what my body was experiencing. Language was dead to me at the moment. The only sounds I could make were whines of encouragement, my limbs clutching to Zaid for dear life as he slowly ripped me apart with every thrust of his hips.

His lips were parted, exposing his euphoric expression as he opened his eyes and glanced down to watch where our bodies met.

"I'll never get enough of this." Zaid grunted out, starting a rhythm that made me see stars, "You're mine, Signe." I nodded, agreeing, because that's literally what monogamy meant, and we had already agreed on that before he decided to split me in half with his erection.

"Uh-huh," I managed to reply.

"You're so beautiful," Zaid grunted with his movements, he glanced down again, "Look at how pretty you look, filled with me like this."

"Jesus," I wheezed. I had desperately hoped he was at least a little bit of a dirty talker, and I was thrilled with the knowledge that he was.

"Remember," Zaid's voice sounded angry, but when he looked back at me, he was smirking, "My name is the only one you need."

I pulled his head down to kiss me, hard. I tugged on his bottom lip before tracing my tongue across the plump flesh, and pulled away just enough to say, "I love you."

"I love you," Zaid replied, wrapping his arms around my shoulders, and rolling us to his side. Only one leg was wrapped around his waist now, and he used his grip on my thigh to keep us connected while he continued to pound into me, "I love you so much." He snuck his other arm around my head, creating a little pillow for my head to rest on while his hand tangled his fingers in the roots of my hair.

I was pinned while he impaled me, and I felt my orgasm approaching rapidly.

My fingers dug into his biceps, my breathing erratic.

"Zaid," I cried.

"I've got you," he murmured into the top of my head, "Let go, Signe."

I did, and I was pretty sure I blacked out a little bit.

After screaming into his shoulder, letting him continue to thrust inside of me as I came, I thought I heard a ringing in my ears. Tears were streaming out of my eyelids. I kept my eyes closed as if hiding from the intensity of the orgasm he was giving me. And giving me. And giving me.

I was still coming, with no end in sight, groaning with clenched teeth and a grip on his arms that was sure to leave bruises.

"Fuck yes," Zaid grunted into my hair with his thrusts, "Keep going." He rolled us so that I was on my back again, still dragging my orgasm out of me as he palmed one of my breasts and lifted it so he could cover the tip with his mouth.

"Zaid!" I gripped his shoulders, still spasming as his tongue started to flick against my nipple, creating more waves of pleasure.

He growled against my breast, fucking *growled* as he impaled me.

"Oh," I realized I was lifting my hips against his, meeting him every time he ground his pelvis against my clit perfectly, "I'm still—"

"Yes," Zaid replied against my breast.

"Come with me," I begged, "Please, come with me."

Zaid released my breast from his mouth with a loud pop, before bracing his forearms on either side of my head and shoving his face in between my neck and shoulder. His momentum increased and became erratic as my orgasm finally, finally started to fade.

"C'mon, Zaid," I begged, "Come inside of me."

At that, he released a shout as he locked his hips against mine and groaned through his release, his face still hidden in between my shoulder and neck. My body convulsed around him with every pulse of his release.

Finally, after emptying himself entirely, Zaid collapsed on top of me.

I held him tight, not bothered by the weight of his body crushing mine.

Feeling him close was all that mattered, as we both caught our breaths.

Some tears were still leaking out of my eyes, his words from earlier ringing in my head.

He was my home. Wherever he was, I belonged. Together.

Chapter Twenty-Six

SIGNE

I FELT something long and hard poking my ass, making me shift under the covers and start to stretch my body. I was coming out of the deepest sleep I had had in a long while.

Large, warm hands dragged themselves up my stomach and ribs, cupping my breasts while I lifted my hands above my head. A warm mouth was leaving suctioning kisses along my neck and shoulder from behind me.

"Good morning, noor al-ein," I heard Zaid's grumbly, sleepy voice murmur against my skin.

I smiled; my eyes still closed as I lowered my hands back under the covers where the two of us were spooning. God, I loved spooning.

"Morning, love," I replied with a yawn, reaching behind me to grab his morning wood that he was already rocking against me.

"Are you awake?" Zaid asked against my throat, his tongue teasing the skin just below my ear.

"Mhmm," I replied, giving him a playful squeeze.

"Good," Zaid sighed. Without warning, I was suddenly pushed onto my stomach and his large body was caging mine in, his erection teasing me. I landed on my face with an *oof* and a startled giggle.

"Do you have condoms in your nightstand?" Zaid asked against my hair.

I gave another *mhmm* as I pointed towards the furniture in question. He shifted above me before I heard the drawer being pulled open and a foil wrapper being plucked out and torn.

I turned my face to the side, brushing my knotted hair out of the way as I glanced up at him hovering behind me. When he asked last night, I had told him I wasn't opposed to morning sex, but the thought of morning breath concerned me. He must have thought this position would avoid that problem, and I was grateful for it.

I suddenly felt his warm hands in between my legs, feeling.

"You aren't ready for me yet," Zaid murmured against my shoulder.

"I've been awake for three seconds," I replied with a laugh. He chuckled against me, the feel of his laughter rumbling against my back before he lightly pinched one of my ass cheeks in reprimand.

"Can I help you get there?" He whispered, kissing my ear and trapping the lobe between his teeth before continuing, "You looked too pretty wrapped around my cock last night." *Jesus fucking Christ, that works,* "I need to be inside of you again."

"You were just—oh—" I gasped as one of his fingers started teasing my center from above me, snaking between my legs in search of my clit. I arched my back and canted my hips to give him easier access, and soon I was gasping into the pillow, "Inside of me a few—oh god—hours ago."

"I belong inside of you, Signe," Zaid replied, I could feel

his lips pull into a smile against my skin, "It's a sin to start my day otherwise."

Wetness started to coat his fingers, and he used that to his advantage to give more attention to my clit. I was grinding against his hand, crushing it between me and the mattress I lay on.

"Oh god, Zaid," I groaned, "Yes."

"That's better," Zaid's voice took on a rougher edge, "Give me one first, Signe."

"How are you so good at talking during sex?" I gasped, my hands clutching fistfuls of the sheets as I started to rush towards release.

"I learned pretty quickly that you liked what I was saying last night," his teeth gently scraped against my neck, and I whimpered from the sensation of it, "And I love telling you exactly what I'm thinking. Like how I can't wait for you to come all over my hand so I can sink into you properly."

That did it.

I was a goner.

I screamed into my pillow, like a lady.

What a wonderful way to start a Sunday morning.

Zaid didn't linger this time, though. This time, he only dragged it on until I was clearly satisfied, left gasping on my stomach.

"That's better." Zaid kissed the back of my neck before I felt him shift above me again, one of his hands on my hips as he encouraged me to arch my back for him.

"You're telling me," I mumbled into the sheets. He just chuckled above me before I felt him nudge my core, "Damn."

"Do you want me to wait?" he asked, his fingertips pressing into my skin with his question. As if he was quite literally restraining himself from taking me right then and there.

"Part of me wants to tease you and say yes," I smiled, squealing in delight when Zaid playfully pressed his teeth against my shoulder, pretending to bite me, "But no, I'm ready."

"Thank god," Zaid growled, giving me no warning before he plunged in.

I muffled my cries into the bedsheet, feeling the blanket of his body heat cover me entirely as he started a slow rhythm that made me concerned about tearing holes into the bedsheets that I was gripping again. After a few thrusts, I felt one of his hands slide up my shoulder towards my neck, gripping my hair gently at the roots and guiding my head more towards the side, making me cry out into the room, "I want to hear you loud and clear, Signe," Zaid murmured into my ear, "don't hold yourself back."

"As if," I grinned, my eyes falling closed. I loved having my hair tugged like he was doing, another thing we talked about the previous night before we had sex for the second time, "Do you—*oh*—do you want me on top sometime?"

"Yes," Zaid emphasized his response with a hard thrust, making me reach my hand up to brace myself against my headboard so my body wouldn't keep sliding up the bed, "But I'm too obsessed with the sight of you underneath me right now."

"Ah," I moaned when he released my hair and used that hand to instead wrap itself underneath my chest, gripping me close to his body by my shoulders. An inch or so higher, and his arm would be wrapping itself around my neck. This gave him a bit more leverage while I still held my hand against the headboard.

"Goddamn, Zaid," I moaned when he somehow changed

the angle of what he was doing, "I'm not gonna—*oh*—be able to walk later."

"Good," Zaid's thrusts picked up, making me turn my head to bite the pillow that I was resting on, "You don't need to get out of this bed." How many orgasms did it take to actually kill a woman? It had been about twelve hours since Zaid and I started doing this, and I had lost count of how many he had given me in such a short amount of time, "You can just lay here, and I'll take care of you," He grunted his words, his grip on my shoulder was tightening, and his entire chest was pressed against my back as he plunged into me, "I'll bring you whatever you need," his hot breath was fanning against my face and neck with his words, "And when you're ready," he paused to groan when I started fluttering around him, my orgasm imminent, "I'll fuck you again—" with a moan, I was already coming right then and there, "And again—until you—ah, shit—" he ground his hips against me, pulsing inside of me as my muscles convulsed around him. He groaned his release into my neck, and I cried mine laying on my cheek.

After a few silent moments, I giggled.

"What is it?" Zaid asked, not moving from on top of me, but shifting just enough so that I could still inhale a full breath of air into my lungs.

"Until I what?" I asked, "You never finished your thought."

"My brain is fried," he replied, pressing gentle kisses against my shoulder, "Something about how you're too perfect to bother getting out of bed or whatever."

"Or whatever," I repeated, rolling over to finally face him. Half of his hair was standing up on one end, probably from sleeping on the one side all night. I grinned and brushed my fingers through it, "Good morning, handsome."

"Morning, beautiful," he reached forward and pressed a kiss against my forehead, actively avoiding my lips and letting me taste his morning breath. He pulled back to look at me, brushing some hair away from my face as he propped his cheek on his fist, his elbow digging into the mattress to support his body as he looked down at me, "I love you."

"I love you, too," I reached up and rubbed my hand on his arm, covering my yawn with my other, "Are you happy?"

"Incredibly," he grinned, and it was so adorable I thought my heart was going to burst, "I feel like I'm dreaming."

"Me too," I smiled up at him, snuggling closer to his chest and tucking the covers around me, "I feel lucky."

"I'm the lucky one, Signe," Zaid pressed his lips into my hair, adjusting his position to wrap his arms around me and hold me snug against his chest, "I know I can't live up to the stamina that Zayne has, but—" I interrupted him by quickly smacking his face with the pillow, humiliation coating my skin as I realized how this was definitely going to be a thing he'd tease me about for a while. He shoved the pillow out of his face with a laugh and held his hands up in defense.

"Just so we're clear," I sat up and towered over him, holding the pillow ready in case he was about to start mouthing off again, "I want you. Just you."

Zaid grinned up at me, something softening the corners of his eyes as he took in my attack-ready position, a smirk on my own lips as I held the threat of another pillow smothering over him.

After calmly tucking his hands behind his head, admiring his view from his prone position on his back, Zaid met my eyes and said, "You have me."

Chapter Twenty-Seven

SIGNE

"Do you have eggs?" Zaid asked a while later, both of us still lingering in my bed, tangled up in the sheets.

"Yup," I raised my hand and pointed to the fridge because that was the perk of living in a studio apartment. Everything was within view.

"I'm going to scramble us some," Zaid announced with a groan as he sat up on the edge of the bed, bending down to pull his boxers back on.

"I think I'm going to hold the bed down a little while longer," I sighed, stretching to fill the space he had just vacated, "I still can't see straight."

He gave me a playful smirk over his shoulder as he stood, bending down to kiss me on the crown of my head once before sauntering into the kitchen in all his naked glory.

Somebody pinch me and wake me up from this dream.

Actually, on second thought, nobody fucking touch me.

I finally reached over and grabbed my phone, scrolling through the hundreds of notifications.

Hold up, *hundreds?*

I sat up, keeping the covers over me because it was chilly without them, and opened up the messages from Michelle first.

> Michelle: I can't keep up with my emails today!

> Michelle: We have bids! Call me!

> Michelle: It's officially a bidding war! Where are you? Call me as soon as you get this!

> Michelle: Oh my god, I have NEVER seen this much interest in a story before! ANSWER YOUR PHONE WOMAN!!

I gaped in shock for a moment, before hitting the dial button near her contact.

My agent answered before the first ring could even finish sounding.

"Thank god, I thought you were dead," Michelle spoke before I could properly greet her, "I was afraid I'd have to turn everyone away and prepare a funeral instead of a pub deal."

"What is happening?" I asked her, putting the phone on speaker and earning a curious glance from Zaid over in the kitchen.

"You're blowing up—again, but more so," Michelle sounded exhausted, like she was frazzled and struggling to summarize things, "Like, way more. Not only are publishers coming back and offering to sign you and your story, but other publishers are sliding into my email with their own bids on your story too."

"What?" I gasped, looking up at Zaid who had the biggest, proudest grin on his face as he cracked an egg in a bowl and lifted his hand to snap his fingers in applause, "How? Why?"

"I had the same question, but when you didn't get back to me yesterday, I decided that I needed to investigate matters myself," I heard the smile in Michelle's voice, "And then I saw your latest post. Or should I say, your man's latest post?"

A blush stained my cheeks, making Zaid hesitate before cracking the next egg. I just stared at him as Michelle kept speaking, "Readers were already obsessed with Zayne, but his video explaining what has been happening between the two of you? Now they're addicted. Ravenous. Obsessed doesn't feel like an accurate enough word. Your story is everywhere, Signe. You went *viral* viral."

I felt tears starting to fill my eyes at her news, my lip trembling because, frankly, it sounded too good to be true, "Because of Zaid's video?" I clarified.

"Not just because of his video. You already had a large following and path to success without him, but Zaid declaring his love for you and his excitement for your story really tugged at everyone's heartstrings. He supported you in the best possible way, it seems," Michelle hummed, "I'm still getting new emails. I'll try to narrow offers down over the next week or so because it'll take time to comb through all of this, but it looks like it's happening, girly. All your hard work is going to pay off big time."

I felt tears start to slide down my face, a wobbly, "Thank you so much," didn't sound sufficient enough for my agent.

"Thank you, and tell your man thanks, too," Michelle laughed before hanging up.

I slowly lowered it and stood from the bed, tears blurring my vision as I found Zaid's t-shirt and slipped it on, my ass still definitely hanging out of it, while I approached him whisking together the eggs.

When I stood at his side, he dropped the bowl and wrapped both of his arms around me while I dropped my head on his shoulder and started sobbing.

"Signe? Love? What's wrong," Zaid's hands were rubbing gentle passes between my shoulder blades, his hug tight around me. I clutched either side of his waist with my grip, using his solid body to ground me while I unleashed a myriad of emotions coursing through my body.

The last forty-eight hours had been a fucking whirlwind, that was for sure.

"I'm okay," I managed to wheeze out in between my sobs, sobs that were slowly starting to mellow out, "I'm so happy I might explode."

I felt Zaid release a heavy exhale of relief, "I thought you were going to be upset that my confession is what went viral and helped get you offers."

"I don't care about that at all," I mumbled against his bare shoulder, "I'm not worried about you stealing my thunder."

"If anything," Zaid replied, "I hope that I helped direct some readers toward your thunder."

"Yeah," I giggled, leaning back and looking at him, "You did."

Zaid squeezed me again, before pulling back enough to press a firm kiss to my lips and murmuring, "I'm so proud of you, Signe."

I sighed, relaxing all of my muscles because of the comfort that was his embrace, "I love you, Zaid."

Chapter Twenty-Eight

SIGNE

WALKING BACK into the office was a big step for me, mostly because I had a myriad of emotions, making every step that I took toward the building that much more difficult. Excitement, anxiety, embarrassment. I hadn't exactly left on Friday on the best of terms, and I knew that I needed to put on my big kid pants and have a chat with Jacqueline about everything.

I just really didn't want to.

But I really wanted to continue seeing Zaid without issue, because I loved him with all of my heart.

The squeeze of his hand wrapped around mine helped, as we both stepped into the elevators that lead to the Sun Steer Technologies suite.

Zaid leaning down to press his lips against the crown of my head behind the safety of the elevator doors also helped.

I squeezed his hand one last time before the doors opened and my front desk was revealed to us.

He held one hand over the doors, keeping them open while I dramatically leaned forward, glancing down the left and right of the large entryway and seeing nobody else.

"What are you doing?" Zaid whispered, leaning forward like I was, to also check our surroundings.

"I'm seeing if she's here yet," I whispered back, finally stepping off the elevator and jogging over to my desk. I reached the elevated lip of it and stood on my tiptoes to look and see if she was hiding underneath it.

She was not.

"Habibti, it's going to be fine," Zaid chuckled as he pressed his hand against my shoulder and pressed a parting kiss to my head again, "You're not the one stepping down today."

"Are you sure that's what you want to do?" I chewed on the inside of my cheek as I turned to face him with my question, "I know you've wanted to step down as CTO for a while now, but—" Zaid lifted a long finger to my lips, smiling as he effectively shushed me.

"Brandon knows this is what I've wanted," Zaid shook his head once, "If he's surprised, or upset, that's entirely on him. I'm willing to take a position better suited for me if he offers, but I'll never struggle to find work elsewhere either."

I stared up at him, in awe that we were talking about him quitting his job to help him reach his own career goals, as well as addressing those pesky unethical power dynamics that Jacqueline had warned him about all those months ago.

After we reconnected in my apartment for the rest of the weekend, I was filled in on some things that were going on during the last few months. Including, but not limited to, how Jacqueline had pretty much warned him off from ever gaining enough confidence to ask me out while we were both employees at Sun Steer.

Which meant that I needed to talk to her and humbly ask that I keep my job for the time being.

At least until my first book was published and I could see how successful it ended up being.

Just behind us the elevator dinged, and Jamie and Mary walked into the office.

"I saw your video," Mary chirped, winking at Zaid and me, "Jamie almost passed out from the cuteness of it."

"She's not wrong," Jamie grinned, a light pink blush coloring her cheeks and brightening her blue eyes, "Nice going, boss."

"I'm not really your boss," he replied, "Not for long, anyway."

"Does Brandon know you're going to quit?" Mary asked him.

"I'm hoping the threat of me quitting will get him to take my requests just a tad more seriously, but I'll let you know as soon as I have updates." Zaid smiled when Mary held her fist out to him to bump, returning the gesture with a chuckle.

I brushed my knuckles against the back of his arm in support, because we were at work, waving bye to Jamie and Mary who continued to their departments of the building.

Zaid wrapped me in a one-arm hug, whispering, "I love you," into my hair before he released me and made his way toward his own office, probably also preparing for his talk with Brandon about changing positions or quitting.

I inhaled a breath to calm my nerves as I settled my things at my desk, including the little snake plant that Zaid had gifted me all those months ago.

Finally, after sitting at my desk for thirty more minutes and not seeing Jacqueline walk through the elevators, I decided to bite the bullet and go to her office directly.

I knocked on Zaid's office door twice when I saw that it was cracked open, for good luck and definitely *not* to delay this conversation before I approached Jacqueline's office next. I gently rapped my knuckles on the wood, before slowly opening her door a little wider and peeking my head in.

Jacqueline was at her desk, her earbuds in her ears as her head jerked up towards me. She sat straighter in her seat and said, "Signe."

"Hi, Jacqueline." I waved awkwardly, pointing to the seat in front of her desk, "Can I come in?"

"Of course," Jacqueline stood from her chair, brushing the wrinkles out of her skirt and patting her hair to ensure her bun was in place. I felt so nervous, and I hated it. I liked Jacqueline, but I was embarrassed to be this kind of person in front of her. She intimidated me.

"I was wondering, um," I tugged on the sleeves of my sweatshirt, "If I could maybe keep my job here?"

Jacqueline was nodding her head before I even finished my sentence, making my eyes widen in surprise, "Your position is yours, Signe. Don't worry about it." She waved her hand away as if the issue of me writing smut about the CTO of Sun Steer wasn't something to concern herself with.

"Oh," I exhaled a relieved sigh, "Thank you so much. I'm so sorry about all of this. For putting you in the position I did. I...I'm just so sorry." I shrugged and folded my arms, not knowing what else to say to her.

Jacqueline nodded once and swallowed, before turning her head to stare at one of the indoor potted trees on the side of the room. She fidgeted with her fingers, lacing them together repeatedly as she stared at the plant.

It wasn't a dismissal, it looked like Jacqueline was working herself up to say something.

So, I waited, and within a few tense moments, it happened.

"I listen to trash music," Jacqueline finally spoke, making me blink my eyes at her in surprise.

"What?"

"Trash music. Specifically, from the early two thousands," Jacqueline's shoulders dropped as she removed her glasses and rubbed her brow with her fingers, "Music you'd hear in like, a club or a rave from twenty years ago. Music with no real deep meaning, just, I don't know, vibes." She looked both embarrassed and defeated as she said this to me. I stared at her, giving her confession air to breathe while also wondering why this was even a confession.

"...I...like trash music too?" I ended up replying.

Jacqueline's dark eyes turned to meet mine, and I gave her a reassuring smile.

She looked hesitant, and I realized that I had no idea who Jacqueline was or what she had to deal with to get to where she was.

"A lot of people hate on artists like Lady Gaga, Kesha, and their early music that made them popular," I lifted a shoulder as I spoke, watching one single stray tear fall from Jacqueline's eye as she quickly wiped it away, "But we all know the words, right? We all get that adrenaline rush when the music others deem 'trash' comes on."

Jacqueline sniffed and nodded in agreement, "Nobody takes it seriously."

"And nobody is asking them to," I stepped towards her, "But people—mostly men—love to find any excuse to tear down and invalidate something universally loved by women, right? Especially if that woman is in a position of superiority over them."

Jacqueline's lip wobbled, before she inhaled a shaky breath, "I know it's silly to be so weird about it." Her voice shook as she tried to control herself, another tear falling,

"But it's so hard to be taken seriously in this industry, to earn the respect of my coworkers. To not be brushed off as someone just feeling emotional or ridiculous because I'm a woman." Jacqueline dropped her head in both of her hands, a soft sob erupting from her body as her shoulders hunched, and I closed the distance between the two of us so I could wrap her up in a tight hug, feeling her body shake as she struggled to contain another sob.

"You don't need to earn my respect, Jacqueline," I felt my own tear fall down my cheek, my heart breaking for this woman who I have judged for being so stiff and rigid and unfeeling, "You don't need to earn the respect of anyone. If people aren't willing to take you seriously or appreciate every part of you, they don't deserve your energy."

Jacqueline sniffed, her hands wiping away at her eyes while still wrapped up in my hug, "I...I do like working here. I like how friendly everyone is with each other," she inhaled another shaky breath, before pulling back from my hug and desperately wiping away at the mascara running down her cheeks, "I'm so sorry I went to Zaid first, Signe. I want to be your friend. I just...I'm *so* bad at being friends with women."

I laughed a little, wiping away my own tears because I was hopeless. If someone cried in front of me, I was going to cry in front of them, too.

"There's no rulebook to follow, unfortunately," I sniffed, squeezing her shoulders before brushing my thumb under her eye to wipe away a smudge of mascara that she missed.

"I wish there was," Jacqueline's shoulders slumped, a self-deprecating laugh escaping her lips, "It would make things easier."

"How about, going forward," I pulled her into a hug again, and this time she wrapped her arms around me too,

"We just talk to each other when we aren't sure where we stand with the other, yeah?"

Jacqueline laughed a little hysterically into my shoulder, before squeezing me in her hug once more, "Yeah, that sounds nice." We stood there for a moment before Jacqueline pulled away and broke the hug again. She waved her hands over her face to dry the tears that dared to escape her eyes during that emotional moment, and I laughed as I used my sweatshirt sleeve to do the same.

"It would make things a little easier, though," Jacqueline smiled as she dabbed her wet cheeks with the back of her hand, "If you refrained from writing erotica about coworkers going forward."

I cackled, embarrassed and thrilled that I was able to have this conversation with Jacqueline. How this could be something we could all laugh about going forward, instead of having it haunt me and potentially ruin my life, or someone else's.

"Oh god," I shook my head as I laughed, my hands holding my cheeks to contain my grin, "I learned my lesson. That's for damn sure."

Chapter Twenty-Nine

ZAID

"You're telling me," Signe stepped in front of me, matching my pace and walking backward so she could give me her playful narrow-eyed look, "That you wouldn't even consider starring in a hypothetical movie adaptation?"

I chuckled and shook my head, allowing her to continue her backward walk down the hallway of my building, "Absolutely not," I reached out to grab her hand before she walked past my door, typing in the code to unlock it, "I'm not meant for the big screen."

"Have you looked in a mirror recently?" Signe asked, "There's a reason you got written into my book. But fine, would you at least consider narrating the audiobook? I know from personal experience it'll do well. 'I need you, I'll die without you'. Ugh, I can see the download numbers now." Her deep voice mimicking my own made me lower my head to laugh at her theatrics, holding the door open for her to walk through.

"Do you really want readers to hear me read your words..." I paused, closing the door behind me as I turned to face her, toeing off our shoes in the entryway, "Or would you like to keep all the dirty things I say to you between us."

She froze what she was doing, her clear hazel eyes widening as she looked up at me. One of her hands was braced on the wall from taking off her shoes without bending down.

After a tense moment, a grin spread across her luscious lips, "That's a good point. I want you all to myself."

I grinned back at her, "Yeah?"

"Yeah," she shrugged out of her jacket and hung it up on one of the hooks, before stepping towards me to help me out of mine.

I exhaled at the feel of her hands brushing past my shoulders as she took my jacket and hung it up right next to hers.

"That's a relief," I sighed, walking up behind her and pressing a kiss behind her ear. She turned around and laced her arms around my neck, stretching up on her toes to kiss my lips. I groaned; my body was still not quite used to being so intimate with her. I shifted my hips, letting her know exactly what she did to me.

Signe pressed her hips against me in response, making me wonder if we'd actually get around to eating dinner tonight like we'd planned, before she whispered against my mouth, "Are we gonna do it in Captain America's bed?"

I chuckled and gave her ass a light slap in reprimand, "I will let you decorate my bedroom however you like, Ms. Lange," I lowered my voice to that tone that I knew drove her crazy. I used my hold to encourage her to wrap one of her legs around me, so that I could grip her thigh, letting me grind up against her.

"I'm not against doing it in a condensed version of

Comic-Con," Signe giggled after I peppered more kisses on her lips, "But like... how permanent is it?"

"Probably until Zeki doesn't care about superheroes anymore."

I was dragging my lips on her jaw when I replied, and Signe made a choked sound that made me stop what I was doing and immediately pull back to see what was wrong.

Her eyes were wide, and her bottom lip was out, and I was so confused.

"What?" I asked.

"You can't be serious," Signe somehow widened her eyes even more at me, "You decorated your room like that to impress your three-year-old nephew?"

I lifted one shoulder, smiling at her reaction to such a thing, "He'll be four soon," I added, kissing her cheek because I swore, I was addicted to kissing her, "That room is the vision of a man in his thirties with no girlfriend and no eye for design, who really wanted to make his nephew smile every time he came over."

"Oh my god," she reached up to grab the back of my neck, taking a turn to pepper kisses all over my face, "I love you so much I think I might explode."

"Maybe we should actually take this to the bedroom then," I caught her lips with mine, savoring the feel of her warm mouth underneath mine, when I suddenly heard the beeping sound of someone typing in a code to the front door, "What the—" Suddenly the door flew open, smacking into my back and squishing me and Signe against the wall.

"Bisbous!" I heard my mother's voice, making my own eyes widen in alarm as I panicked with the knowledge that I was just dry-humping Signe before she intruded.

"Mama, what are—" the door pulled back, and to my

horror, both of my sisters and my parents were now filing into my apartment. Everyone carrying bags of groceries, except for Raina, who had pulled the front door closed and revealed Signe and me. Signe, who still had her one leg wrapped around my waist.

"Oh shi—" Signe scrambled off of me, her own face turning beet red just as I felt my own embarrassment coat my skin.

"What are you two, sixteen?" Raina asked with a raised brow.

"We weren't—well—" Signe flapped her hands a little bit before holding her hand out to my sister, "I'm Signe."

"I know," my sister replied, supporting my newborn nephew wrapped to her chest with a hand under his rump, and using the other to shake Signe's hand, "I have been following you since day one."

"Oh god," Signe turned to look at me with a look of horror, which made me throw my head back and laugh at the hilarity of this moment.

"Tariq!" Raina called over her shoulder, "Come meet my brother and his girlfriend while they're stuck behind the door here." A young, tall black man with dark, short hair, dressed in a white t-shirt and cargo joggers stepped up beside Raina, resting one of his hands on her shoulder while smiling nervously at Signe and me.

"Nice to meet you," he nodded at the two of us, before turning to my little sister and murmuring, "Let them out, you monster."

"Zaid!" My mother gasped, gently pushing my sister and her boyfriend to the side, and opening her arms wide, before hesitating and noticing the state of us. "Were you not expecting us?"

"Uh, no," I shook my head, "I was not expecting visitors." I stepped forward to place a hand on Signe's lower back. My mother didn't appreciate a lot of visible PDAs, even when my sisters gave quick kisses to their partners in greeting or farewell, she always looked away. I had only seen my parents kiss a few times in front of me growing up, usually when they thought they were alone.

"Susu!" My mother called, making my sister snap her head up from whatever food she was preparing at my kitchen island, "You didn't tell your brother that we were coming?" My mother placed her fists on her hips with her question.

"Whoops." Salma winked at us, making Ben chuckle as he stepped next to her to help her with the food.

I leaned down towards Signe, whispering in her ear with both of my hands on her shoulders, "Is this okay?"

She placed both of her hands on mine, something my mother noted when she turned back around to face us, "This is fine," she turned to look up at me, "Should I go home?"

"No, no, no," my mother stepped forward and took hold of Signe's hands, pulling her out of the entryway and into my kitchen with the rest of my family, "I want to officially meet and get to know the woman my son was hiding from me."

I furrowed my brows at her wording, "I wasn't hiding Signe from you," she stopped to give me a disbelieving look, to which I rolled my eyes and admitted, "I just didn't want you to scare her off too soon."

"If you would have told me you were seeing someone," my mother wrapped one of her arms around Signe's shoulders, "I wouldn't have paraded another young woman in front of you both." At that, my mother turned to face Signe. They were similar in height, and neither had to look up or down at each other, "If I had known my son was in a relationship with you, I would have never done such a thing."

Signe gave her a small smile with a nod of her head, "That's okay, I appreciate you clarifying that."

My mother smiled, wrapping Signe in a tight hug and saying, "I just want him to be happy."

"I do, too," Signe replied, sending me a grin over my mother's shoulder.

I felt my body relax little by little, having Signe meet my family and having them accept her with open arms. I wasn't sure if my mother knew exactly what brought Signe and me together, and frankly, it was fine if she never really did.

"Stop hogging her," Raina complained from her spot at the island, chopping vegetables with my dad and Ben on either side of her, "I want to talk to Signe, too."

Signe blushed again before the excited squeal of Zeki filled the space. We all turned down the hallway, where he was running towards her with one of my Spider-Man action figures in his little hands.

"Signe!" Zeki squealed as he lifted his arms up to be held.

She laughed and obliged, pointing to his toy, "Who is that?"

"Spida-man," Zeki held the action figure with both of his chubby hands, bouncing in Signe's arms with the energy of a three-year-old who was still deep in his superhero phase.

"He's a pretty cool guy," Signe smiled up at me, and the sight of her holding my nephew so comfortably on her hip made something warm bloom in my chest. A vision I would love but wouldn't push her for. She knew where I stood, and I was more than willing to wait for her to decide whether that was part of our future.

I had already waited this long to have Signe in my arms, and nothing, absolutely nothing, was worth letting her go.

Chapter Thirty

SIGNE: MONTHS LATER

"How are presales going?" Jamie asked as she slid into the seat next to Mary. She leaned forward and smacked a quick peck on Mary's cheek, who had a mouthful of waffles and was leaning over her plate of food like it was her last meal.

"They're going," I smiled. I tried not to focus too much on how the book was doing. I still had just under a year before it was officially published, but when I hit a number in presales that I only ever dreamt of having, I realized keeping track of all the numbers was a surefire way to send me into an imposter syndrome spiral.

"But you're still not ready to quit, right?" Mary asked around her mouthful of food, a threatening glare narrowing her eyes. I nodded at her, even though I still didn't plan on working at Sun Steer forever, I wanted to wait until I saw how my book did once it was published in the world before I quit. I had a three-book deal with my publisher, and I knew that I could still fulfill that obligation and keep my General Manager position just fine.

Once Zaid finally had a firm talk with Brandon about how he was desperate to step down or quit, Brandon finally started to take the option of hiring someone else as CTO more seriously. Apparently, that casual conversation we had in Zaid's car on the way to the airport had some weight, because a month ago it was announced that Mary's hot cousin—excuse me—Leo Turner, would be filling the position of Chief Technology Officer.

Sun Steer was still rapidly growing, adding a couple more teams of software engineers to the workforce to keep up with sustainability. Zaid would be working alongside Nikhil now, managing a team of engineers on his own, and having more opportunities to build and write the software that started it all.

I could see how much happier he already was, even though Zaid still had a couple more weeks as CTO to give Leo time to make the move from the UK to the US. The fact that he could see a light at the end of the tunnel really affected his mood.

Stepping down from CTO would also mean we could sneak off and have our own little lunch dates more often, since we would still be working at the same company, and I was confident that everyone there knew that Zaid and I were together.

"Hi Jacqueline—whoa," Mary sat up from her crouched position as the chair next to me squeaked and Jacqueline threw herself into the seat.

"I'll take a mimosa," Jacqueline called over her shoulder to the waiter who had just walked up to take her order. The waiter widened their eyes before nodding in appreciation, "On a Tuesday morning in your work clothes. Respect."

Jacqueline gave them a smile before she slumped in her seat.

"Is everything all right?" I asked, knowing that

Jacqueline needed to be asked directly about herself, to share how she was feeling or what was going on in her life.

I still knew very little about her, but I loved that she was going out of her way to be part of the women friend group at the office. Alice had joined us on these weekly brunches we started having at a cute little café that had opened a block away from Sun Steer, before she suddenly quit and took a better offer at Blix.

The social media company that Jacqueline and the new CFO, Nicole, had come from.

Mary was annoyed that she was once again the only female identifying software engineer, and that Nicole hadn't taken us up on our offer to join us for these weekly brunches.

It took Jacqueline some time to warm up to our friendship, so I was willing to give Nicole the same.

"I swear, your cousin," Jacqueline pressed her lips together while resting her elbow on the table and pinching the bridge of her nose, even going as far as to rub her perfectly groomed brows to ease some sort of frustration she was feeling, "Is the most annoying person on the planet."

Mary just laughed, "What did he do?"

"If I get one more goddamn email from him asking for more information on benefits, explaining how they work, or however else he is actively choosing to avoid looking it all up on the app himself, I'm going to scream," Jacqueline grumbled, only perking up when the waiter returned with her mimosa. She didn't let the waiter set the glass down on the table, instead opting to take it from their hand directly.

They just laughed a little as they sauntered off to check on the other tables.

"He's not the most organized," Mary shrugged, "But he's very talented, and great with people. You'll love him once you get to work with him outside of your email exchanges. I promise."

Jacqueline shook her head once, clearly disbelieving everything Mary was saying, and took another large gulp of her mimosa.

My phone vibrated in my pocket, so while Jacqueline continued to grumble, I pulled it out to read the text I just received.

> Salma: My coworker just told me that she got approved to be an ARC reader this morning!

I smirked; I had little to no control over who got approved to receive advanced reader copies of my book to review, but I responded with a variety of excited and celebratory emojis anyway.

> Raina: What the hell? Why didn't I get approved?

> Me: You still don't want to read it, I promise.

> Raina: I can be objective! And just skip past any scene with Zayne.

> Salma: That's half the book, you doofus.

> Me: I'll be sure to get you an ARC for the next one, Raina, I promise.

I had already started drafting a second novel, something my publisher had been on me about for a few weeks now. I was nervous about diving back into that fictional world again, mostly because of all the anxiety I felt when writing it in the first place, but Zaid made sure I stayed motivated.

Really motivated.

Sure, most of the incomplete draft I had of book two was just smut at this point, but writing was writing, and I could always go back and piece the plot together later. There was still value to me being able to slap words on a page to get the creative process going again.

My phone buzzed again, this time from my favorite man in the world.

Zaiddy: Guess what I just found.

He then sent a picture of the scream mask he had worn in his office last Halloween. I giggled, ignoring the curious looks from the women around me, as I typed my reply to him.

Me: Don't lose it this time.

Zaiddy: Is this seriously a thing?

Me: Put it on tonight and see for yourself.

Zaiddy: Whatever you want, habibti.

I was confident I had officially peaked in life.

Hearing him call me endearing terms like "love of my life" or "light of my eye" or "my moon" in Arabic would never get old. Neither would reading those pet names from his text messages. Or in the cute little handwritten notes he'd leave next to me any time he went into the office before me, and I was still asleep.

Zaid Ansara wasn't perfect, but he was pretty damn close to it.

Because he was mine.

And even though we wouldn't be living this picture-perfect life forever, taking turns staying the night at each other's places, going to work together, and leaving together most days, I was excited to see what came next for the two of us.

Looking back, I was glad that I had the insane idea of writing him into my first published novel because even though it was probably one of the most anxious seasons of my adult life, it landed me here.

I didn't want to be anywhere else.

THE END

Acknowledgments

First, I want to thank you, for reading this book. I don't know how you found it, or why you picked it up or downloaded this story, but you are the only reason I am able to keep doing this. Thank you for taking a chance on me.

I'd like to thank my sensitivity and authenticity readers for educating me on how best to write Zaid's character and family dynamics. For being willing to brainstorm with me and answer any questions that I had, which were quite a few.

I'd also like to thank my beta readers, for encouraging me to write four books now. For being that perfect balance of gassing me up, while also helping critique my work so that these stories can be the best they can be.

I would specifically like to thank my editor, Yara, for pushing me and finding all possible weak points in the story. For pointing out where some scenes could use some more tension and how to take advantage of it. My storytelling is improving because of you, and so is my confidence as a writer. Additionally, you're a wonderful friend. I hate that we live on opposite sides of the world, but I'm so grateful that the internet gods brought us together.

I'd also like to thank my friends (Jayden, Genna, and Shirley) for getting excited over any new developments I have to share when it comes to writing love stories. It's a little thing, but the constant support and positive excitement help elevate my mental headspace during the writing process. Thank you for helping me maintain enough confidence in myself to keep going.

Thank you to my family members (my mother-in-law Kelly, my cousins Jordan, Megan, and Kristi. My aunt Emily as well as my sister-in-law Emily, and sister-in-law Kat) and everyone else who has helped proofread or simply bought and read my stories from afar. Familial support means the world to me. Thank you all so much for everything.

Thank you to all of my author and writer friends that I have made since starting this journey. Being available to answer my questions, to letting me spiral about meeting deadlines. Thank you specifically to Stella Stevenson for suggesting the brilliant title for this story, and to Melissa Whitney for helping me troubleshoot my back cover blurb when after the dozenth try, I wanted to pull my hair out and scream.

I'd like to thank my husband Clayton for learning more about romance reader spaces with each book I write and publish, to better understand and support me when I spiral about decision making. Thank you for holding my hand on this journey. Thank you for everything you do for me as my partner, as a parent, and also as the family IT guy. Also, thank you so much for helping me brainstorm and create Sun Steer Technologies for the rest of this series. The only reason anyone talks about the inner workings of a tech company in this book is because you taught me. Thank you.

Also by Andrea Andersen

Up next:

MELTED BY A MAN

The WHAT IT MEANS interconnected standalone series:

WHAT IT MEANS TO BE WHOLE

WHAT IT MEANS TO BE BRAVE

WHAT IT MEANS TO BE FOUND

About the Author

Andrea is originally from Oregon but now resides in southern California with her little family. When she isn't curled up on the couch writing love stories, she can be found rewatching her favorite TV shows or taking too many naps.

www.andreaandersen.com